Researching Enterprise Development

Dialogues on Work and Innovation

The book series *Dialogues on Work and Innovation* presents empirically based studies as well as theoretical discussions on the practice of organizational renewal.

Its publications reflect the increasingly urgent need for the development of new forms of work organization. In today's interdependent world, workplace reform and organizational effectiveness are no longer solely the concern of individual organizations; the local and the global have become closely interconnected.

Dialogues on Work and Innovation mirrors the fact that enterprise development and societal development cannot be kept separate. Furthermore, the Series focuses on the dialogue between theory and practice, and thus on the mutuality of knowledge and action, of research and development. The *Dialogues* stress the critical significance of joint reflexivity in action-oriented research and the necessity for participatory processes in organizational change.

Volume 14

Researching Enterprise Development: Action Research on the cooperation between management and labour in Norway
Edited by Morten Levin

Researching Enterprise Development

Action Research on the cooperation between management and labour in Norway

Edited by

Morten Levin
Norwegian University of Science and Technology, Trondheim

John Benjamins Publishing Company
Amsterdam / Philadelphia

∞™ The paper used in this publication meets the minimum requirements of American National Standard for Information Sciences – Permanence of Paper for Printed Library Materials, ANSI Z39.48-1984.

Library of Congress Cataloging-in-Publication Data

Researching enterprise development : action research on the cooperation between management and labour in Norway / edited by Morten Levin.

p. cm. (Dialogues on Work and Innovation, ISSN 1384–6671 ; v. 14)

Includes bibliographical references and indexes.

1. Research, Industrial--Economic aspects--Norway. 2. Technological innovations--Norway. 3. Organizational change--Norway. I. Levin, Morten. II. Series.

HC370.R4 R47 2002
388'.007'20481-dc21 2002-034216
ISBN 90 272 1784 X (Eur.) / ISBN 1 58811 334 5 (US) (Hb; alk. paper)

John Benjamins Publishing Co. · P.O. Box 36224 · 1020 ME Amsterdam · The Netherlands
John Benjamins North America · P.O. Box 27519 · Philadelphia PA 19118-0519 · USA

Table of contents

Foreword

This project was made possible by a grant from the Norwegian Research Council under the program Enterprise Development 2000.The first ideas for this book were presented at a meeting between involved researchers in this program. A proposal was written and funds were granted. The work was initiated in the fall of 1999 and was finished by early summer 2001. The results from Development 2000 are reported in detail in *Creating Connectedness*, edited by Bjørn Gustavsen, Håkon Finne and Bo Oscarsson (2001), published in the same book series. The book *Work Organisation and Europe as a Development Coalition* (Ennals and Gustavsen 1999) preceeds this project.

The current book presents learning and reflections from key participating researchers.

The development of the book took 6 months involving researchers from seven different research institutions scattered all over Norway. A total of 14 researchers took on the responsibility of writing the history chapters, while a core group of five cooperated in the whole writing process. The leading idea in the writing project was to create a structure that would support collective reflections. Ideas were developed jointly, cooperation emerged, and critique and support were encouraged in this group.

The book has been a collective learning experience, creating new cooperative links.

Chapter 1

Researchers on research

Morten Levin

Introduction

This is a book about research. It is about researching a large, multi-site research project. It is about telling the stories of seven different research groups within the same program. It is about the collective reflections and research process of a group of researchers. It is about a Norwegian national program on enterprise development. This book conveys the participating researchers' stories about how the program developed, and a collective reflection process aimed at making sense of the aggregated learning from being active in this program. The book will accordingly convey the history of how the research developed in the seven participating modules of the program. In addition, the researcher group, who have written the individual case stories, engaged in a collective reflection process in order to extract the learning from the total program. That is the researchers' research on their own research.

The book does not promise to deliver on all possible interpretations of the title "Researching Enterprise Development". This is not a book about all bits and pieces of enterprise development. The book will focus on issues that the participating researchers found to be of vital importance in enterprise development. The issues that make up the second half of the book emanated from discussions in the author group, and the second half was written as a co-operative effort.

Norwegian Work Life

Modern Norwegian Work has emerged as an integrated part of the creation of the welfare-state. In the reconstruction period after World War II, political processes were dominated by the very influential social democratic party. An important element of the power platform for the party was based on close co-operation with the Norwegian Federation of Trade Unions (LO). Today approximately 60% of the working population are members of national trade unions and LO is by far the biggest single entity. An important aspect of the reconstruction of Norway was to secure a stable and predictable relationship between the parties on the labour market. With the Social Democratic Party in charge, the groundwork was in place for a tripartite structure. The Federation of Business and Industry (NHO), and the Federation of Trade Unions were invited by the ruling government to jointly discuss issues of common interest. These consultations were especially important in the initiation phase of the collective wage negotiation processes. In addition to this, the general relationship between the social partners on the labour market was more characterized by co-operative arrangements than hostility. The general climate was certainly in favour of management and union co-operation, with the government as the more or les neutral third party. This largely co-operative climate is probably one of the most striking features of Norwegian Work life.

On the other hand, this extensive co-operative structure has not ruled out conflicts, but it situates conflicting issues in a more general co-operative environment. It was unproblematic to have a functional co-operation even though traditional conflicting issues related to wages, benefits and work environment were present. This separation of the arenas for conflict and co-operation might be explained by the way the collective bargaining process takes place.

Every fourth year, the Federation of Business and Industry and the Federation of Trade Unions, negotiate the renewal of the general agreement that guides the relationship between management and unions at company level and the more overall relationship between parties, including how wage negotiations should be organized. The general agreement also has an appendix that deals with how the parties are encouraged to co-operate on enterprise development. This addendum is an agreement on enterprise development (HFB agreement), which spells out how the social partners at company level are encouraged to jointly create developmental processes. A major function of this agreement is the legitimisation of joint labour-management organization developmental efforts. The HFB agreement is handled by its own board, and will fund expenses related to initiate local developmental activities. This can for example be to cover the costs of running a first search conference aiming at shaping a common ground for joint activity. Such a conference can last for a couple of days, and the focal point for developmental activity at company level is jointly decided upon.

The negotiations for a new contract, starts quite routinely as the parties set up a negotiating meeting, after an internal preparatory phase both within the Federation of Business and Industry and the Federation of Trade Unions. As already indicated, at a preliminary stage the government will call for a preparatory discussion on the constraints and possibilities for the Norwegian economy related to the upcoming wage negotiations. At this stage, potential contributions from the government could be negotiated. This could include extended benefits in healthcare, social security or extended holidays. If this "conventional" negotiation process does not lead to a new contract, the parties are called to a public mediation process. This is the second stage. The public appointed mediator would now be in charge of the negotiations, and he or she is expected to actively shape the ground for new solutions. The conventional way of doing this is the present "sketches" indicating potential solutions. These "sketches" are often creative suggestions to balance key issues both for the employers and the management. The mediation process operates with a specific deadline, so the parties cannot use the mediation as a filibuster. The outcome of the mediation will either be a new collective agreement, or a strike or lock-out. The final possibility for the government to intervene is to pass a new law in the Norwegian Parliament, which has happened on rare occasions when key societal functions are threatened.

The Norwegian Economy is dominated by small and medium sized companies. There is hardly any single production facility that employs more then a couple of thousand workers. More typical are production sites that employ between 50 and 200 persons. The industrial picture is of course dominated by heavy reliance an the oil industry, but traditionally energy consuming raw materials have been important. Successful operation on international markets is dominated by niche products, often with an advanced technological content. In the geographically widespread country, there is no dominating industrial concentration. Raw material production has created many company towns located close to accessible hydroelectric power generating plants. In the South Eastern part of the country (near the capital of Oslo) there is a concentration of petro-chemical plants.

Another interesting characteristic of the Norwegian industrial landscape is the relative stronghold of two regional industrial clusters, both built on networking between small and medium seized companies. One cluster is located in the South-West and the other is to be found in the North-West. These networks combine economic activity with knowledge creation processes, having both a focus on money and on competence. The networks have risen from local culture and are well integrated into the broader local business and public activity. The South-West network is built around mechanical production in general, and its core element was how the different production facilities co-operated on joint knowledge development. The North-West based network had both a focus on knowledge development and on joint business, either as suppliers to each other or in joint ventures with a focus on serving market demands. Through this network a regional leadership developmental program was launched as an integrated element in regional competence development.

These regional networked economies have developed out of local needs and possibilities. Today it is clear how these efforts shaped the ground for a modern regional economic development, focusing on networking production systems combined with joint efforts in knowledge creation.

Enterprise Development 2000

The program has a long history of negotiation and recruitment of actors in order to create support for this program. A key networker in this process was Professor Bjørn Gustavsen, who managed to pull the interested parties together and get enough support to have it funded. The first official invitation to potential research groups was sent from the Research Council of Norway (NFR) on July 13, 1994. Fairly soon, four groups were granted module status, while the next three group had to live through hard and complex negotiations before they could enter the program.

Enterprise Development 2000 (ED2000) was planned as an action research inspired program to enhance organizational innovation processes in Norway. A detailed description of the program is found in Gustavsen et al. (2001). We will not go into detail here, but just give a brief outline in order to attract the reader's attention to the broader picture. The overall aim was to make Norwegian industry competitive on the global market. At the outset, a popular phrase in the proposal was to support "concept driven" change processes. The first program brochure in English states on the cover page: "Enterprise development 2000–Conceptually managed productivity development and organizational renewal in working life." This rhetoric faded gradually as the program became operational. A cornerstone, both in the program's developmental phase and in the operational mode, was the close co-operation between the Trade Union Council and the Confederation of Employers. This social institution of formalizing co-operation between labour market parties in participative approaches to enterprise development dates back to the aftermath of the first action research in Norwegian industry (Emery & Thorsrud, 1976, Herbst, 1977). In recent years this institution (HFB agreement)[1] has played a key role in participative modes of organizational change in Norwegian work life. The board of ED2000 had many key HFB players in addition to research and business representatives.

ED2000 became a regionalized program, where the seven modules were located in all major research sites in Norway.

The program eventually had seven modules in operation. These modules emerged from a negotiating process with a program board that was active in designing co-operation between research institutions. Two modules were located

1. The HFB (Employers-Workers Joint Action Program — Enterprise Development) agreement was negotiated the Trade Union Council and the Confederation of Employers in 1994. It the followed a former agreement installed in the 1980's. The HFB agreement is basically a joint effort by management and trade unions to mutually engage in enterprise development. This participative approach is supported by funds diverted equally from the trade union and employers side. If a company decides to engage in a participative approach to enterprise development, the social partners can jointly apply for funds to this activity from the board oversee this HFB agreement.

in the capital Oslo. The Work Research Institute, which is a state supported institution for research on work life, made up one module. The other Oslo based module was a combination of the Institute for Applied Social Science (Fafo) and the Norwegian School of Economics and Business Administration (NHH) in Bergen. The module had only one researcher in Bergen, while the rest resided in Oslo. Fafo was also responsible for the Fafo/NVF module located in the regional business environment of Ålesund. This module was linked to a regional learning network (NVF), and also co-operated with a network of regional researchers. In Kristiansand, Agder Research (AF) was responsible for the southernmost module. In the oil capital Stavanger, Rogaland Research (RF) was in charge of a module working on the construction of business networks. The Trondheim module was a co-operation between the Norwegian University of Science and Technology (NTNU) and The Foundation for Scientific and Industrial Research at the Norwegian Institute of Technology (SINTEF). Finally, the Tromsø module was linked up to the northernmost University in the world, and involved researchers both from Nordland Research (NF) in Bodø and from Fish Research Institution and NORUT Research, both located in Tromsø. As can be seen from the map of Norway, the modules pretty much covered Norway from North to South and from East to West. This picture ties in pretty nicely with the important regional perspective of the program. The program was intended to sustain business development in the whole country.

At the program level, it was a stated goal to create a national momentum for work life research, where the regional dimension became a clear political leverage for this type of activity. The national program had a superstructure where all module leaders met twice a year. The intention with these meetings was both to co-ordinate the activities, and to have an arena for professional discussions. It turned out that the basic function of module leader meetings was to support information exchange and practical problem solving. Only to a lesser extent did these meetings created a ground for intellectual exchange. The most important function was probably to make it possible for module leaders to get acquainted with each other. At first, the tone at these meetings was highly competitive, but as time went on larger areas of co-operation became visible. It made it easier to co-operate and compete at the same time, as this potentially could create a win-win situation. Co-operating on certain issues would enhance the competitive edge on others, and competition might enhance co-operation.

The changing program

ED 2000 was not a program that found its form from the first day of operation. Neither the program founders nor the involved researchers had a clear conceptualisation of what the essence of the program was and how it should operate. The first two years were characterized by negotiations between modules and board/ secretariat, making entrances into company life, creating relevant and acceptable roles for the researchers and finally creating a sustainable research praxis. All these processes revolved around the need for and the strong imperative to engage in developmental work with businesses "out there". This period could be labelled a learning process. For sure — the program was a learning program. Its mode of operation changed fairly much by "walking the road". ED 2000 as a program capable of redirection was not an important argument in the initial program memorandum, but, through a fairly unorthodox mode of operation by the board and secretariat, thus became an important feature that adjusted and developed the program quite substantially.

The researchers, the modules and the board/secretariat created roles that eventually integrated reasonably well. However, the complexity of this process exceeds the meaning of the simple term "learning". Usually, we conceptualise learning, and especially organizational learning, as a sort of straightforward process where the most challenging issues are to take on new modes of acting while letting older habits faded away (Senge 1990, deGeus 1997). This is a too narrow conceptualisation to describe the operational characteristics of ED 2000. Political controversies, differences in values and research paradigms, and the conflicting interests created, in addition to the conventional jargon of learning organization, created the dynamic that shaped the change processes in the ED2000 program. These aspects highlight some of the more problematic and undeveloped questions related to "organizational learning". In this book we intend to present histories of research on enterprise development that reflect a much more complex understanding of participative development than what can be understood as learning processes.

The process creating this book

The book revolves around these processes of development that shaped the program that was concluded in 2000. The book project is constructed as a participative writing process. The idea of this book was first launched during the module leaders meeting in April 1999 held in the city of Kristiansand and hosted by the Agder module. The first reactions were positive, and the editor (who also proposed to create the book) wrote the first draft of an outline. This was passed back to the participants shortly after the meeting, and within a short time the module leaders responded favourably. The board and secretariat of the program were equally favourable, and by the beginning of the year 2000, funds was granted for the book project. The potential authors had already met once during the module leader meeting in fall 1999. The first and very preliminary drafts were discussed at that meeting, mainly in order to get a first understanding of the development of the work in each module. Already at that time it was evident that this material was very rich and varied. No better ground could be found for the construction of a joint reflection process aiming at producing a book to communicate these insights.

The team of authors met for the second time in February 2000 in the town of Hell, some few miles north of Trondheim. Each participant was asked to bring a first draft of the module history. The meeting lasted for two days, and the main focus of the communication was to learn and discuss the individual module history in order to extract the main research and reflection issues. This was a collective process where all authors participated actively. The second stage was to develop the major themes for the reflection part of the book. Through an in depth discussion several themes evolved. The main topics were identified, and authors volunteered to start working on drafting outlines. These outlines were shared and discussed, and the authors teamed up to write the chapters as they appear in this book.

A second major event in the making of this book was a workshop where a group of seven authors participated. This seminar was held at Cornell University in August 2000, with seven researchers participating. The module histories were discussed, and based on this, the group embarked on the reflection process. A three day long discussion resulted in a new structure of the second part of the book. The present structure of the book results from the discussions which took place at this meeting.

The focused issues

Several issues emerged through the participative process that was described in the previous section. Through discussions in the author team, they were clustered around seven different themes. Each of these issues was subsequently made into chapters, each linked to a broader question. These questions are the nuclei for the reflection processes that are communicated in Part II of the book. In the following paragraphs the questions are presented, the relevant issues are given a brief introduction, and finally the link to the actual chapter is created.

A major question that is pertinent to raise, given that ED 2000 was a national program, is: Why create national programs involving a number of different stakeholders? One could imagine that running a research program in itself is a task of sufficient complexity, so why bother making it a national enterprise? The involvement of quite diverse modules, both with respect to professional background, experience in action research related work, and having a very different population of enterprises to work with, would obviously create a messy situation. First of all this would probably generate the most difficult situation for the board/

secretariat as they would have to administer and integrate quite opposing and divergent research activities. The generative question is accordingly: *What are the key issues at stake in constructing a national program for enterprise development?* In Chapter 10 "The changing program: Controversies and cooperation" — this question is placed under scrutiny. Questions about managing and leading the research program arise in this context. Can research programs really be directively steered or controlled? If not, how do research programs really develop?

ED 2000 aimed at creating a research praxis that was expected to closely link researchers to the ongoing business activity. This involved new demands on the participating researchers. Some of the involved researchers had a long history of working in action research programs; for others this was a novel experience. The issues at stake were diverse. The "hard-core" action researchers were faced with the challenge of transcending old modus operandi, whereas those who were unfamiliar with the demands for active, concrete, and constructive involvement in the field stumbled on other obstacles. An obvious, but not clearly stated aim of ED 2000 was to support the development of researchers that managed both active and constructive involvement and who had the ability to produce "scientific" work communicable to the community of fellow scientists and researchers. This transition involves the changing of the current research paradigm. The following question can accordingly be stated as: *Can researchers move beyond the paradigm created through their initial training?* In Chapter 11 "Creating new research practices" an answer to this question is sought.

The modularisation of ED 2000 was probably motivated by two separate factors. First, developing regional knowledge resources would potentially be helpful for local economic activity, and skills in enterprise development were considered to be important in that regard. Second, through linking regional actors closer to local economic activity, new and potentially fruitful cooperation between diverse professions might arise. Collaboration might be established between academic departments and research organizations, between researchers in separate professions, and between different strata in the higher education system. The potential underlying idea was that a regional setting would enable this process, simply because the willingness and the ability to experiment could be higher regionally, as the vested interest in professional disputes was less than in the higher status national institutions. An important question to raise is: *Does it makes sense to regionalize enterprise development?* Much of the work in ED 2000 was constructed around networking. The program itself could be seen as a networked system of researchers engaging in the same issues. Another important concept in the program was to develop learning networks. Our first question related to network issues is: *What came to be the characteristics of these networks?* is our first question related to network issues. The second question is: *How did these networks support enterprise development?* The answers to these two questions can be found in Chapter 12 "Networking as an action research practice".

One central argument in creating ED 2000 was to enhance the organizational innovation processes. The point was that the program through its mode of operation should increase the participating companies ability to innovate, mainly in terms of shaping new participative structures that outperform older organizational models. The essence is to investigate and to understand how participative approaches to organizational change might support the participating companies' ability to innovate. This lead to the following question: *Did the research program really promote and enhance innovation capability at company level?* This discussion is located to Chapter 13 "Enhancing Innovations — a Core issue of ED200".

An important value statement in the program has been the commitment to democratic change. Most of the underlying conceptual thinking behind the program (Gustavsen et al. 1997, Gustavsen et al. 2001) points to the importance of creating participative processes as a vehicle for change. The process conveys a democratic rhetoric that should be possible to trace in the activities of the program, both on company level, at the networking level and among the engaged research team. The multi-dimensional aspect of participative process, to include the research team and the whole program structure, seems to be important in order to genuinely be able to support democratic change. On the other hand, is it also self evident that all structures in business life, as well as in research, has existing power structures that are hard to overcome? Accordingly, perfect participative governance or participative research are utopian objectives potentially disconnected from everyday life. The question for research will accordingly be: *What are the challenges, possibilities, and limits of democratic change?* These discussions are found in Chapter 14 "Democracy, participation and communicative change: When democracy becomes a mean and not an end".

Finally, the fifteenth and final chapter of the book pulls the different threads together and communicates insights for action. The title is "Research on enterprise development: Lessons learned".

A guide to the book's lay out

The book has three sections. This prologue gives both an introduction to the participative way this book has been developed and it works out a first introduction to the ED 2000 program and its key research questions. In Part I, the individual developmental histories of the seven participating research modules are presented. The narrative is chosen as the format for the presentation. The intention is to write stories in the narrative form in order to give the reader a "flavour" of the processes that shaped the development of each research module. Our idea was to utilize the richness of the narrative form to be able to convey complex and dynamic stories. In Part II, the intention is to convey the collective learning on the core research question. The format of this section is to use the rhetoric and the language of the research report, connecting the empirically based reflections with theoretical linkages in order to convey our collective learning to the reader. In the epilogue the threads are pulled together, presenting a position on future action and research on enterprise development.

Part I

The emergent research program

Stories of research — learning from diverse experiences

Morten Levin

In this section we present the stories of how the program evolved, seen from where the action was. The intention is to create an understanding of this national program, through understanding how the involved researchers and the program board participated in shaping the direction and contents of the program. ED2000 was dualistic in its nature, combining a directive board with great local freedom. The demarcation line between what could be up to decided at a local level, and what was under the power of the board, was never clear. The board imposed certain demands on the seven participating modules, but it never exercised a strict controlling regime when the research was up and running. Given this overall structure it was obvious that local adaptation, creativity and initiatives would colour local activity. Those stories are what will be communicated here.

The modules had very different points of departure. Rogaland was the first module that got a green light to start research, and this module also managed to obtain substantial additional funding from other relevant resources. The two modules that Fafo were engaged in had to pass several obstacles before they were in operation. The module that was run in co-operation with NHH was created because of pressure from the board, while the Fafo/NVF module had to pass several phases of negotiation before grants were given. The Trondheim module and the WRI module in Oslo, both connected to the institutions that had initiated action research in Norway, also had to overcome a long struggle before the funding eventually was secured. The Tromsø module was included, as this university is central for Norwegian fisheries. Finally, the Agder module fought a hard battle to be included in the program, and after very effective lobby activities, using both the local business life and local politicians, entered the program one year after the first module was included. More than 40 researchers have been engaged in the program, most of them part-time, and not during the whole period. The core research group of 20 has been connected to the program over the whole period of operation.

What follow is seven stories of how enterprise development and research evolved under the umbrella of the ED2000 program. These stories are written differently. Some of the authors present the history of their module in a narrative form, while others lean more towards a conventional presentation of a research process. Despite the differences in form, the underlying idea is to give the reader an understanding of how the research and developmental work appeared in the different modules, providing a basis for understanding how a research practice has been shaped. The presentations both accommodate the individual writing style, and they also convey what the researchers in the module considered to be key issues in ED2000.

Chapter 2 is written by Bjørn Gustavsen, who was one of the key actors making ED2000 happen. He developed ideas of a national program on enterprise development, and he was able to enroll other actors in a network strong enough to get the project off the ground. Gustavsen tells this story as from his experience in this chapter.

The presentation of the work in the program starts with *the Work Research Institute* (WRI) in Oslo (Chapter 3). This module was considered to be one of the most important, as the research group at the outset viewed the program to be pretty much in line with the core activity at the institute. WRI had developed core concepts like dialogue conferences and development organizations, which were central in the vocabulary of the ED2000. By first being introduced to the work in the WRI module, the reader will get an understanding of both development organizations and dialogue conferences. This will provide a good basis for understanding the work in the other modules. The module had a very difficult initiation phase. Long and complex negotiations with the board took place before the module was up and running. Later the board intervened again to influence the leadership and the organization of the work in the module. The story conveys this difficult process of first conceiving oneself as the backbone of the program, to being a module that attracted more interest than usual from the board throughout the entire program period.

Chapter 4, "Filling the knowledge gap", is in stark contrast to the previous chapter, as it presents the work of the last module that entered the program. *The Agder module* started their work more than a year after the first modules got off the ground. Sustained lobbying from local politicians and the social partners on the labor market resulted in funds granted for local research. The module made its first entry into action research on developmental processes in business life. At the local level, this resulted in an effort to shape co-operation between consultancy like approaches and a more conventional social science research. These contradictory positions created both successful corporate interventions, but we also learned about the inherent conflicts that emerge when action and research are merged in a co-operation between different researcher and consultant roles.

In Chapter 5, the history of the northernmost *module located at Tromsø* is presented. Research and development activity were closely connected to the regional fishing industry. Participating researchers in the module came both from disciplinary orientated departments at University of Tromsø, and researchers with experience from applied research in the fishing industry. None of the researchers had any formal training or experience in action research. The work in the module started with a heavy focus on quality assurance systems, but it gradually shifted towards broader developmental issues. The researchers in the module struggled both to create co-operation between researchers from different disciplines, and to make action research work.

Chapter 6 "Fragile coalitions" is the story of the Fafo/NHH module, which was created as a consequence of the board's insistence on shaping a co-operation between these two institutions. Both institutions had displayed an interest in working with large multinational corporations in the perspective of trade union and management co-operation. The module was granted funding when they came up with a joint proposal. Five companies were enrolled in development coalitions where management and trade union representatives were encouraged to co-operate on enterprise development. Two coalitions broke down, while three survived and prospered throughout the program period. This story presents the of the Fafo researchers' side. This story is written in a format where the introduction is much like a conventional research paper, but the descriptions of the life of the coalitions approach a more narrative form.

Chapter 7, "Networking industrial development", communicates how the *Rogaland Module* managed to combine financing from ED2000 and external sources to almost double their activity. The Rogaland module was the first to formally receive the grant from the board of the program. Network and networking became their focus of interest. The research group had two approaches to their network activity. First, they supported the creation of a network in the region where the dominating offshore yard became the linking pin and driving force. The other activity was aimed at revitalizing a 40 years old industrial network, making the members take on new perspectives, among which participation was a key ED2000 issue. The chapter is written by two members of the local research team, and reflects on the modules' development as a collective group effort. Much of the energy in the writing process was focused on the actions, challenges and pitfalls in their networking activity both as "midwives" for the new one, and as "reformist" for the already existing one.

Chapter 8 is devoted to a presentation of the regional learning network in northwestern Norway. The Northwest Forum module was build around a management training program aimed at creating a professional leadership in the regional economy. The activity in the module was built around the network created through this leadership program and by involving different research institutions. Ph.d. students were both affiliated with the Norwegian School of Economics and Business Administration (NHH) in Bergen and the Norwegian University of Science and Technology (NTNU) in Trondheim. In addition, the module cooperated with local colleges and research institutions. The focus of the activity in the module was to create a knowledge bridge to international, national and regional knowledge organizations. The Institute for Applied Social Research in Oslo, together with the local network (organization) running the leadership development program, was responsible for the activity in the module.

Finally, Chapter 9 presents the work in the Trondheim module. This module had to work hard to get off the ground. The first two proposals were not accepted by the board of ED2000, and it was not until a perspective of creating a research praxis linking engineering and social science was introduced that money was granted. Trondheim is the Norwegian birthplace of action research in industry, and having to fight to get funded felt a little awkward for the involved parties. The module developed a strategy for in depth action research in three companies, but in addition an extended network for knowledge exchange and learning emerged. This network was operated and developed in a co-operation between actors from enterprises and the local researchers. In addition to this activity, the module also paid attention to making it possible for students at NTNU to learn how to participate actively in developmental work.

There is of course no common strong thread in the histories of the module. The diversity of both perspectives and modes of working was a characteristic trait of the program. Diversity, even though it was not flagged as a key feature of the program, turned out to be a trademark. The board had ideas of what the program should look like, and they used their influence to shape ED2000 in the desired direction. Still, the diversity emerged as a consequence of the structure of the local economy, as an effect of the professional backgrounds of the involved researchers, and the great variety in the professional platform of action research. Some of the participants had years of experience, while others had never worked as action researchers before. Given this perspective, ED2000 renders a fascinating story of how to develop skills and proficiency in doing action research in industrial settings.

Chapter 2

Creating a framework for enterprise R&D

Bjørn Gustavsen

Introduction

The research program known as "Enterprise Development 2000" (ED2000) began in 1994 as a joint initiative by the Norwegian Confederation of Trade Unions (LO), Norwegian Confederation of Business and Industry (NHO) and the Research Council of Norway. The main purpose was to explore the potential for increasing Norway's visibility and competitiveness in the global economy by improving the existing, unique co-operation between management and labor.

While the tradition of co-operation characterizing industrial relations in Norway was viewed as providing a good platform for the continuation or creation of productive and innovative enterprises, each of these groups, independently and collectively, recognized that the tradition itself might be in need of renewal and innovation.

Arising from this awareness, the ED2000 program included about 80 enterprises as "first line participants" and, indirectly, a much larger number as the result of network relationships. When counting the number of people working within the participating units, nearly 15,000 workplaces were involved in ED2000. Over 100 researchers, largely social scientists from the field that can be called "research on organization", were in contact with the program, half in a deeper and more lasting way. Of these, approximately 15 were doctoral students.

Since ED2000 drew to an official end in June 2001, the LO and NHO has undertaken a new initiative to broaden the activities started in "phase I".

The variety of approaches that could be taken in any effort where research is a main factor, made it necessary to agree from the beginning on the perspective of the research, and the role of researchers. Even though research is conducted in a program where change and development are major issues, the research approach may not be particularly influenced by the context. In this case, research can be compared to a hammer: it can be used for many different purposes but is not, in itself, much affected by these purposes. It has its own goals and criteria, forms of work, patterns of evolution, and so forth. From another, almost opposite, perspective, the research activity is part of a family of activities where the context determines which activity is mobilized and, in turn, the challenges to be confronted and resolved.

Given the specific nature of ED2000 as a development-oriented joint venture among social scientists, management and labor, a context-sensitive perspective could hardly be avoided. Emphasizing this perspective is important, not only to help understand ED2000, but to understand social research in general (Toulmin and Gustavsen 1996). Rather than free-floating reason arising from nowhere to create order and method in a chaotic world, research is seen as "reason from the inside"; reason that has to emerge as a response to a particular situation and its inherent challenges.

To understand the elements of reason that came to characterize the design of ED2000 and the challenges facing the researchers, it is useful to know a few details concerning the background and intentions of the program.

The evolution of ED2000

The roots of the ED2000 program date from the 1960s, when Norway was the site of a series of experiments on new forms of work organization. These experiments were developed by researchers in co-operation with labor, business and industry; a co-operative venture which came to acquire a dynamic of its own. The ups and downs of this co-operation through the years are described in Gustavsen (1996) and Gustavsen et al. (1998 and 2001).

In the early 1980s, the NHO and the LO made an "Agreement on Development" (HFB). In this Agreement the parties expressed their mutual wish for more dynamism and innovation among the membership enterprises, and offered some support in this connection: Provided the parties could agree locally on a joint effort, financial support could be given to conferences, projects and project co-ordinators. Criteria for what could be considered a "joint effort" were introduced, and all initiatives had to be approved by a body, such as a work environment committee or a co-operation council, with equal management and worker representation. Insofar as possible, the principle of *broad participation* was to be applied to these efforts. Broad participation was defined as "the active involvement of all concerned on a project level"; basically, the development and execution of whatever the local parties decided to do (for a presentation of the Agreement see Gustavsen 2001).

During the 1980s the Agreement was used primarily to support conferences where management and employees got together to discuss the challenges the enterprise was facing, and what could be done locally — and co-operatively — to meet these challenges. Most of the conferences were organized by single enterprises and support was given after a decision by a board established specifically for the purpose of managing the Agreement. To some extent projects and project co-ordinators were also supported, most of these on the level of the individual enterprise as well.

An evaluation, conducted in 1990 in connection with a revision of the Agreement, judged the initiative successful in terms of generating interest and discussion. Nearly 1000 decisions regarding support had been made, and several hundred enterprises had used the Agreement measures. The impact on each user, however, was judged to be modest. In many cases, there was little or no follow-up after a conference and only 20 to 30 enterprises could be identified where more substantial changes had occurred. As a result, the LO and NHO decided to strengthen the Agreement in several ways, including:

– Emphasizing the inter-relationships of labor and management co-operation, enterprise performance and overall patterns of value creation in Norwegian society.
– Encouraging the national unions and employer confederations (the members of the LO and NHO respectively) to develop initiatives within their own areas; in essence, expand their networking.
– Using resources or establishing partnerships other than those traditionally associated with the Agreement, the LO or the NHO.

One such partner was the research community, in particular, social science research on organization that could provide new insights on labor-management co-operation as well as other areas of concern such as work organization and networking. Even with this new awareness of the role research and researchers could play in the quest to strengthen the Agreement, it took several years before Enterprise Development 2000 could actually be launched.

One reason for the delay was the need for extensive discussion of this and other partnership options by the Agreement Board itself and broader circles in business and industry, labor and management. Despite the fact that there were previous examples of researchers working well with the parties locally, there was concern about the ability of researchers to communicate effectively with workers, to understand and actively use the agreement system, and to engage in the long-term process of developing new support resources in co-operation with LO and NHO.

Another reason for the delay came from the research side. The emergence of the concept for ED 2000 coincided with a major reorganization of all research types and groups in Norway. Ultimately, five different research councils were merged to form the Research Council of Norway. Each of these former councils was transformed into a division within the new council and Enterprise Development 2000 had to come to terms with two of them — the Division for Industry and Energy, largely oriented towards what is traditionally known as "applied technology", and the Division for Culture and Society, basically a successor to a former council for applied social research and social planning.

The research profiles of these two areas were — and are — radically different. The research orientation in Industry and Energy is towards practical success and user value. Research questions are dealt with in a pragmatic way. In contrast, the Culture and Society division carried with it the traditional social science debate on "good research" coupled with only a modest interest in user value and practical results.

Co-ordination

When ED2000 was launched in 1994, the program emerged as a joint venture involving four major types of interests and perspectives: those of the employers, those of the unions, those of a modern version of "applied technological research", and those of a similar version of "applied social research".

There were two mediating mechanisms: the Agreement on Development co-ordinating the labor (LO) and management (NHO) parties; and the Research Council of Norway, coordinating its own divisions. However, neither of these mechanisms could handle all coordination problems. As a result, ED 2000 became "four partite" as much as "tripartite".

In addition, each of the four major interest groups was, in essence, an umbrella over other parties, not always in agreement among themselves or with their leadership. For example, the LO and NHO each has a large number of members, national unions and employer organizations respectively, who do not necessarily see eye to eye on all questions.

The main goal of ED2000, which was strongly supported by all parties at the time, was to help Norwegian enterprises become more competitive in the global marketplace. More importantly, to pursue this goal, an orientation towards issues of organization was given priority from the start, departing from the Agreement on Development and the implied co-operation between labor and management.

Thus, with the idea of co-operation and broad participation as its foundation, ED2000 was expected to branch off into a broad range of themes and areas of exploration. These themes had different contexts, in that some pertained to goals and others to means but, in general, each could be placed into one of three categories:

- Work organization and other issues pertaining to "internal organization".
- Enterprise "improvement systems" such as total quality management, business process re-engineering, just-in-time logistics, etc.
  Many of these systems were or were about to be introduced into the operation

of many Norwegian enterprises, raising questions, for example, of how well a system worked in a Norwegian context and if such programs could be implemented in ways consistent with the historical patterns of co-operation between labor and management.

– Relationships or issues of common concern between and/or among enterprises; for example enterprise clustering, networking, regional economies, etc. The LO and NHO felt strongly that there was now a need to think in terms of some kind of cluster or network formation of enterprises. This concern seemed to stem from the period when enterprises related individually to the LO-NHO Agreement, making it necessary to handle a large number of cases.

There was a strong feeling among the parties that new elements of organization had to be introduced at many levels. If Norwegian enterprises were to be supported, one-by-one advances would be hard to make. This concern prompted an in-depth discussion concerning the platforms for networking; in particular, whether or not these platforms should be industry-based, or go across traditional industry boundaries and be more pluralistic.

The initial preference was for industry-specific networks, primarily because labor-management relationships were historically organized according to industries, and it would be easier to carry on this tradition than to introduce a new principle. However, there were also indicators suggesting that networks of enterprises from different branches might be more fruitful, at least for certain purposes. Nordvest-Forum (Chapter 8) had been founded by this time and seemed to make advances with a heterogeneous membership. Experiences from Sweden also gave some support to the idea of heterogeneous networks (Gustavsen 1997). Ultimately, the discussions ended by keeping both options open and letting events decide.

The themes of the program were generated as “opportunities” rather than “musts” because it was important to all four interest groups that participants at the local levels should determine decisions regarding agendas and methods. In Norway, the notion of “participation” as applied to labor, management and the workplace means not only that employees should participate in whatever happens on the workplace level, but also that the local representatives of labor and management should themselves decide what is to happen. In other words, they should be neither forced nor persuaded to accept an agenda from “outside”. Whatever they choose to do should be a natural response to local circumstances. However, it was generally agreed that once the local participants committed themselves to a certain development agenda, ED2000 researchers could make contributions, including contributions that could lead to a change in this agenda. Nevertheless, such changes should emerge from joint learning in a development context, not because research suggests a “better answer” on day one.

Funding and organization

From the experiments in the 1960s, enterprise development in Norway has been recognized as a national need. Thus, when it became a reality, Enterprise Development 2000 was accorded full recognition as a research and development program, national in scope and purpose.

Financial support was secured by the Research Council of Norway from its Division for Culture and Society and its Division for Industry and Energy, from the LO and NHO, and from funds remaining from a previous program.

A program board was established, with two representatives from industry (one of whom was to chair the program), two from research, two each from the LO and NHO, and one from the Norwegian State Fund for Economic and Regional Development (SND). The Research Council never participates in program boards but has observers present during the meetings. The secretariat consists of one program coordinator, two representatives each (different from the board members) from the LO and NHO, and one research director. In this structure, it is interesting to note not only the strong position of labor and management, but also their sharing of operational tasks.

Despite the fairly broad framework, the research purposes for which the funding was to be used were quite clear, but the board needed to determine how and with whom the research should be undertaken. The Research Council's Division for Culture and Society, for example, had a tradition of funding "research-driven" programs for the purpose of doing analyses and writing reports. Within the Division for Industry and Energy, the tradition was to give funding to a business or industry and let it determine the direction and/or use of the research; in other words, a user-driven program. To conduct ED 2000 as a traditional social science program was out of the question since the whole initiative emanated from a need to step-up the speed and quality of development processes in Norwegian enterprises, and no one thought that purely making more studies could do this.

While a user-driven approach seemed to be the most viable, it also raised some serious questions:

- Were the enterprises sufficiently well oriented in the world of research to be able to define fruitful projects and pick the right partners?
- Would the program be able to make itself known to the enterprises in the first place?
- Even if the enterprises would be able to define projects and pick research partners, what would the situation be like for the research partners?
- Would a more or less haphazard group of research institutions get a more or less similar portfolio of projects for each to handle as well as it could?

– Insofar as certain ideas — such as the notion of networking between the enterprises — are to be pursued in the program, who should pursue or construct them (for instance build the networks)?

With these issues in mind, the board saw, from the beginning, the need for a developmental perspective on the research side as well as on the enterprise side.

The board was also hesitant to place totally on itself the entire burden of deciding what enterprises to support. In particular, the industry representatives wanted an intermediary to work between the board and the enterprises, get into closer contact with the enterprises, and make a judgment on development potential based on more familiarity than what would be possible for the board.

Ultimately, discussions of these concerns gave rise to what became the core characteristic of the program: the idea of a *module* — a combination of researchers and enterprises working together within some kind of common framework. By creating several research modules, geographically spaced, the program ensured for itself a set of "local agents" that could work on behalf of the program to contact enterprises, develop projects and inter-enterprise co-operation and, in general, accept responsibility for the fieldwork of the program.

The program aimed, in principle, at offering the research groups funds to cover about half of their costs associated with participation in ED 2000. The program wanted the research groups to mobilise other money as well, to avoid a complete reliance on ED 2000 and a likely termination of module activities when the program came to an end.

No economic support was offered directly to the enterprises. They were expected to cover their own costs, or, in other words, they were expected to use ED 2000 to initiate and strengthen development activities that would have had to be undertaken anyway, and not to use the program as a source of financing. Enterprises who wanted direct economic support could turn to the LO-NHO agreement on development, in many cases also to the State Fund for Economic and Regional Development (SND). Many ED 2000 users also did. Even in these cases, however, external support was marginal compared to the economic interests generally involved from the side of the enterprises.

Broadening participation

While the program was originally intended to have a budget of approximately NOK 25 million per year for a five to seven year period, the actual budget was slightly more than half this amount. This made the number of modules a critical issue. On one hand, the limited resources would offer reasonably comfortable frame conditions for each module only if there were not many modules. On the other hand, the need to find as many partners throughout the country as possible, and to involve as broad and varied a range of enterprises and other participants as possible, required numerous modules, therefore less money for each.

The decision to create seven modules — stretching the resources to their absolute limit — reflects the importance the board placed on making the ED2000 program as far-reaching as possible. Clearly, despite the fact that this decision would create some extra burdens for the research groups, the board did not want to launch "just another program". Though there were various predecessor programs, in Norway and elsewhere, which had been reasonably successful in operational terms, most failed to establish a more permanent platform for the broad use of research in enterprise development. With its strong links to the labor and management confederations, the board, from the beginning, had to use its mandate in such a way that a stronger, more tightly organized coalition could be formed among labor, management and the research community — a coalition with the potential to continue beyond ED2000.

To achieve this, the board established broad participation in the program as the most important prerequisite. Unless a substantial number of people, businesses and industries could be included, research would not be recognized as a useful, long-term resource for enterprise development.

After reviewing a number of examples of individual success stories, where single enterprises had made major strides, but few others had been convinced to follow suit, the board had limited faith in the value of these "star cases" to generate wide-spread interest. Rather, it was thought necessary for the program to communicate directly to a broad range of enterprises and workplaces. In this context, "communication" meant actual involvement in the program, and not simply information about the program.

Finally, given Norway's geography (vast), population (spread out and small), and fairly traditional industrial base, the board felt a regional approach, rather than building a single, national coalition, would be more appropriate and, potentially, more robust.

To compensate for the strained economic conditions to which this focus would expose the modules, the board made the following commitments:

1. To level out annual budget variances in order to provide as much stability as possible. (In addition to a narrow budget, the program was also vulnerable to more or less unpredictable annual variations.)

It seems unusual that a development program such as ED2000, with direct involvement from the labor and management, could not get adequate economic support in a country that is one of the richest in the world. Furthermore, the country has a strong need to create new industries to supplement the predominant oil and gas exports and, even more importantly, to increase productivity to counter the growing shortage of labor. As ED2000 began, however, little attention was given by the government or industry to a "post-oil economy" and no other framework existed to explore new initiatives. The chief labor-market challenge was full employment, not the critical labor shortage that was starting to reveal itself, but was not really recognized.

The budget of the Research Council of Norway is decided year-by-year by parliament, and too often research is at the losing end of the political infighting. In the beginning, ED 2000 could not muster sufficient political resources to avoid such forces. Towards the end of the program period and in the context of a new initiative, the labor and management confederations have become much more vocal, publicly and politically, because they see ED 2000 as sufficiently successful to be worthy of stronger support. Before the program proved its worth, however, it was not possible to generate a stronger political mobilization, and thus stronger financial support, from the program's participants.

2. To refrain from using annual variations in the grants offered each of the modules as a steering mechanism.

Even with a planned duration of seven years, money had to be allocated annually and there was a certain tendency in research management to use this as an opportunity to send signals to the recipients. The board wanted to ensure that each module had optimal opportunities for developing its own partnerships and forms of work. However, since budgetary variations were not used to evaluate the modules, the program came under pressure to apply other means of evaluation.

3. To support and encourage cooperation and exchanges between the modules.

The board wanted to give each module access to a broader discourse than what was possible solely within each module. Although this measure actually came to bear fruit — as evidenced by this book — it was also hampered by a lack of adequate resources.

4. To secure a better institutional platform for workplace-oriented research if ED 2000 is sufficiently successful to legitimate this move in the eyes of the membership.

Today we know that the board actually fulfilled this commitment. The initiative called "Value Creation 2010" is unfolding as this is being written. As indicated by the name, if this initiative is successful it implies a 10-year time horizon, more money and more differentiated activities in what could also be called "ED2000 phase II". Among other aspects of the new initiative is a special doctoral program for researchers with a background in action- and development-oriented studies. (For a short presentation of the new initiative, see Gustavsen 2000a.)

Addressing potential tensions

Broadening the scope of participation in ED2000 made it necessary for the board to acknowledge the fundamental, often long-standing, differences inherent in the perspectives of each of the four major interest groups — labor, management, applied technology research and applied social science research.

Despite a history of established cooperation among and between these interest groups, there was still not a full merger of interests. Significant, identifiable distinctions existed, for example, between:

- Management and employers, workers and unions.
- National headquarters and local branches of the NHO as well as the LO.
- A labor relations system with historic roots at the peak of Norwegian national development and one in the process of globalization.
- The basically inward-oriented research traditions of the social sciences and the results, user-oriented traditions of technological research.
- The descriptive-referential approach preferred in most social research and the development, action-oriented use of this kind of research implied in ED 2000.
- General, well-known, well-tested approaches to development and decentralized, variable innovative systems.
- Labor, business and industry in the old economy and in the new.

Although these contrasts in perspective could be easily identified in the early phases of ED2000, it was far more difficult to predict what the coalitions and participants would look like at the end of the program, five to seven years ahead in time. It could be assumed that the four major interest groups would be present in approximately the same way but it was far more difficult to predict what coalitions would be of critical importance when the program was drawing towards a close. For instance: Would the cooperation between the LO and NHO have been strengthened in a smooth and conflict-free way, or would new problems have emerged as a result, for example, of the ongoing process of globalization? What would the relationship be between the technological and pragmatic orientation of the Research Council's Division for Industry and Energy and the tradition of discussing "research qualities" pre-dominant in the Division for Culture and Society? Even if, by the end, ED2000 could be seen as successful, this was no guarantee that it would be worthwhile using it as a platform for further activities. Naschold (1993) makes the point that there is some degree of inward orientation in the Scandinavian countries in this field, and a corresponding neglect of what happens internationally. There is little reason to celebrate a 10% increase in productivity if all competitors can note an increase of 20%.

The board found it difficult to prepare for a discourse on the "scientific merits" of ED2000. This was considered the responsibility of the modules, and it was difficult to predict the kind of discourse that might occur. The social science community, for example, continually criticized the use of "action research" or similar involvement from research. To bypass this critique, the board located the ED2000 program under the umbrella of the Division for Industry and Energy rather than Culture and Society. Administratively, although the divisions were jointly responsible for the program, ED2000 could be attached to only one of them. But, by aligning the program with Industry and Energy, the board ensured that ED2000 would have a pragmatic context where user value would be at the core and sent a clear signal of its own preferences.

The board took two other, pro-active steps to minimize or eliminate the potential for disunity. First, it established an international benchmarking group to continuously assess the current status and direction of ED 2000 against developments in other countries. The group was formed with representatives from Sweden, Germany, Finland, the United Kingdom and France, having backgrounds in research and development. Second, the board determined that the LO and NHO representatives in the program's secretariat should spend as much time as possible in the field and, in this way, monitor membership opinions as closely as possible. These actions firmly anchored ED2000 to two points of comparison and reference — international trends and membership opinions.

The research environment

For the research groups that came to join the program, this was what they joined as it looked in the beginning. As a context for research and associated development it was perhaps even more "constructivist" than what is common for efforts of this nature. If we look, for instance, at the Work and Technology program in Germany (Fricke 2000 with further references), each project, of course, needs to fit into a specific enterprise context and to create a forward momentum. It is also quite clear, however, that "conventional research" is expected to do this to a greater extent than was the case in ED 2000. This can also be said about a parallel program initiated by the Ministry of Labor in Finland (Alasoini & Kyllønen, 1998), and most of the one dozen or so programs run from the early 1980s to the middle 1990s by the Work Environment Fund in Sweden. The orientation in these programs is often associated with the notion of "design" while ED 2000 is associated with the notion of "dialogue" (Naschold 1993, Fricke 2000). Even a design-oriented program needs dialogue with the users to enter their world and to maintain flexibility in the way in which the design ideas are implemented. However, the basic set of ideas concerning what "new reality" to create is often expected to exist before the user contact is established.

In ED 2000 there were no workplace-oriented design criteria on the program level. If any of the research groups wanted to put such criteria up front in their efforts they were free to do so, but, from its very conception, the program emphasized the need to listen to the users. The goal was always to phase in the efforts of the research in as seamless a way as possible in user-driven processes.

In fact, establishing dialogues was one of the pre-defined elements in ED 2000. A *dialogue*, in the sense of ED 2000, was no elementary "you and I" conversation relying on psychodynamic or similar processes. The dialogue between the parties within each enterprise was part of a broader, social dialogue with history based in the agreement system, as well as in strong traditions. As demonstrated by Jurgen Habermas (Habermas, 1981/84) and other communication theorists over the last few decades, this is a field of its own, not least in research terms, and not an appendix to other issues such as, for instance, the design of a production system.

Even with an orientation towards constructive dialogues rather than predesigned solutions, a very strong communication theory could easily become problematic as well. One reason design theories need to be implemented with care and caution is, among other things, to avoid "foreign ownership" of workplace ideas and hierarchies, passing over, for example, local leaders or influences (Leminski 1997). In much the same way, highly elaborate theories of communication can easily function as communicative straitjackets, rather than as opportunities for liberation. At a program level, every effort was made in ED2000 to ensure that the basic rules of the original LO-NHO Agreement on Development were applied, leaving further elaboration to the research groups.

Given these variations in the nature of research itself, and the decentralized nature of the program's organization, it is reasonable to wonder why ED2000 was developed as a research program involving researchers, as opposed to a program using other types of business-, industry- or labor-specific resources such as consultants.

It is common to assume that the main focus of research must involve "large questions", "universal reason" and/or "big leaps forward". Research is something we call upon when facing the deepest challenges of culture, society and economy with a need for a completely new understanding that can deal with the challenges in one sweeping movement. As pointed out by Toulmin (1990, 1996), among others, this kind of role for research is mostly an illusion. Instead, researchers actually plod along, facing numerous smaller questions and coping with them as well as possible. To see how well they have coped, researchers cannot avoid looking at the consequences of their efforts. In most cases, these are on a practical level. However, if research generates findings, for example on "innovation systems", it will be hard put to maintain credibility if no innovation ever comes out of the proposed system.

The ED2000 board recognized from the beginning that research resulting in great but unapplied claims was not needed as much as research that was able and willing to enter the processes of everyday life, characterized by numerous challenges and, generally, incremental changes. Although each step forward may be limited in meeting these challenges, it does not mean they are easy to make. A small challenge and a modest step ahead can demand as much in terms of work and intellectual effort as a big one. The difference is that, by definition, a small challenge is one of several challenges rather than the one and only challenge. Dealing with it does not mean a great leap from being in deep trouble to being on top of the world but, if the small challenge is not addressed, success in other areas may be in vain or impossible. To move forward, many steps need to be taken simultaneously.

In a sense, these points are trivial and acknowledged by many, but the demands they impose on research are less well recognized. Even in a world where numerous researchers on organization write about "networks", they write as if a single researcher can grasp and understand everything there is to know about networks. Insofar as there is a need for research on networks, however, it is likely to be because an individual is unable to independently study the field and develop adequate perspectives. Contributions from many points of view are needed, and no single mastermind can pull them all together. Rather than assume they are the only ones able to grasp an idea (or worthy of doing so), researchers must recognize they are simply one of many participants in any endeavor. Then and only then will they recognize that the main task of research is not to make grand theory, be it about networks or anything else, but to use its knowledge, competence and methods to help sort and understand details within specific contexts and, in the end, help work out solutions to a broader range of problems and challenges.

In a development coalition such as ED2000, it is vital that research and each of the other interest groups try to see the links between the different processes and solutions, draw the benefits of interaction, and create an overall movement, where all elements work together to form a forceful whole. The essence of ED2000 in general, and the associated research in particular, was the belief that this movement must grow from the bottom up, and not be imposed from the top down, before any dialogue among participants could begin.

Ups, downs and successes

The ways in which the various research groups that came to join ED 2000 related to these points of departure emerge in the narratives that follow. Many issues that arose for the modules as well as for the program are discussed, including some of the decisions made by the program board during the span of ED2000 from 1994 to 2001. For any program of this scale and scope, there were, of course, many expected and unexpected ups and downs. Ultimately, however, the framework for Enterprise Development 2000 as it was conceived in the beginning and continued to develop, gave the program its character and set the course for the modules that formed its foundation.

Since this is written after most of the assessments and evaluations of the program have been completed, it can also be added that the program turned out to be a success. Almost all of the participating enterprises developed their patterns of labor and management interaction, with special emphasis on broad participation, and with strong positive results to show for the effort. Some of the most notable carry-over effects of improved participation can be directly related to improvements in productivity (about 80% of the cases), quality (70%), product development (45%) and marketing (25%), just to mention some of the dimensions that were measured. For a presentation of all the studies used in the process of benchmarking the program see Gustavsen, Finne and Oscarsson (2001, pp. 39–70).

Perhaps the most important positive result of ED 2000 was the establishment of a series of new social relationships, not only between researchers and enterprises but also between and among these groups, the LO, the NHO and other private and public economic entities. This spirit of co-operation and trust was evidenced, for example, by the active participation of the LO and NHO, and the decision by the board to use the personnel resources each could provide in the field. Representatives from the LO and NHO were in direct contact with their members to acquire independent information about project activities, their impact and their value. Even if researchers could have investigated these issues, the findings would hardly have carried the same legitimacy.

The value of "development coalitions" in the Norwegian economy was significantly strengthened by their visibility in the ED2000 program. The discussions that follow, however, will show there was no uniform pattern to these coalitions and no universal model of any kind that was applied across the table. Each coalition involved a unique set of participants, challenges and processes — in fact, a reflection of a modern economy. Now, each coalition must continue to contribute to (it is hoped) a dynamic economy, not by adopting uniform or independent solutions but by working together — inside or outside Enterprise Development 2000 — and contributing its best rather than contributing the same.

CHAPTER 3

Developing development organizations

Øyvind Pålshaugen

Introduction

The launch of Enterprise Development 2000 was welcomed by the Work Research Institute (WRI) in Oslo, especially by the group of researchers to which I belonged. The general reason for WRI's appreciation of the new program is easily understood. For almost thirty years WRI had been occupied with action research in industrial work organizations and other organizational structures. Over these years the institute had experienced many ups and downs, and ED2000 was considered a journey upwards. As a condition for financing work-related research projects, ED2000 required that these projects be closely connected to or, at best, parts of practical development processes in the enterprises. In other words, ED2000 could rightly be considered as a program to enhance action research — the primary purpose of WRI.

The reasons my group was in high spirits were more specific, best reflected by our name — The Enterprise Development Group. The connections between the group and ED2000 were more than the similarity of names. For more than a decade we had been undertaking action research projects in collaboration with enterprises that were carrying out development projects, with financial and institutional support from the Norway's two main labor and management organizations, the LO and the NHO respectively. Thus, our research practices and relationships were already well established in what was to be the institutional framework for the research projects of ED2000.

Not only our research practices, but also some of our theoretical achievements were re-confirmed by the launch of ED2000. For example, the memorandum defining the main goals, objectives and strategies of the ED2000 program included a comprehensive overview of the requirements and conditions which the various research groups were expected to meet. It was encouraging to find that the first of the six goals that were also to serve as the foundation for six corresponding topics of research was "To establish or further the development organizations in the participating companies"; a goal which has guided our work for many years.

To understand our excitement on this issue, however, it is important to know that the concept of "development organization" was first explored by our group at WRI in the late 1980s (Pålshaugen 1998). We began working with the concept in connection with practical enterprise development projects in progress at the time, grounded in task-oriented organization theory. In essence, the concept was derived from the distinction between operational tasks — those performed throughout the value chain — and development tasks that attempt to improve the conditions for performing operational tasks. The development tasks are not directly linked to the value chain. If operational tasks create added value, then development tasks are those aimed at increasing the opportunities for creating this added value. This distinction led us to conclude that an enterprise should try to organize changes in improvement and development tasks just as carefully — and thoroughly — as they organize changes in operational tasks to improve performance and productivity. In other words, optimizing an enterprise's operational organization requires optimizing its development organization, and vice versa.

This does not mean that an enterprise should necessarily spend a lot more time on improvement and development tasks. On the contrary, a development organization is created to implement the tasks more effectively. Instead of organizing this kind of work on an ad-hoc basis, development organization was conceived as a means for carrying out a strategy of continuous improvements. To produce positive results in reality, not just in theory, development organization requires the active participation of a broad spectrum of employees. Their firsthand experience is essential to design a strategy of improvements and to determine the best ways to implement it.

Of course, those of us who had developed this concept were impressed with it. We had to admit, however, that not many others seemed to recognize its potential. Researchers who appeared interested, seemed to misunderstand or not understand a concept that, to us, seemed quite simple. Often the concept of development organization was regarded as a synonym for "project organization", regardless of type of tasks normally associated with a "project". As a result, the distinction between operational tasks and development tasks was often blurred and the strategy for improving the performance of development tasks on a practical level was out of sight.

What we thought in the beginning

In our view, the launch of ED2000 was a consolidation of the kind of action research strategy that had led us to the formation of development organization as both a practical and theoretical phenomenon. Since a primary task of research is to gather new knowledge and insight without repeating itself, we viewed our future action-research tasks within the new (and better) framework of ED2000 as the next phase in the evolution — the transcendence — of our own approach. This meant that we had to be innovative on both the practical and theoretical levels.

On the practical level, we recognized that the conditions for further development would depend on the enterprises with which we were to collaborate, and our relationship to them. The prospects for creativity on the theoretical development level were even more open. First, it was not possible to know in advance what new knowledge the research might provide, even though the kind of knowledge being pursued was guided by the general research themes outlined by ED2000 and our own research strategy.

Second, and perhaps less obvious, was the fact that we could not know beforehand what research projects or experiences would be worth writing about afterwards. The review of any research endeavor depends on the nature of the experiences, their interpretation, and an ability to distinguish new knowledge from existing knowledge (Pålshaugen 1996). In other words, there are pieces of the research puzzle that must be kept open until the very end — the process of writing. At least, that's what we thought.

What we did in the beginning: establishing collaborative relationship

Regardless of the theoretical outcomes of our projects within ED2000, or the way in which they might be used, the theories had to be generated from the enterprise development projects. These projects were to be carried out in collaboration with enterprises, and in accordance with the guidelines of co-operation established by the LO and NHO in the "Agreement on Development" (summarized by Gustavsen on page 18). Thus, the projects had to fulfill the criteria of the enterprises, the research sector and the Agreement that had, as its general objective, "to add and increase value by means of broad participation."

If the main concern of the enterprises was that the collaboration with research should be practical and useful, to us at WRI the main concern was that the development work should **not** be carried out in ways that were of only local interest. Beyond the practical work of fulfilling the various local conditions and objectives, we felt we had an obligation to acquire insights — both practical and theoretical — that could be generally applied in settings other than those in which they originated.

Potential tension between local practice and general knowledge is exactly what our action research strategy was designed to deal with, and is one of the main reasons why a vital part of our research approach involves organizing dialogues among participants at all levels. As a result, the ED2000 focus on dialogues was crucial for us and, together with the criterion of broad participation, became the basis for the formation of the locally generated development organizations.

Another potential for discord was the difference between enterprise interests in the short-term, and our research interests in the long-term. The process of forming and effectively using a development organization definitely required co-operation for more than just a year or two.

To determine if long-term, mutually beneficial collaborations were possible required more than simple dialogues with representatives of the management and unions at an enterprise. Even if these initial dialogues were important, what really mattered was that we were invited afterwards to make a practical contribution to their development work. Clearly, to establish long-term collaborative relationships both the research community and the enterprises had to be willing to invest time and resources in a somewhat risky undertaking.

At WRI, we did not have to start the work of seeking enterprise partners from scratch. We already had a number of such relationships from earlier projects, particularly in the technology industry. In fact, we had good working relationships with LO and NHO representatives in this sector as well as a number of enterprises. It was natural, then, that the board of ED2000 asked us to approach several enterprises participating in a program, partially funded by the Research Council of Norway, for the combined development of technology and productivity.

Of the 20 to 25 enterprises we contacted by letter or in person, 15 invited us to discuss the prospects for ED2000 collaboration in greater detail. Almost without exception, our distinction between operational tasks and development tasks was welcomed during these dialogues. The enterprises had no difficulty recognizing that development tasks had to be organized in parallel with daily operations, in order to ensure that the operational needs and conditions were met successfully and cost-effectively. It seemed as though both labor and management were, to some extent, aware of the differences, but never quite succeeded in pursuing the practical consequences.

To acknowledge the practical potential of a development organization was one thing, but to actually take a step in this direction was not that easy. The possibility of doing so was discussed in only a few of these initial dialogues. In half the enterprises we visited, the management had no interest in broadening the participation in development work. For those managers who took some real interest in trying such a strategy, a number of questions needed to be answered before the concept of development organization could be considered more seriously.

These questions pertained primarily to the ways in which a local process of enterprise development based on broad participation would be initiated, implemented and sustained. The questions posed required practical answers, and usually served as the point of departure for a dialogue between the enterprise and us. When the enterprises asked us to return for further discussion, we could be even more specific about designs and working methods that had the flexibility to meet local needs (Engelstad 1996; Pålshaugen 1998). Generally, these were variations on the idea of "dialogue conferences"; a working method based on carefully organized dialogues among the participants of the development project. Eventually the dialogues lead the participants from discussions of relevant steps to collaborative actions implementing them. Dialogue conferences, in theory and practice, are an important part of our action research strategy. It was natural, therefore, that they were also the focus of our earliest contacts with enterprises expressing interest in ED2000.

Dialogue conferences — beginning to move from talk to action

Long before ED2000 was conceived, our research at WRI determined that dialogue conferences were one of the most comprehensive, effective ways of minimizing the ever-present underlying tension between those defending local practices and those seeking change. In almost any context, with or without reason, those seeking change are perceived as "outsiders" imposing change for the sake of change, rather than encouraging change to better meet the local needs. Our motives, as researchers, are often viewed with such suspicion, as are, unfortunately, the motives of upper or new management.

The crux of the dialogue conference, as we designed it, is a general format that can be shaped and adapted as necessary to fit the local context. Participants from an enterprise create most of the *content* of any dialogue conference, within a general framework created by us. In this sense, a collaborative relationship also becomes complementary.

Typically, a dialogue conference lasts two days. The number of participants ranges from 20 to about 100. Depending on the size of the enterprise and other local conditions, the participants may be a representative selection of employees and managers at the enterprise or everyone may participate. Formally, a dialogue conference consists of group discussions with plenary sessions at which important results from the group discussions are reported. In the course of a conference, four to five sets of group discussions and plenary sessions are completed. The group discussions are, by far, the most crucial. The plenary sessions serve as devices to link the parts to the whole. The plenary is a forum for mutual information (from the various groups) rather than a forum for lengthy discussions.

In general terms, the "variables" influencing the design of the group discussions are the topics to be discussed and the composition of groups. Each of the group discussions is designed according to the general principles of task-oriented organizational theory; in this case, the topic to be discussed is considered the task to be confronted. The composition of each particular group in the discussion of each particular topic depends on who should participate in the process of solving a particular task and how best to ensure their cooperation. This task-oriented perspective is also infused with perspectives on organizational democracy. Those who are most directly affected by solutions to the tasks or topics under discussion should have an equal and legitimate voice in finding the solutions. The essence of any democracy is that no single participant can be the only judge of what is best for the all. The overall task of a dialogue conference is the same as that of any democratic organization and, it is hoped, any work organization: to identify topics of concern and work together towards mutually agreeable solutions.

From the 15 enterprises that invited us to an initial dialogue on enterprise development, 10 were interested in getting a firsthand impression of what a dialogue conference might be like. In the end, five of these wanted us to collaborate with them in arranging a dialogue conference as a way of mobilizing support for enterprise development projects and getting them started. These conferences turned out to be quite different in purpose and format as well as in content.

The most demanding challenge was to design a dialogue conference in collaboration with a "high tech" enterprise that had been given the go-ahead to create a prototype of a New Sea-target Missile (NSM) having the characteristics of an unmanned aircraft. The original construction team of 90 engineers increased to approximately 200 in the final stages, all with graduate degrees in engineering. The total timeframe for the project was 8 years.

Analyses of earlier, similar projects using sequential steps from model development to production had shown that a concurrent engineering approach might be significantly more cost-effective. Thus, to minimize costs for the transition from developing the prototype to producing the missiles, the NSM project was organized to take advantage of the benefits of concurrent engineering. Our challenge was to design a dialogue conference that would help improve the understanding, acceptance and implementation of this approach.

The technological and organizational dimensions of the NSM project were quite complex. The organizational form was a kind of matrix created by the axes of the enterprise's line-organization and the NSM project-organization. This consisted of roughly 30 subprojects, clustered in six main project groups. To ensure that members of each of these subprojects understood the place and importance of their work in the total NSM project, the project management needed to provide some schematic descriptions that would show the interconnections of the subprojects developing the various components and emphasize the customer's very stringent requirements. In addition to these *process descriptions*, the project management needed to establish a so-called *system process* to handle the multitude of internal dependencies and interfaces of the missile.

The complexity and magnitude of the NSM project demanded that everyone involved have an understanding of not only the technological challenges confronting them but also the organizational interdependencies, if they were to have any chance of successfully fulfilling their parts of the total task. To cooperate in solving the technical problems, the engineers had to work by means of technical specifications. To cope co-operatively with the organizational challenges, they had to work mainly by means of language. Therefore, part of our task was to organize a dialogue conference to help the participants use language to create common, or at least overlapping, pictures of their respective parts of the NSM project.

To do this, we designed the first three sessions of the conference to examine the socio-technical dilemmas of the NSM project. We decided upon this approach after casual conversations with a variety of NSM project members from all levels and subprojects. As is often the case, however, the topics discussed in the remaining two sessions and the composition of those discussion groups were determined "on location" as natural consequences of the earlier discussions.

This dialogue conference involved 90 NSM project members. In the first group discussion we briefly presented to the participants the four main reasons why the NSM project was organized the way it was. Then, they were asked to discuss the main problems and challenges this way of organizing might create in the course of the project. This was chosen as the "kick off" topic because it was clear, at this early stage of the project, that there was no general understanding of the organizational form of the project, and no commitment to this form.

In the second session, the strategy of concurrent engineering was the point of departure. The main, general parameters of a process of concurrent engineering were presented and the participants were then asked to discuss what they considered to be the critical parameters that had to be specifically addressed in practical ways in the process of organizing and implementing the project.

In the third session (which ended the first day) the general benefits and features of a concurrent engineering strategy were discussed along with some of the group-based work forms that might be required. Based on the existing process descriptions, the participants were asked to suggest the types of working groups and processes they felt should be applied in the NSM project, to ensure the success of the concurrent engineering approach and the project itself.

Among other objectives, the group discussions on the first day were intended to create or confirm a commitment to the project strategy by appealing to the creativity of the individuals and the design teams. The second group discussion worked well. The third did not; largely because the process descriptions available at that point in the project plan were incomplete or imperfect. Thus, in the fourth group discussion that opened the second day, the participants were asked to discuss what they considered to be an optimal *overall* process design.

In the fifth and last group discussion, participants were asked to suggest better ways of organizing the work, after the conference, of creating new or better process descriptions and ensuring that those people most concerned with these descriptions would have a say in this effort.

The views contributed by the conference participants regarding the challenges of effectively organizing the NSM project, coordinating the working methods and improving the process descriptions by broadening the input had been turned into constructive contributions. In addition, the dialogue conference helped engineers at all levels better understand the need to take advantage of the benefits offered by a concurrent engineering approach.

While these improvements in understanding and attitude are important on a personal level for the participants, a dialogue conference is also designed to generate outcomes on a practical level. Most important here is the last session of group discussions. In the NSM-project conference, for example, the last group discussion laid the foundation for decisions to be made *after* the conference, regarding the development and improvement tasks to start working on, and the way these efforts should be organized.

In designing the NSM-project dialogue conference, four types of tasks were given priority:

- Working out ways to improve the *system process*.
- Working out ways to improve many of the singular processes and incorporate these improvements into the *process descriptions*.
- Organizing discussions for members of the NSM project who did not participate in the dialogue conference; focusing, in particular, on improving their understanding of concurrent engineering and the reasons why this strategy is appropriate for the project.
- Implementing in the enterprise as many as possible of the proposals for improvement identified at the dialogue conference.

Organizing these improvement tasks in parallel with the processes by which the missile prototype was to be created, constituted the initial form of the local *development organization* of this enterprise.

In the early phase of enterprise development, a dialogue conference creates the foundation for the first version of the local development organization. In the course of our collaboration with this high-tech enterprise three more dialogue conferences were held. Each had different participants, purposes and outcomes. The form and content of the development organization were constantly revised to better fit the priorities of the current development and improvement tasks as they were identified.

The purpose, format and outcome of a dialogue conference vary as an enterprise itself continues to develop and, of course, from enterprise to enterprise depending on the type and history.

For example, in collaboration with a more traditional industrial enterprise producing lamps for the retail market, we designed a dialogue conference to create the foundation for a development process that would result in a more flexible work force and reduced production costs. Participants included managers from all levels and shop stewards from all departments. In accordance with the management's strategy only 25 employees participated from a total workforce of 110. Management preferred to involve the workers in only a limited number of development tasks that might be emerge from the dialogue conference because these tasks had to be defined in cooperation with the local union.

One project group was established to work with competence development and another group was assigned the task of refining the procedures of adjustments in the production process. These two groups constituted the main part of a limited development organization at this enterprise. Among other obstacles, the groups struggled throughout the period of our collaboration to find the time and resources to work with the development tasks.

In contrast was our experience with an engineering enterprise, producing special fittings for utility vehicles (buses, trains, ambulances, etc.). We had collaborated with this company for several years; it had already established a rudimentary development organization on the basis of an earlier dialogue conference. The second dialogue conference, now conducted as part of ED2000, was aimed at reorganizing the departments of various support functions such as construction, maintenance, warehousing, etc. in order to integrate each department into one of the four profit centers of the enterprise. Thus, the dialogue conference was regarded as part of the development organization; *that is*, as one of the tools to be used for identifying development tasks that might, at any time, be given priority within the development organization.

At the other extreme in the spectrum of acceptance, a dialogue conference arranged in collaboration with an enterprise producing military equipment resulted in the top manager's expressed desire to terminate the collaboration with us. Middle management and the union were eager to continue the collaboration in an effort to come to grips with the various development tasks identified at the initial dialogue conference. While the top manager appreciated the commitment to future development tasks that resulted from the dialogue conference, he did not want to be compelled to use the proposals when deciding the development tasks to prioritize. He later admitted that he had wanted the conference to create more of a "feel good" atmosphere among his work force, from which he could benefit when making organizational and staffing changes. As this manager later learned, this is **not** the rationale for a dialogue conference.

In the course of 1½ years under the ED2000 umbrella, our gradual, confidence-building approach recruited five enterprises that signed a letter of intent for long-term collaboration with us on enterprise development. The conditions for collaboration were clearly stated and in accordance with the goals of ED2000: the local needs of the enterprise had priority; the practical steps to be taken should also be of general interest; and participation, based on dialogue and interaction, should be as broad as possible.

In addition, the letter of intent confirmed that the enterprise was responsible for the practical progress and content of the development project, while our task as researchers was to provide the relevant practical means and strategies required to facilitate the development process. It also stated that any research publication written as a result of this collaboration should address the research community, and any other documentation of the project was the responsibility of the enterprise itself. This point was made to emphasize the importance of presenting something new to the research community, rather than simply a review of something already widely known.

Differing points-of-view and expectations

From our point of view, the time and work we had spent in creating the relationships with these five enterprises for the purpose of the ED2000 program was quite successful. The letters of intent were signed not only because of an interest in or agreement with the intentions of ED2000, but also because the enterprises were able to see, firsthand from the dialogue conferences, some potential in this approach to enterprise development projects. To us, the letters of intent acknowledged that both the enterprises and the researchers had passed the "initiation" tests and become partners in practice. We knew, after years of similar experiences, that establishing such trust was an essential precondition for the success of any long-term action-research project

We also knew that establishing trust between labor and management within an enterprise was just as crucial as a development project based on broad participation. Management, union members and other employees are almost always sceptical about entering into this type of project. Therefore, at the beginning of a project, it is very important that they share experiences that give them the confidence to work together, and prove they can do so effectively. A dialogue conference is designed to provide a forum for these kinds of experiences, and we had succeeded in convincing at least four of the five enterprises with which we had been working of the value of such meetings of minds.

Of course, we could have wished that the number of enterprises wanting to collaborate was greater. We knew from previous experience that any collaborative effort can end abruptly, and we couldn't afford to put all our WRI research eggs in one ED2000 recruiting basket that totally consumed our resources. Furthermore, our basic research practice was based on the premise that our primary task was to support the creation of better practices in enterprise development and, in the process, increase theoretical understandings. As a result, we assumed that the task of "industrializing" these practices and methods would be mediated as specified in the LO-NHO Agreement of Development and other institutions already part of the overall infrastructure for supporting enterprise development.

In fact, all the action-research projects of the WRI Enterprise Development Group during the last decades have been conducted from the strategic point of view that the Group was part of a greater infrastructure supporting enterprise development based on broad participation. Thus, from our perspective, the practical means for broad participation had to be general, in order to make them generally applicable. To a great extent these practices depend on dialogues, and experience has shown that the extension of these practices to other enterprises is generally not achieved by simply sharing information or insights. Even the extension process involves some degree of dialogue, and in the last ten years the Agreement on Development has given the LO and NHO greater responsibility for initiating forums for these kinds of dialogues. Initially, we saw ED2000 as having similar responsibilities and, in any case, our research group had neither the resources nor the institutional foundation for creating such forums.

Once these forums were created, regardless of how or by whom, we regarded them to be arenas in which we could contribute our experience and expertise from other collaborations with local enterprises in the quest to help extend the now-proven practices to others. For us, then, the point was to try to acquire knowledge and practices that would be worthwhile taking into other arenas. However, even though an increasing number of enterprises showed an interest in involving the employees in enterprise development, there were still major deficiencies in their competence and capabilities that reduced the likelihood they would actually carry through with their intentions. We felt one of the reasons for these deficiencies was a lack in the practical means and theoretical perspectives available. From this point of view, we were rather confident that in the course of the first 1½ year of ED2000 we had succeeded in starting to develop development organizations in these five enterprises.

We soon learned that the board of ED2000 viewed our efforts quite differently. Given our long history in action research on enterprise development, the board expected us to recruit many more than five enterprises in this amount of time. From its "total program" point of view — to ensure that the program would be as broad in scope and participation as possible — the board was less concerned about the quality or sustainability of the research relationships we had worked to establish, than about the quantity and diversity of the relationships.

In addition, some board members regarded ED2000 as a program to advance *reforms of research* as much as reforms of working life. From this perspective, the objective was to bring social research in closer and more collaborative relationships with enterprises and, simultaneously, stimulate greater communication, cooperation and integration among the researchers and research groups in this field. More specifically for the Enterprise Development Group, this focus seemed to support merging us with another group at WRI, the Process Industry Group. This group was also engaged in action research in collaboration with enterprises, but most of its work was in the oil and process industries. From the program board's perspective, integrating the groups would mean that the ED2000 module at WRI would include a greater number of collaborating enterprises and, thus, an expansion of our module's relationship to a wider range of business and industry, labor and management.

As the leader of the Enterprise Development Group, I was not quite convinced of the synergy benefits of such an integration. Though in many respects the practical means and the theoretical perspectives pursued by the Process Industry Group were similar to ours, our strategies were quite different. We felt an integration of the groups could result in a "disturbing" process rather than a process distributing ideas. Viewed from the outside, however, the similarities were more striking than the differences, especially to the ED2000 representatives from the LO and to the confederation's representatives on the board at WRI.

Ultimately, mediated by an initiative from the research director of ED2000, we began the integration process. Progress was very slow, however, and eventually strained the patience of the ED2000 board, to such an extent that it issued an ultimatum to conclude the merger of the two groups by the end of the year (1996) or lose further financial support from ED2000. The deadline was met and the two groups were totally integrated; an event that, in retrospect, marks the end of the beginning, but by no means the beginning of the end of our participation in ED2000.

Towards a new beginning

After the reorganization and enlargement, the Enterprise Development Group represented sustainable relationships with a number of enterprises in several industrial sectors, including technology, oil and processing industries. To the satisfaction of the ED2000 board, the participation of a larger number of enterprises was ensured, and we could now concentrate on the quality of these research-to-enterprise relationships. In particular, we were able to focus our efforts on those enterprises already seriously engaged in broad labor-management participation. Thus, the demands by the ED2000 board to merge the two WRI groups resulted in improving conditions for the pursuit of our primary research tasks and the challenges of publishing the results.

The details of these research achievements — both practical and theoretical — are, and will continue to be, presented in numerous publications (Gustavsen 1998, 2001; Pålshaugen, Qvale, Engelstad 2001, etc.). One result for our now-expanded research group at WRI may not be discussed as thoroughly, but is no less significant: ED2000 enabled a number of research groups to enter the field of action research on enterprise development, encouraged their expansion in the area, and/or reinforced their already existing research activities.

As mentioned at the beginning of this chapter, the most obvious reason for the WRI Enterprise Development Group's early embrace of the ED2000 concept, was that we considered the program a way of extending the use of action research in the field of enterprise development, and to do so by working with labor and management, the LO and the NHO in a format as partners, not adversaries, in the collaboration.

Far beyond this, however, the achievements made by **all** research groups involved in ED2000 represent not only an extension of the number of researchers and research institutions in this field, but also an improvement in the quality of our work. We have gradually come to this realization in a way that has also served as a kind of challenge to the way we conceptualized our own role and research strategy at the time ED2000 was launched.

For many years prior to ED2000, action research in Norway was the domain of researchers from WRI plus the Institute for Social Research in Industry (IFIM). The researchers at IFIM had close ties to WRI and the action research approaches were not too different. Both groups were well aware that a variety of approaches existed and could be applied to research on enterprise development. Nevertheless, this remained an awareness in theory, not practice, because there were few practical examples of such action research carried out from a really different approach. ED2000 totally reversed this situation by enabling a number of different research groups to enter into a number of practical projects on enterprise development, each using different approaches, but all within the same institutional framework.

The assortment of projects conducted by the many ED2000 research groups has helped us all understand that research and development on enterprise development can take on a number of different forms. We have learned that this form is not determined by any single factor, such as conditions at the local enterprise, the topics of the development process, the research approach and so forth, but rather by the differences created by the local combinations of all such factors.

It is exactly these particular combinations of factors which create the need of each particular form of R&D-project performed by each of the modules. In this way, through the experiences we have made, the real plurality of the field has come to the fore as a *practical* situation, not only as a theoretical horizon.

This new plurality in the field has contributed to a better understanding of our own role. We have experienced that if the action research projects at WRI should contribute also to the reform of work life this can not be done only as an effort to expand and improve our own approach. It is necessary to enter into dialogues and forms of cooperation with other research approaches on the premise of a kind of mutual acceptance of both the legitimacy and the necessity of pluralism in this field.

Both the researchers in the different research groups and people working in other parts of the infrastructure to support enterprise development have had some chance to experience this pluralism in the course of ED2000. These experiences have made it easier for all to acknowledge the *complementary role* of the different research approaches. It has also become easier to realize the complementary role of other actors within the institutional framework to support enterprise development, like the regional infrastructure, the parties at the branch level etc..

Thus, the institutional framework and the organizing of ED2000 have enriched our experience of in what ways the various relationships between the different actors and institutions to support enterprise development is complementary. Of course, the real 'test' of the quality of the support given to enterprise development by any of the actors within the infrastructure, is the practical impact these efforts have in the enterprises. That's why no particular research approach not any particular institution within the infrastructure can claim to be the most effective one *in beforehand*. From this it follows that the 'mechanism' of enhancing and improving the contributions from the various actors within the infrastructure has to be one of *dialogues* between them, on the basis of the collaborative relationships to enterprise development each of the actors are involved in.

In the course of the run of ED2000, a certain number of such dialogues was organized. Needless to say, we experienced these kind of dialogues as being rather rudimentary and fragmentary. However, by some occasions, for instance the conferences for all the researchers of ED2000 and in the seminars which have been organized around the production of some anthologies, where researchers from different research groups have participated, we experienced fruitful discussions on this topic. Nevertheless, by means of these conferences, meetings and other more or less ad hoc-based communication and exchange of experiences in the course of the running the ED2000 program, we gradually made the experiences I have tried to tell of.

These experiences indicate that for a future research program, it will be of great importance from the very beginning to create a kind of infrastructure for dialogues to *improve the infrastructure in accordance with the different kinds of experiences made at the enterprise level.* Of course, these kind of dialogues can not be pursued on behalf of others. They have to be undertaken by some of those who actually make the various kind of experiences at various places and levels in the course of the run. The question of how to organize these kind of dialogues have to be figured out in one way or other by those who participate in them. The way of organizing them of course has to be subject to continuous improvements. Thus, in the end we seem to have learned that the distinction between operational tasks and developmental tasks may also be applied to research programs: In addition to the operation tasks pertaining to the running if each of the research projects, it is also necessary to organize the development tasks pertaining to improvement of the common infrastructure of these projects at the program level.

Chapter 4

Filling the knowledge gap

Harald Knudsen and Hans Chr. Garmann Johnsen

Capturing the nerve

In addition to co-authoring this narrative, we have shared responsibility for the Agder module of ED2000. The challenges of this discussion and our project are, undoubtedly, similar to those faced by our ED2000 colleagues in each of the other ED2000 modules and projects: identifying and distilling the threads of common concern that connect people — all having different perspectives, philosophies, and expertise resulting from different sets of theories, personal values, desires, and intentions — with one another.

An excerpt from one of our working journals reflects the depth of mutual commitment and trust required from all participants in the program willing to take the risks and confront the challenges.

> Our research leader for the project, OB, called about 10.00 am, reporting that he was at the steel plant yesterday and had talks with the plant director, the shop steward, the personnel and logistics manager, and a lot of other people. OB used first names for all of them and most were known to me from previous meetings. He explained, "The shop steward called me late last evening, about 10.30, and we talked again this morning. He hadn't slept too well and, frankly, neither had I." I asked, "Is he up to it; is he ready to go on?" "I think so", OB answered, "but it's really tough. The old climate of distrust *sits in the walls*, as they say at the plant. And it's not easy for a shop steward to go for real participation and cooperation when most of the rank and file still believe in confrontation and tough negotiations."
>
> I told him I could understand these concerns but asked "what about you? Do you really believe the plant manager can handle it? Are you sure that it's not just another game? What about his position in the management team? Does he have the necessary authority to get the other managers to cooperate?"
>
> "I hope so", said OB. "I am quite convinced that he himself is serious, but it takes a god-like authority to make the rest of the bunch conform. Some of these guys never even go out in the factory and they have repeatedly told the workers that their recommendations are not wanted. All technical problems, for example,

are to be solved by the engineers; all administrative matters are to be settled from above, and so forth. Basically, the messages are 'We leave you alone, you leave us alone' and 'we have the power.' So, how can you change that? Of course, they are not all the same. Some of them are actually quite eager to invite participation."

I expressed my concern, "If you invite somebody to trust someone, you have to be reasonably sure they won't feel deceived afterwards. I mean, if the shop steward decides to continue with our project, he will really be taking a big risk. Of course, the worst would be if the plant manager were playing games. But it's almost as bad if members of the top management team are being arrogant or if they are unwilling to co-operate, share information and give the teams a share in their power. If that happens, the shop steward is dead meat! He will be the Chamberlain of the steel plant. A fact which I am sure he knows and is probably why he called you so late last night and so early this morning."

"You're right; that's exactly how it is and he knows it."

"So what did you tell him?" I asked.

"I told him that no one in this world could give him the kind of guarantee that he really needs, but that I would support him with all my personal integrity and whatever my word is worth. I told him that if the top leadership team fails to deliver, I would share the frustration and the blame. I told him I will confront them but I won't be the only one doing so, the plant manager will react in the same way. I also told him that what we need now is not an affirmative answer on the whole ED2000 process, but an indication of their willingness to continue the process."

"I like that", I answered. "Without you, the project wouldn't have one chance in a thousand. Call him up again and tell him that you have spoken to us, and that we are also part of this — if the support of a college professor and a researcher makes any difference!"

This conversation took place in February 1998. It is an understatement to report that our ED2000 project had turned out to be a bit different from what we had originally expected.

The first round of bidding

In early 1994, the Agder Research (AF) learned that a new, national work-relations research project was being framed. AF wanted to be part of it. As a separate research institution, however, AF was too small to compete, and joined forces with Agder University College (HIA). Working co-operatively in this coalition, Hans Christian Garmann Johnsen, a senior researcher at the Agder Research, served the project as an active researcher and, for most of the time, administrative leader. Harald Knudsen was the "fronting scholar" and formal research leader of the Agder team, hired on a part-time basis from Agder University College.

The project agenda called for new perspectives on work relations, and action research focused not only on the quality of work life, but also on efficiency and competitiveness. It called for co-operation between researchers and major companies in the region.

The AF and HIA together brought in specialists on organization development, innovation, internationalization, corporate strategy, and systems thinking. The team produced an application in which all these perspectives were put into an overall frame of learning and improvement. Numerous companies were also contacted, 15 of which decided to participate in the project. The application also had the support of the leading business network in the Agder region, the "Competence Ring South".

When it turned out that the ED2000 board did not grant the funding, members of the Agder team felt hurt, and a loss of pride. As time went by, both the AF and AUC groups got busy with business as usual. The potential of ED2000, however, was never out of mind. Eventually, the Agder leaders met in Oslo with representatives from the Trondheim module (which had also been passed over) in an attempt to co-operate in seeking a share of the ED2000 budget. But, the attempt failed — the specialists on co-operation weren't really able to co-operate! Despite these setbacks, the Agder leaders did not give up the quest; they continued to work systematically to secure funding for the proposed research. They contacted the regional offices of the LO and the NHO and obtained the local support of these two organizations which, on the national level, were an integral part of the program. They also mobilized the "Competence Ring South" network, contacted political insiders in the Research Council of Norway and sought support from others in the field of work-life research.

Gradually, the team was able to move Agder into a more favorable strategic position. A decisive element in this strategy was to contact the Rogaland module and suggest co-operating in the research. The Rogaland module had focused on the introduction of modern management concepts, such as Total Quality Management (TQM) and Business Process Reengineering (BPR). Their research objective was to study the impact of such concepts in a Norwegian work life and business culture. By co-operating in the pursuit of this objective, Agder and Rogaland would provide a broader platform for research and a greater sample size for conclusions. (Unfortunately, as will be seen, the Agder companies did not go for such a "concept-driven" development process.) In June 1996, as a result of strong lobbying efforts by AF combined with contacts in Rogaland, particularly Rogaland Research, the ED2000 board requested a new application. This application was successful and funds were granted to the ED2000 Agder module.

A “lutefisk” dinner

By the time our proposal was accepted, the Agder module was over a year behind the other ED2000 modules in getting started. Furthermore, we had to have several meetings just to re-establish the AF/AUC coalition and the Agder module team. All of us were, at the time, part-time participants. We had discussions on action research, on communicative action, participation and work life. We also tried to form a common theoretical and ideological platform — a task that proved to be not so easy. There were differences of opinion regarding the real core issue of the project: Was it the application of ready-to-use management concepts (TQM, BPR)? Was it the development and application of AF’s homemade analytical tools and systems? Or, was it trust building and the human side of participation?

The ED2000 module leader meeting in Stavanger, in October 1996, was a turning point. Again, an entry from our module’s working journal (Harald’s) summarizes the crossroads the program seemed to be at.

> By October 1996, I had become sufficiently involved with our module team to see the differences of interests, ambitions and orientations that were present in our home base.
>
> The two-day module leader conference in Stavanger was, in my case, an important moment of truth. Most clearly, the meeting brought home the impression that the other modules were, to put it mildly, still rambling, although very busy with their “impression management”. It seemed to be important to give the impression of efficiency and motion, while, at the same time, voicing the problems of getting the work done.
>
> Several modules had received negative evaluations of their first-year effort. Getting bad grades is never fun and living with a threat of having your funding cut off is decidedly less so. I decided I wouldn’t want the Agder module to end up in the high-risk category.
>
> A long discussion focused on the importance of benchmarking. The ED2000 program needed an objective evaluation of the effort from an outsider. However, a questionnaire put together by the benchmarking group was effectively massacred. It seemed that one of the benefits of being a year late in getting started was that we in the Agder module hadn’t been pressured to administer this questionnaire among our business partners.
>
> There was also strong agreement among the leaders that ED2000 had a responsibility to investigate the role of women in the work place and the challenges of cooperation in women-dominated work environments. But, there was an even more overwhelming agreement that nothing could be done in this area since all ED2000 money was already committed to predominantly male environments. (At this point I felt a certain guilt, since the resources of the Agder module as yet were not committed and since I knew that our effort, in line with the others, probably would end up saying rather little about issues important to women.)

> However, at the dinner in the evening of the first day of the conference, I sensed a somewhat different spirit. While I am being a bit facetious about the negotiations during the day, I am serious about the dinner. Excellent "lutefisk" from Voss, chased with equally excellent aquavit from Loiten and beer from Tou. More importantly, after the often heated debates of the day there was an atmosphere of open, honest exchange. A group of dedicated researchers sitting together, tasting good food and drinks, and voicing their opinions about ED2000 and its board, to be sure, but also about philosophies and issues related to participation, communication, ethics, and enterprise development. I liked it! And I was drawn to the project.

We cite this (and other) personal experiences partly because, as the Adger module developed, it became more and more apparent that individual involvement, experiences and style had a decisive impact.

From a theoretical perspective, we started with the traditions of work-life research, participation and action research, and we adopted a Habermasian perspective of communicative action, including the practical tool of *dialogue conferences*. We believed that a good dialogue conference could be a wonderful tool for putting issues on the agenda. We also believed, however, that the real work would be a longitudinal process of building openness, trust and involvement, and of handling setbacks, unruly emotions and differences of opinion — elements that pass before and after the Habermasian communicative action.

From a practical perspective, we realized that balancing two only partly overlapping "ideological" orientations among the Agder team members required a great deal of diplomacy, especially from the module leaders. AF, for example, had a strong drive to develop practical tools for intervention and change but there was also a fairly strong reaction against the systems- and control-driven organization. The two orientations, however, were definitely overlapping and all members of the team would argue that we needed both systems and involvement. Nevertheless, it was clear there would be differences of preferences, priorities, and approaches.

Getting started

During the first months of the project, we prepared for our presentation to the business community and for signing co-operation contracts with individual enterprises. Our first presentation conference was held in January 1997. Of the 50 companies invited, more than 35 attended. In addition to presenting the Agder ED2000 module and inviting enterprises to participate, the shop steward from Siemens, Trondheim, gave a talk about their experience with self-managed work teams. A representative from the ED2000 secretariat gave a presentation on the goals and scope of the national program.

The presentation conference was deemed successful, in the sense that there was a positive atmosphere and a nice group of attentive listeners from the business community (top managers and some union representatives). However, only one company responded directly by inviting us to visit and talk to a broader base of employees before it would consider signing a cooperation contract. After several weeks, an agreement was signed with this enterprise (a high-technology, defense-oriented company) but it dropped out of the program before the process really got started.

During the spring of 1997, we visited a number of enterprises and co-operation contracts were signed with seven. One of these seven also dropped out after several months. The remaining group of six included two factories from the processing industry (later referred to as the steel plant and the chemical plant), two companies from the service industry (one hotel and one grocery chain), and two companies from the public service sector (telecommunications and energy). In each case, the ED2000 projects were scheduled to start by August 1997.

Responsibility for a project was generally given to the researcher who had "sold" the co-operation agreement. Most of the research teams consisted of two people — the person who had finalized the agreement with the enterprise and a (usually junior) partner. However, other members of the Agder module team took part in various phases of the projects and in different roles (as interviewers, process observers, trainers, technical experts, etc.). All together, 13 people were part of the module team between 1996 and the year 2000, with a maximum of eight people involved at any one time. Once a project's research team was defined, the next step was to establish an "in-house" project team specific to each enterprise.

The first practical task of the research team was to conduct eight to twelve in-depth interviews, analyze the results and review them with the in-house project team. About half of the interviewees were selected by management and half by the labor union. Usually, the results of the interviews were presented as a strategic SWOT analysis of the enterprise, emphasizing the strengths, weaknesses, opportunities and threats that were identified. As a result of these interviews, three areas of interest and/or concern were selected as main themes for the dialogue conferences

To "sell" the co-operation contracts, we defined a list of standard services that would be included as project activities. In addition to conducting the preliminary interviews and dialogue conferences, and analyzing the feedback from them, we offered to administer simple versions of the AF "customer barometer" — indicating customer satisfaction and loyalty — and the "internal-climate barometer" — indicating employee satisfaction and loyalty. We also offered to pay the fees for two people to participate in leadership training seminars arranged by the Kristiansand Management Institute (KMI) and for two days of KMI tailor-made, in-house leadership training for twenty people. Finally, we offered 50 hours of consulting, mentoring and meeting services.

Dialogue conferences were mandatory in all projects but the selection of participants varied somewhat. Normally, about 50 people, representing all groups in the enterprise, were invited to participate. In the case of the hotel, the CEO and the union agreed to start in one division of the organization. In the case of the grocery chain, two stores were selected.

At the dialogue conferences, the research team highlighted findings from the initial interviews. Group work, focusing (for example) on the gap between "what is" and "what ought to be", was followed by a plenary session to present and discuss the results. These questions and comments, in turn, defined the substance of the next group-work session focusing, for example, on the need for change. A summary plenary session and dinner concluded each conference.

The conclusions (often in the form of flip over pages that gradually papered the walls of the conference rooms) of the group work and plenary sessions were reviewed and summarized in a report from the research team to the in-house project team. The in-house team would study the report, examine the critical comments, and explore a number of the ideas generated by the work groups for changing and improving attitudes, strategies, processes, communication, and so forth. Ultimately, the in-house team would make a list prioritizing the suggestions for change.

Compiling this list marked the completion of phase 1 of a project and was essentially the same in all Agder-module enterprises. Phase 2 included taking action to make the changes and implement the improvements. Not surprisingly, this phase differed a great deal among the enterprises as a consequence of the difference between the questions raised at the dialogue conferences and the kinds of priorities listed by the in-house project teams. Also, it was in this second phase that the "systems first" versus "involvement first" orientations came to play an important role.

The Agder module adapted a method of intervention that combined Norway's tradition of co-operative participation in the workplace and the emphasis on communication within this tradition, with ideas taken from modern research and business strategies, as well as ideas from more fundamental pragmatic philosophies and personal ethics.

Project scenarios — Adversaries, advocates, advisors

During the summer of 1998, a young doctoral student from Bergen was invited to take a critical look at the status of our projects. His analysis concluded that our progress (or lack thereof), and the depth of change brought about by the ED2000 effort in the individual projects, reflected the kind of business the enterprise was in, the type and level of union involvement, and the nature of the history of this involvement. For example, the two projects from the processing industry, as well as the energy company, were put under the heading "comrades in conflict" — reflecting strong traditions of union involvement. The two projects from the service industry were described as "hostages and apathy" — reflecting the tradition of weak unions and lower levels of competence. Finally, the telecommunications company was described as "administrators in harmony" — reflecting a minimal level of union involvement and the strong position of administrative managers.

From crises to cooperation

In the two processing industry projects, the ED2000 research teams had to cope with classic, strongly polarized labor-management environments. The steel plant, for example, went from one crisis to the next, and was plagued by the company's long history of union-management conflict. Despite this history of confrontation, however, the plant had solved some very fundamental technological problems and by 1997 was a profitable operation.

At the time of the dialogue conference in October 1997, conflicts concerning a profit-sharing/bonus system, redundancies and possible outsourcing of maintenance activities, were still quite visible. Thus, the main themes for the dialogue conference that emerged from our previous interviews were: trust building and team building; responsibility and power; real participation and involvement.

While the dialogue conference was successful, problems materialized soon afterwards; among other things, the in-house project team failed to follow up. In the period following the dialogue conference, the internal climate was rather cold. Only the push of the research team kept the project alive. It would be an overstatement to say that there was a continuous dialogue, but at least there was occasional contact between the researchers and the shop steward, the plant manager, and key members of the staff and the union. While the exchanges between the groups and the individuals could hardly be called "communicative action", at least there were some exchanges.

In January 1998, however, the union decided to freeze the process. In a letter to the Agder module research team they expressed the concern that only company goals were being considered and nobody in top management cared about the goals and interests of the union. A period of intensified contact followed. Our research team had to use every trick of the trade to get the process back on track. Two overriding objectives emerged:

- The union saw a chance to get rid of the threat of outsourcing.
- The plant manager and the top management team saw a chance to rationalize production and add a new furnace, without expanding the work force. The development of self-managed work teams was seen as an instrument for increased production efficiency.

Finally, in late February 1998, after numerous discussions similar to the telephone call highlighted at the beginning of this chapter, and a great deal of personal mentoring, the plant manager stated explicitly that he was no longer committed to outsourcing maintenance work. The project was back on track.

Since then, there have continued to be many ups and downs, but the combination of persistence, personal mentoring, training sessions, committee work, analysis and planning, trust building and the establishment of a new steering committee with real top-level responsibilities, has slowly added momentum and increased co-operation. Since the spring of 1998, the steel plant's vision has been "Together we will make our company the best". The slogan today, "Best 2002", means that both labor and management are working co-operatively to make the company the most productive of its kind in the world by the end of 2002.

An unexpected nose dive

Although also in the processing sector, the start-up phase for the chemical plant participating in the Agder ED2000 module was less marked by conflict. The CEO was very active in informing groups of employees about visions and goals, both for a new IT communications system and for a new production unit. Also, the dialogue conference was seen as very successful, perhaps more positive and productive than in the steel plant. The research team was very optimistic about the future of the enterprise development process at this plant.

From this glowing beginning, however, things turned very gray. A difficult wage negotiation process took place during the spring of 1998 and the workers felt that top management was not really listening to their demands. Several groups of mid-level employees felt the same. Even worse, the union felt that key people in the management team were not making any attempt to implement the ideas or embrace the philosophies that emerged at the dialogue conference; in particular, sharing information, improving contact and cooperation in personnel management, building trust and creating a cooperative atmosphere.

On the first of July 1998, the second-in-command of the union board announced in a letter to the Agder research team that he was resigning from the in-house project team, because "the company shows no intention of taking the viewpoints from the dialogue conference seriously." The letter effectively marked the end of the ED2000 project at the chemical plant.

What went wrong? If we look at trade backgrounds and industry characteristics, the steel plant and the chemical plant are both from the processing industry and exponents of a traditional factory culture. Historically, the lines of demarcation between workers and managers have been very clear. A traditionally strong union culture, emphasizing bargaining strength and concerns about rights and duties, reinforced this tendency towards polarization.

In both projects, the ED2000 concept and purpose was very tough to accept, marked by a high level of mutual scepticism between labor and management and, subsequently, by failure to establish mutual levels of trust. At the chemical plant, the belief that these issues could not be overcome in practice, not just voice, finally led to the union's decision to pull out. In stark contrast, the steel plant has become the "winner" among our projects in the Agder module. A winner, not in the sense that the project has been successfully completed, but rather in the sense that the trust-building and team-building efforts are still going on, gradually affecting more and more parts of the organization at deeper and deeper levels. Now, as the original planners of the ED2000 program had hoped, the objectives, ideas and ideals of the steel plant project are spreading to a sister company in another part of Norway. Perhaps, as a next phase, this ED2000 project will lead to the transformation of the corporate headquarters in a bottom-to-top process.

The same researcher from the Agder module led the chemical and steel plant projects. Despite the fact that they were similar industries, the research team was not able to bring the union at the chemical plant back into the ED2000 fold. Whereas a key message to labor and management — in line with the project's "involvement first" orientation — was to engage in trust-building processes, developments at the chemical plant made it clear that such a message needed to be guided by words of caution and patience. Involvement nearly always means that one person or position may (or will) be more vulnerable than another, increasing many risks including the feeling or fact of being hurt. We attempted to clarify this for the union at a "reconciliation meeting", where representatives were told that unless they really believed that top managers were sincere about their desire for change, and about their willingness and humility to learn, the union should not come back! The union leaders remained firm in their opinion that key managers were incapable of sincerely pursuing the ideals and values we had been advocating. They also did not believe that the in-house project team would be capable of effecting the necessary changes and developing the right team spirit. Suffice to say, the union did not come back. The leaders were not willing to risk being vulnerable, and the message was expressed literally: "You cannot change these people."

Unfortunately, as evidenced by symptoms that include conflict, waste, and absenteeism, the chemical plant continues to have problems today.

From theory to theory, not theory-to-practice

The two service industry projects, involving a hotel and grocery chain, reveal quite different stories from our experiences in the processing industry, as do the projects from the public services.

One major difference was that neither the hotel nor the grocery chain had very strong union traditions. Both groups employ many women and, in general, their workforces have not pursued higher levels of education. Because the grocery chain operates with low mark-ups and narrow operating margins, it tends to pay low wages and encourages little personal involvement. The proportion of employees with vocational or professional training is greater at the hotel chain but, even so, they are part of a culture with a strong tradition of top-down decision making and little systematic effort at empowerment.

In each of these projects, preliminary interviews were conducted, dialogue conferences were arranged, and ideas for improvement and change were followed up. In each project the process went on without major problems and without the kind of "struggles" encountered in the steel and chemical projects. The shop stewards and union leaders tended to play very minor roles, whereas top managers were quite active in structuring the process and voicing their priorities. Participants in the hotel and grocery projects generated very long lists of problems and tasks. While many problems were solved, the general impression is that there was very little change in terms of employee empowerment and real participation.

After completing phases 1 and 2, the projects more or less "died away", without serious prospects for more profound, transformational change. In the case of the hotel project, a new CEO took control just as phase 2 ended. He made it clear that he wanted to personally take charge of the change processes, and that he did not see any need for support from our research team. The regional director of the grocery chain had been the interested, active initiator of the ED2000 project. When he was promoted to another position in the corporate hierarchy, no one was tagged to continue the enterprise development process.

Transforming public agencies into private companies

The Agder module's projects in the public-service sectors of telecommunications and energy were distinctly different from those in the hotel and grocery arenas. In fact, in many respects they were quite similar to the steel and chemical plants. For instance, the telecommunications and energy industries both have a tradition of strong unions. Even as the energy company grapples with the problems of deregulating the electricity market in Norway, it is preserving the culture of a strong union coexisting with the culture of a traditional public bureaucracy.

Although the tradition of a strong union also typified the old publicly-owned telephone company, the telecom enterprise that participated in our ED2000 module has continued to go through a number of mergers and reorganizations that are pulling the working culture more in the direction of "high tech" information technology. As a result, the power of the union has gradually weakened and the impact of professional management has strengthened.

Even with their union histories, the relationship between labor and management in the telecom and energy enterprises was quite mellow, especially compared to the steel and chemical enterprises. In fact, the relationship seemed marked more by steadiness and cooperation than by confrontation, hard bargaining and polarization. The impact of technology and reliance upon middle levels of management were also much more noticeable. In fact, at the time of the ED 2000 project, more participants (especially at lower employee levels) seemed disillusioned by the erosion of regulation and public protection than concerned about union militancy.

Dialogue conferences for the telecom and energy projects were followed up with programmed, prioritized change. In phase 2, the telecom implemented a list of concrete solutions to practical problems that had been identified. Company managers were happy, because the project and the processes initiated were accepted as useful tools that aided their capacity for problem solving. The conclusion of phase 2 marked the end of the telecom's ED2000 project.

At the energy company, phase 2 was followed by studies and seminars focusing on strategic development and market orientation. While the follow-up was seen as useful, we have reason to believe that the process was insufficient when considered in terms of the deeper, broader cultural transformation that was needed to meet the demands of deregulation and privatization. In essence, the follow-up phase was "phased out" before the process really got under way.

Overcoming a deadlock of our own

By early 1998, four research teams were engaged in development processes in the companies that signed ED2000 cooperation agreements with the Agder module. At the same time two doctoral candidates were starting their work.

The mid-term evaluation by the ED2000 secretariat reported that we were doing well, considering our late start in the program. However, the secretariat expressed concern that we had not made more progress in the academic aspects of the research effort. They also questioned the extent to which we had managed to engage the regional business network, the "Competence Ring South". In other words, we had concentrated our efforts on the practical development work relevant to each project and, so far, had contributed less than expected to academic analysis, and to inspiring other enterprises in the network.

The reasons for these deficiencies were reflected in the internal organization of the Agder module. The research leader, Harald Knudsen, had only limited time available from his position at Agder University College and depended on an administrative assistant to handle daily operations. The Agder Research was organized in a number of small centers, and the ED 2000 project became a dominant activity in one of them, in essence adding that center's manager as a third member of the ED2000 leadership team. This "triumvirate" structure involving the research project leader, the administrative project leader (Hans Christian Garmann Johnsen) and the AF-center's leader created a great deal of confusion for all members of the Agder module team.

Each of the leaders had different opinions on the theories applied, resources allocated, and the final authority in discussions. The deadlock this situation created became increasingly frustrating for the leaders and the team members. One of the young researchers, concurrently starting on a doctoral program, quit. In addition, the research teams became somewhat polarized, each working from different theoretical perspectives. One team, for example, emphasized engineering and strategic approaches, while another focused on values and trust.

The deadlock was broken by a series of events that included receipt of the mid-term evaluation (mentioned above) requesting more academic research, reorganization and re-staffing at AF, and application of our own dialogue-conference strategies at the biannual meeting of ED2000 module leaders, board and secretariat. As hosts of this meeting in April 1999, the Agder module team decided to stage a session where a typical situation from companies in the Agder project was role-played by two project researchers. The session generated a very positive response from the audience and, ironically, this helped initiate a broader, more open debate within the Agder team concerning ideas of democratic dialogue, forms of participation and involvement, and so forth. We took one step further in questioning and clarifying the ideological and philosophical foundation of the ED2000 program.

A learning experience

As the projects began to show results (both positive and negative) we needed to reconsider our basic concepts of organizational change, to evaluate the ED2000 process and to discuss our experiences. To appreciate the results of these discussions, it is important to remember that the common thread in all six Agder projects was the view of ED2000 as a communicative development coalition program that included a set of standardized initial interviews, dialogue conferences, and procedures for follow-up activities. The initial interviews were considered very important. Some participants may hesitate to speak freely as members of a larger audience, such as a dialogue conference, but they may be willing to do so in an interview. For the research teams, one-on-one interviews provided one way of gaining an advantage and a preview of problems, ideas and hopes, before staging the dialogue conference. The whole ED2000 process at Agder and each of the other modules was based on the idea of workplace and enterprise development through cooperation between researchers and practitioners, and upon strong, internal commitment to broad participation. The underlying idea was that the enterprises themselves should define development issues.

Our experience from ED 2000 tells us that change agents, academic or not, need to be perceived and judged more like leaders than like candidates for a certain notion of academic licensing. Transformation in an organization is, to a great extent, dependent upon the personal qualities of the change agent and upon the strictly personal relationships and feelings of trust between the change agent and key participants in an enterprise.

As researchers, our involvement in the ED2000 program created rich opportunities for learning about enterprise development by working directly and closely with the enterprises themselves. Our reflections on these experiences focus on possible answers to two major questions:

- From a practical point-of-view, why did a fairly standardized procedure lead to such differing results?
- From a philosophical point-of-view, to what extent and under what conditions does the "communicative method" or the "communicative concept" really lead to the exposure of salient and sensitive issues, and to the deep transformation of an enterprise?

We have focused our analysis of these questions and the Agder module's experiences in ED2000 on three factors that, in one way or another, influenced each project:

1. The "ideological" orientations of the research and/or in-house project teams.
2. The organization culture, traditions of unionization and the level of antagonism in the enterprises.
3. The personal qualities and character traits of the project members and of the top management and union leaders.

In the context of the ED2000 program, long-lasting change depends, to a great extent, on empowerment and involvement. Deep personal involvement by members at all levels of an enterprise's organization is a prerequisite for productive and innovative change. Empowerment, openness, and trust are, in turn, prerequisites for such involvement.

In organizations marked by long-standing antagonisms, extensive involvement is possible only when "the other side" is seen as, potentially, a reliable partner. The initial decision to enter into an enterprise development contract, such as we offered, and the subsequent decisions to continue a project, despite periods of frustration and setbacks, critically hinge on the belief that each party is just as committed as the other to honoring psychological contracts and continuing the empowerment processes. The single, essential ingredient necessary to instill and maintain this belief is trust.

In a working climate that has been traditionally adversarial, the trust-building effort, directed at inter-personal and inter-group relationships, will take a long time. Furthermore, the building process requires great amounts of stamina, humility, and willingness to learn. Help from an objective, outside resource, in our case an Agder ED2000 research team, is an enormously important element for success.

For the research team to succeed, the researchers, like labor and management at the enterprise, must be personally as well as professionally committed to the process and to the values underlying empowerment. In the terminology of the Agder module, such a focus and level of longitudinal commitment requires a "people first" orientation. It will not come about as a by-product of a "systems first" orientation, and it will certainly not emerge automatically as the result of some action research initiative.

The "people first" orientation and the need for empowerment, openness and trust must be explicitly recognized by members of the in-house project team as well as by the research team. To get everyone "on board", the initial dialogue conference can be of great help but it will not automatically result in an understanding of the need for trust or in the initiation of a trust-building process. People at an enterprise may not always feel free or qualified to speak about such needs (trust, reinforcement, commitment, etc.) and researchers with a "systems first" orientation may not perceive such needs. To further compound the problem, representatives of labor and management (too often opposing factions) may not be willing to take the personal risk of expressing a need for trust building. Too often, declaring such a priority is incorrectly perceived as admitting a personal shortcoming; for example, not being sufficiently trusting or trustworthy.

Ultimately, this means that the classical "decision to participate", including the "inducement-contribution contract", needs to be taken one step further; in fact, going beyond financial or psychological contracts. An informal contract, agreement or understanding has to be accepted by the parties, each saying essentially: "We don't quite know who you are and how much we can trust you, but we are willing to give it a try, provided that you, as the project research team, will use your authority to safeguard the process."

Therefore, in addition to a people first orientation, a project researcher also needs to have a personality that, in itself, builds trust; traits such as openness, friendliness, personal confidence, expertise and experience, an appealing leadership style, emotional intelligence and trustworthiness, to mention just a few.

Each of these factors — a people first orientation, a mixture of personal characteristics — is highly personal, highly relative and also contextual. While other aspects of enterprise development, such as re-engineering business systems or organizing network conferences, may lend themselves to general conclusions based on objective criteria, the turn-around of an enterprise culture marked by antagonism and distrust may not.

Based on some historical evidence (especially in Norway), the ED2000 program and the Agder module have assumed that academic research institutions may assist an enterprise in its quest for excellence, by helping to build partnerships between labor and management, employees and managers. Our observation, so far, is that research institutions may provide all kinds of technical assistance, within their domains, but that building partnerships and trust among those in an enterprise requires competencies, and an innate knowledge, far beyond that acquired in the pursuit of proper academic credentials.

Chapter 5

Enterprise development in Norwegian fishing industry

Jarle Løvland and Lene Foss

Introduction

The institutions which made up the Tromsø module were invited by the Norwegian Research Council (NRC) late in 1994 to participate in ED2000. This led to co-operation between several units located at the premises of the University of Tromsø. Our story is of a newcomer to the Norwegian work research scene. The story of the Tromsø module is influenced by conditions related to an action oriented research program in an industry which is unfamiliar with this type of approach, as well as the disciplinary disputes and problems arising when trying to constitute a "new" research practice in an environment with heterogeneous research institutions and disciplines.

Research organization and reorganization in Tromsø

The researchers in Tromsø joining the program came both from the university and external applied research institutions. From the beginning of the 1970s, both the University and the Norwegian College of Fishery Science (NFH), as well as several applied research institutions (Norwegian Institute of Fisheries and Aquaculture — NIFA), were established to support competence building and industry development in Northern Norway. During the 1980s, research foundations within social sciences, marine biology and information technology were established in connection with the University of Tromsø. The fishing industry plays a crucial role in the economic system of the region, and a political consensus was developed that facilitated the buildup of research capacity and competence at a rapid speed throughout the 1980s. Tromsø soon became the regional center of research on the marine fisheries sector, medicine and social sciences. In early 1990, research and development activities in Tromsø were reorganized. This process was to a large extent initiated by the NRC, which advocated a stronger co-operation between the research institutions. This meant merging activities of the fishery related research in NIFA with activities at (or related to) the University of Tromsø. After a short and intensive merging process around 1990, the research foundation NORUT was established, forming an umbrella organization over all the applied research institutions in Tromsø. The intention was to offer and co-ordinate a wider range of basic and applied research to users than was usual when the institutions operated on their own. Hopefully this would make it easier for users to relate to a wider set of research disciplines. This idea coincided with the basic idea in ED2000 of improving the relevance of regional R&D environments to local users. However, when trying to establish a joint industry oriented research program in 1992, consisting for the most part of the same research institutions as participated in the Tromsø module, the NORUT research group found that the process halted, as the former independent institutions were not willing to co-operate closely in designing the program. These factors seemed to fuel the internal competition for funding among the institutions, overshadowing the possibilities for co-operative research processes and a regional industry orientation. The ED2000 initiative and the ongoing local integration process formed a golden opportunity for the university and the applied institutions in Tromsø to increase their national and local relevance, in addition to taking part in the Norwegian system of work related research.

Enterprise development setting prior to ED2000

After our first application, the feedback from NRC was an instruction to cooperate with another research group (Nordland Research) localized in Bodø, based on their research and education in management. The reason for this instruction was that both module applications were very similar, with respect to the empirical setting and research problem focus. The co-operation was established from the start, and lasted until 1998, when the research team in Bodø decided to withdraw from the program.

Tromsø was a new actor in Norwegian research on organization and management. The success of becoming a module in the ED2000 program depended largely on strong industry support. In the following, we give some examples of the ties between the fish processing industry and research that influenced and shaped our approach to the program. One important influence was the ongoing Norwegian adaptation process to the internal European market. The process affected the fish processing industry, as exports to Europe amounted to more than 60% of the production value. The fish processing industry adopted this change process at an early stage and created a close relationship to consulting companies and relevant areas of the R&D environment in Tromsø to support the implementation of formal quality systems and training programs related to this process. The Fish Producers Association (FPA) was central in co-ordinating this process. As the initial phase of consultant supported quality development work in the fish processing industry faded out around the middle of the 1990s, the producers association (FPA) started another development project. Much of the resources in the initial phase had come from external sources like consultants and R&D institutions, but now attention shifted towards increasing the internal resources of the enterprises for development. This process was necessary in the fish processing industry, with its very small administrative resources compared to other industries. A "middle-management school" was established to train middle managers to organize and carry out development work, especially related to quality improvement. This process was carried out, with engagement from the R&D environment that later became the Tromsø module, as researchers were engaged in lecturing and guiding the participants both theoretically and in relation to the applied project work of the students. Another influence was the development of formal qualifications among workers in the fish processing industry. This activity also was co-ordinated by the FPA since the early 1980s as a follow-up activity to a governmental committee, pointing out the lack of formal competence and training at all levels in the industry. This process partly was evaluated and supported by the research environment in Tromsø. On the one hand these ongoing development processes and ties to the fish processing industry influenced the choice of research perspectives in the design of the Tromsø module in 1994. We also felt that a major difference from other ED2000 modules was that there existed no formal network organization between the companies. The R&D institutions forming the module had to develop direct relationships with interested companies. Given the scattered localization of the industry in the rural and coastal areas of Norway, we had to spend a lot of money on transport. The goals of the ED2000 program and the focus on broad participation in enterprise development were very relevant to the situation in the Norwegian fish processing industry.

Developing a common action and research perspective

The process of forming the Tromsø module was heavily influenced by the heterogeneity of the participating R&D institutions and professionals. The point of departure was based on institutional organization theory, with a focus on organizations in the public sector and the overall management of the fisheries sector. Through increased enterprise development activity, these institutions shifted their orientation towards the private sector and the fish processing industry in particular. NIFA and NCFS formed an industry oriented approach, based on their long time engagement in the fishing industry, both in applied research and in higher education.

Their disciplinary basis was partly institutional organization theory and economics (NCFS), and partly management science, business administration and marketing (NIFA). It is obvious that this heterogeneity made up a broad and complex platform for developing joint perspectives in the module work. This heterogeneity was also manifested through several methodological issues that had to be clarified before entering the process work in the enterprises. There were methodological differences between economists and organizational theorists. The former advocated a more traditional, positivistic approach to the research process, whereas the organization researchers were more positive to action-based research design. As such, the latter group was more in line with the expectations of established Norwegian work research. The economists were also more oriented towards the use of quantitative designs than the other disciplines, and they stressed the normative orientations of productivity goals for, and measurement of the economic results of, the enterprise development processes. The Tromsø module started out based on a group of R&D institutions with very different research practices, methodological backgrounds and professional views on the role the researchers should have in collaboration with the enterprises. As the design of a joint research program started, the challenging question was: How could one possibly combine such divergent perspectives and experiences within one common framework? Even when facing the same empirical context, researchers would identify quite different "main" problems. Earlier experiences had shown that these problems would be solved without having to create a general consensus.

"The integrated approach" — Combining three research perspectives with action?

The diverse disciplinary background meant that the process of creating an agreement on fundamental research topics, and the approach to the work, demanded considerable time and effort. Therefore, what was to become "The integrated model" took more than one year (1994–95) to develop. The approach involved combining perspectives both from institutional, organization and economic theory to form a multi-method approach to ED processes. This approach emphasized that enterprise development among the module researchers should be based on a thorough understanding of both the intra- and interorganizational aspects of the companies, their resources and their internal and external relationships. At the same time, the benchmarking perspective with emphasis on organizational learning and productivity improvement through external comparisons with other companies would be an important reference for setting priority areas of enterprise improvement. By combining the qualitative approach from the intra- and interorganizational field with the more quantitative methods related to productivity enhancement and organizational improvement, we argued that the module and the companies would benefit from the disciplinary heterogeneity. In addition to that, the module would then provide a rather different approach compared to the other modules. When communicating with the program secretariat and the other modules, we perceived that this difference was appreciated as both innovative and relevant. However, the module's design goals and perspectives proved to be both ambitious and hard to fulfil, because of the different research traditions and multi-methodological approach involved. The task of co-ordination was not made easier by the co-operation imperative with the research environment in Bodø, a city 400 miles south of Tromsø.

Taking the negative collaboration experience in 1992 into consideration, the fact that these institutions together with the university and the NCFS now managed to reach a compromise with the title "Enterprise and productivity development in the Norwegian fish processing industry", as our common framework and application for ED research, was almost felt like an research achievement in itself. Five researchers, 2–3 doctoral students, and numerous other students doing thesis work in relation to the enterprise development were involved in the project. The most substantial contribution was the external legitimacy created by apparently combining quite conflicting research professions to form a new alliance with the potential to address the relevant goals of the ED2000 program. Integrating the different perspectives in actual research activities soon proved a difficult and complex task. Were these three approaches really different perspectives, or just different focal structures and processes taking place at both the intra- and interorganizational level? The intraorganizational perspective focused on processes at the network level (in relation with contact and relationship analysis), whereas the benchmarking perspective dealt with both intra- and interorganizational processes. This underlines both the opportunities and problems related to dealing with heterogeneity. It also indicates the successful symbolic and rhetoric power of the integrated approach in creating external legitimacy and difference.

Relationship building and interaction with the enterprises

The recruitment of the enterprises was a new and difficult step for our module. The enterprises in the fish processing industry were familiar with technological R &D, but they were less familiar with social science researchers, especially in the field of organizational development. We did not succeed in recruiting any firms from the Tromsø area. Ironically, these firms, both white fish processing enterprises and shrimp businesses, have managers and employees who were educated in Tromsø (at the NCFS) and who know the R &D environment in Tromsø well. Generally companies would avoid such projects as the ED2000, because of the fear that it would impose strategic and competitive risks. It is possible that the enterprises located close to the R&D institutions felt they could achieve more by using direct and informal channels, and by accessing the institutions without projects as a reference. We were more successful in establishing contact with enterprises in the county north of Tromsø. This region was heavily dependent on the fishing industry. We ended up enrolling two whitefish processing firms and one shrimp business. Later in the program, we recruited 3 more firms in the benchmarking area. One firm in the south was recruited because one of the researchers knew this firm from an earlier action-oriented project. We also recruited two enterprises in Nordland. The benchmarking approach, with its focus on "learning from the best", seemed to be easy to sell as the imperative for productivity enhancement and economic performance. Some firms felt that the focus of benchmarking in internal resource building for competition as too sensitive. Instead they applied instead an internal focus with no direct relationship to other firms in this process. It was fairly easy to recruit three firms that were interested in this way of guiding and monitoring the internal development processes in a combination with external comparisons and learning processes. The enterprises were very eager to participate at the start, but the relations changed gradually as the researchers focused more on methodology and did not support short-term needs for improvement. The large geographical distances involved in serving seven firms in three different counties soon proved to be difficult. The consequences of this, in combination with a fragile research team with high "turnover", was that it turned out to be impossible to devote one team leader to each enterprise with consequent follow-up visits several times each year. In retrospect, we see that it was too ambitious, having so few researchers, to try to cover enterprises within such a wide geographical area, and at the same time doing action research. The result was that we lost trust and relations with two of the firms. Part of the explanation was also that these two companies engaged in merging processes where "*the relation with the R&D environment imposed a security risk*", according to one of the leaders. . A third company dropped out due to expansion and external strategic adaptation process. We worked with these companies for a full year. The three companies located north of Tromsø were engaged in the project in all five years of operation. Common for most of the firms was their interest in the intraorganizational issues. We started the work in the firms with issues related to organizational structure, information and communication, and issues relevant to the operator level. The reason for this is obvious. The intraoganizational perspective contained elements that were familiar issues in a factory setting: How many vertical levels should this enterprise have? Does the spread of information work well in this firm? What are the problems at the operator level? How well does the new middle-manager function? Does the leadership have legitimacy? Are there any arenas for communication between the leadership and the employees? Is there a potential for teambuilding at the operator level? The module therefore used the 2–3 first years in each firm to perform analysis on intra-organizational issues and to develop common perspectives with their representatives on how to move forward. The process of one of our main collaborators illustrates our approach and methods in dealing with the needs and preconditions for OD.

Modes of engagement

The firm, "Fish Processing Ltd." is a relatively large fish-processing firm with 100 employees. In two shifts the plant produces from 12 to 15 ton daily of frozen fillet, single frozen fillet and fresh fish. At the time of engagement with "Fish Processing", they had started to reorganize leadership functions. The top manager, the production manager and the quality and personnel manager meant that the "bottleneck" in this reorganizing process was the middle-management level. The firm had recently established some visions and goals, and the management wanted the members of the organization to develop values, norms and a state of readiness so that one could obtain these goals upon entering the new century. The firm's participation in ED2000 was in the top manager's view a possibility to *"be supervised, to make plans and to evaluate their choices"*. The ED2000 participation was, in other words, to be used strategically in an organizational development process of implementing their existing strategy visions. The research module had its first visit to the firm in October 1995. We interviewed 12 persons, three from the administration, six from the fish processing unit and three from the production unit, using a 10 page interview guide. Analysis of the data showed an overall lack of joint and collective identity. One of the informants said that *"This is a firm that in reality consists of three firms: an administration, a raw material acquisition unit and a production unit"*. The interviews revealed that the "we-feeling" stopped on the borders between these three units and that the employees in the different units had limited knowledge of the work operations in the other units. The language clearly marked lines like "*we*" and "*them*", "*upstairs*" and "*downstairs*". Our analysis concluded that several factors contributed to the lack of "we-identity" in the firm. Among these, the information system was one factor that matched our focus in the intraorganizational perspective. Our initial study showed that the managerial level claimed that they paid attention to information, but that it got misinterpreted at the lower level of the organization. One informant illustrated the situation like this: *"There is a communication failure between the administration, shift manager and down to the production level. A couple of things get lost on the way here."* On the operator level, employees complained about receiving too much written information, and that face-to-face communication from managers to employees rarely happened. The researchers suggested that a next possible step was to study the managerial level's actual communication with the rest of the organization. With whom did they talk? Which medium for communication did they use? What did they talk about? And to which degree was the communication directed initiated by themselves or initiated by other members of the organization? In January 1996, the top manager, the production manager and the quality and personnel manager wrote a field note of their internal communication. One of the reasons for the information and communication problems seemed to rest in the fact that the formal structure was not adjusted to the tasks that the employees had to fulfill. The vertical distance in the firm was too long, and the result was that some of the information got "lost" on its way either way up or down in the hierarchy. Concerning the information at the horizontal level, in-depth interviews revealed that there were not enough arenas for communication between employees, especially at the middle management level. Formal meetings at the sub-managerial levels were non-existent. The analysis of the field notes revealed that the production manager was the one that had the highest percentage of use of telephone, use of fax, face-to face interaction, gave general information, and task-oriented transactions with the other organization members as well as with the concern group. We concluded that the production leader had relations that not only suited a production leader, but also a sales manager and a purchasing manager. Some of this was traced down to the external pressure that the production leader had, from the industry group that the firm belongs to. As a result, the firm chose to reduce the number of levels in the organization. The situation for the production leader improved, as the industrial group took over functions like sales, and accounting was transferred to the concern level. The story of this firm reveals that the intraorganizational issue was a good starting point both for the firm and the research group. It allowed the firm to pick an immediate problem they were facing in the organization, and it allowed us to get to know the organization, its people and its work. The firms' need for focusing on organizational design was of immense help for us in moving to themes that needed more knowledge of how the organization functioned, its history and the internal relationships between members of the organization. One firm wanted to develop teambuilding at the operator level, another wanted feedback on leadership styles at the top and middle management level. These issues required more trust between the research team and the organizational members, and were a natural follow-up after diagnosing the organizational design. The incremental step towards issues that were related to the enterprise and their environment and benchmarking, seemed to be the way our research group navigated between the three cornerstones in our theoretical framework. The time frame was significant here — at the time when the interorganizational themes were academic labels, both firms were interested in this, as we already had analyzed and developed the enterprise "from within". The interorganizational perspective developed in a different manner than the other modules. Our firms stated openly that they would learn from other's experiences when the researchers drew these parallels — but they did not see any value in being integrated in a network with other firms and taking part in development work through such a system. This insight made us work with the interorganizational perspective in a way that allowed us to study networks from the firm's point of view. We did this in several ways. We started off with mapping the degree of external relations at different hierarchical levels, i.e. top-management, middle management and at the operator level. The very first issue on the interorganizational theme based on the field notes was purely descriptive. The researchers analyzed the frequency of contact with certain constituencies such as customers, suppliers, regulative actors etc, and the frequency of the themes they communicated on. Characteristics of the relations such as weak and strong ties were measured. The results were reported back to the two firms.

The work based on the interorganizational perspectives has to a large extent been driven from network theory, marketing and cognitive theory. It has allowed us to focus on explicitly theoretical grounded questions, and to use extensive data collection methods, such as a one-month self-reported field note by organizational members. The development focus has been to involve the participants in constructing their own field note — and in that sense increase their attention concerning who they talk to, what they talk about and what they get out of it.

Communication

In many ways, communication is a term that both characterizes the relationship between the researchers and their approach to the field setting. As we experienced the first couple of years as difficult — with many changes in the research team and several firms leaving the project, we felt that the latter part of the program was more consolidating. Firstly we had to learn to speak to each other — and to understand the paradigms of the different disciplines. One of the consequences of the very strong efforts on the intraorganizational theme in the initial phases of the program, was that the three researchers working within this area worked together out in the field, and thus they could exchange experiences and learn from one another. These three researchers who worked together wrote the majority of the 44 confidential reports the module has produced. We also recruited a new researcher in this area, and several graduate students.

The interorganizational theme involved work and analysis of the survey — and half the team ended up analyzing and writing about the results. In the latter part of the program, a marketing researcher, who worked with cognitive models, enhanced the module. When we tried to incorporate the market aspect and a cognitive perspective into the research module, we managed to combine structural network theory and cognitive theory on the field note data — and these analyses were more relevant for the enterprises. The managers found it useful to be questioned about their market orientation. The result of using heuristics in their perception of contact frequency had immediate consequences, as they became aware of their overestimation of market contact and underestimation of contact with suppliers.

Regarding our approach to the field, our mode of communication differed from dialogue conferences. Since most of us were new to action research, we needed a mode of communication that resembled traditional research methods, like observation, interviewing etc. At the same time we wanted the benefit of the participatory action research involving that the knowledge of the actors in the field to be an integrated part of the development process. This resulted in a mode of communication that was "rich", in that it followed a process where the knowledge of the researchers and the knowledge of the participants built on one another in a sequence. Our work with internal and external field notes are examples of this process, where the informants and the researchers in co-operation chose categories that were both of theoretical and of practical for the informants . The process of developing the internal and external field note schemes was very similar to that of two academics writing an article together by sending it back and forth to one another. The differences lie in the way of communicating, and in understanding what the right terms and needs in the field are, and at the same time develop the field notes as scientific research tools. In this manner, the researchers and the employees in the enterprises not only learned from one another, but also managed to obliterate the "myths" of research as an abstract activity performed by scholars who never are in contact with the "real" world, and whose work are of little practical use. The researchers learned how the subjects in social science research have qualified opinions about their own behavior and the work community they are a part of, and how valuable their contribution is to the understanding of barriers in OD processes. The fishing industry is characterized by small administration and "self-made" managers, production workers of many different nationalities. Many workers are untrained and have low degree of education, and thus a central objective was to improve the communication between the two parts — managers and union representatives in the enterprises. In many firms, there was a pretty cold atmosphere between managers and union representatives, each blaming the other for not thinking about the financial future of the firm vs. the work/health problems for the employees. In the intraorganizational part of the project, we aimed at increasing the enterprises' communicative design logic, where the objective is to secure legitimacy by a communication enhancing structure. This was done (in the enterprises) by suggesting arenas constituted by employees depending on their competence and involvement. In practice, this was implemented by ED boards,[1] WE boards,[2] and more practical development groups. In one firm where an ED board was established, an interview one and a half year later illustrates the communication between the various parts of the firm represented in the board: "*We have got a useful meeting arena and another information channel to a wider audience of the employees. At the same time it is "narrow" enough to make it possible to pass information in a decent way. Issues get through there. Information about absolutely everything of interest for the firm internally and for the industrial group as such is conveyed. I do think that it spreads further (to the rest of the organization). We use the ED board to plan the new production locality and the production lines. We have one rule — to avoid discussing wages — and we have managed that. A nice warm atmosphere, active participation and great interest. We have come closer to one another, the climate has changed*". Our experience is, however, that spreading information from the different communicative arenas to the other parts of the organization is often difficult when the rest of the workers hardly participate in development processes. The following quote illustrates that although the mentioned ED board functions well internally, it is not quite as "understandable" for the rest of the workers at the operator level. "*I do not know what it is, but I have heard about it… I have read the minutes, but forgot what it said. It is a good idea to have such an arena. I think it is needed. But the ED board needs to be more exposed. What it is, how it shall be used and when. I have seen that the union representative attends it. But I do not know what he does there.*"

One lesson from developmental activities and the creation of new developmental bodies like the ED board is that their success implies a tradeoff between their internal capacity to co-ordinate development processes effectively, and their external legitimacy towards other employees to create a common basis for enterprise-wide development.

Professional differences and disputes — The benchmarking experience

The benchmarking perspective on enterprise development was taken forward right from the initiation of the ED2000 program, as a mean to achieve increased

1. An ED board is an enterprise development board, which is mandatory in firms with 100 employees or more.

2. An WE board is a work & environment board, which function is to improve the work climate and environment.

competitiveness among the enterprises. In the Tromsø module program it was focused as a research perspective, because productivity research already existed as an activity in the R&D environment. It also happened to be the research area of the first module leader, who was an economist at NFCS, and had a long record of researching productivity measurement in the fish processing industry. Consequently, the initial benchmarking approach was significantly altered by the researchers from a learning and process perspective, towards an econometric line of research with an emphasis on quantitative measurements and the use of secondary population data from industry survey data that NIFA had been preparing for more almost 20 years. A doctoral student was recruited and the work started, with a focus on basic methodological development. This framing of the research indicated an approach quite opposite to the action-oriented processes that were undertaken and not well received by the other researchers in the module. The methodological distance between the economists, management science researchers and sociologists, political scientists and organization theorists seemed enormous. During the initial relation building process with the company, we carried out interviews with a stratified sample of representatives from management, union representatives and employees within different departments or functions. In this process, the benchmarking activity was presented to the participating companies with a fairly good response. The results of these interviews and meetings were communicated back to all employees. However, within the research group it became increasingly more difficult to integrate the diverse approaches suggested by the integrated model into a holistic approach to enterprise development, as the productivity measurement activities and methods stayed very much outside the process of the organization researchers' work. The cross-disciplinary communication between economists and the other researchers polarized and gradually ended. Another background for this conflict was that the non-economists felt that they did not receive sufficient feedback and information from the processes within the other modules in the module leader meetings. In line with this process, distrust was building up, and the conflict level escalated quickly and reached a peak in 1997, when the module leader chose to step back and withdraw from the module activity. This controversy revealed our basic problem in dealing with disciplinary heterogeneity. The problem was in part related to methodological differences between economists and organization science. The economists advocated the use of quantitative methods and secondary population data instead of in-depth qualitative action methods, which they did not regard as adequate to ensure productivity enhancement and increased competitiveness. It was also related to the institutional division lines, where NCFS and NIFA were more positive to the economist and management perspective, whereas there was little support among the researchers with a background from the university within social sciences. In a way it ended up as a competition between the hard and soft methods. The problem became even worse as few of the researchers in the module really looked into each other's methods, to explore the possibilities to let these two perspectives on enterprise development play a complementary role in the action process. The losers in this academic dispute were the participating enterprises, which had indicated an interest to develop benchmarking processes and productivity enhancement. As the clear-cut productivity measurement approach was terminated, we had to reconsider the research strategy and it was decided to change the approach to a more applied form of benchmarking, emphasizing on organizational learning and process orientation. This was more in line with the enterprises' direct needs. However, even with this approach during the last three years, it was difficult to establish relationships between this research activity and the rest of the module in the concrete action directed at the enterprises.

Relevance of research knowledge and co-operation with enterprises

The Tromsø module chose to focus their research activity in the fishing industry both because of knowledge about the industry, as well as the researchers perception of enterprise development needs with reference to management science, which formed an important basis for the module research. The enterprises themselves surely had the expertise and responsibility to decide on issues like what kind of underlying competitive strategic choices should be supported by the enterprise development processes. By focusing on the enterprises' development needs, the researchers had to deal more explicitly with the issues of *relevance and strategic fit* of their research knowledge to support the processes and priorities chosen by the enterprise leaders. Clearly this meant that we had to step back in areas where we lacked relevant competence and training in facilitating these specific processes. We also experienced, in two of the original enterprises, that the researchers were thrown out when the enterprises engaged in sensitive strategic processes. In one case this was related to a merging process aimed at establishing new seafood concern. This had the effect that all enterprise development activities and co-operation with researchers lost priority. We also had the impression that communication with researchers was considered a security risk that they were not willing to take due to the critical necessity of trust needed from the new partners and owners. We experienced a similar problem of getting access to enterprises when we approached an enterprise within a fishery concern group. After a few positive meetings and discussions, the enterprise suddenly just dropped out of the communication. The general experience was that enterprises that were part of concerned groups were more difficult and demanding to cooperate with than the individual enterprises were. The breakdown of co-operation can be seen as a consequence of our internal disciplinary heterogeneity and mixed methodological platform with weak practice in action research. The fact that we did not use many of the methods established within work research, also caused problems, as the researchers were perceived to be oriented towards the leaders. Generally our experiences indicate that we did not anticipate that the increasing restructuring activity in the fish processing industry would demand a longer common history of co-operation with these enterprises, and a higher level of trust in order to be a relevant partner in such strategic processes.

Enterprise development — An invisible field of research?

Enterprise development was launched as a new arena for many research disciplines in Tromsø, giving an opportunity to channel work in research institutions towards a major industry in our region. This argument was important when many new disciplines were mobilized to create the module. In retrospect, it is fair to say that the new research area only to a modest degree has been integrated in the existing institutions and disciplines.

One reaction is that enterprise development is not seen as a focal research area, but more like an applied process where researchers tend to operate like consultants with few meriting options. The idea of different disciplines sharing a common context (the fish processing industry) has not seemed very appealing, as the rather laborious and integrated work process (including many interactions with enterprises), is considered more demanding and less meriting than the single person projects. In this situation, the module researchers have not spent much time on marketing their research alternative, as most of their time and consciousness has been directed towards the enterprises. To a certain extent this use of time, effort and expansive relation building process seem to have yielded the opposite result in the researchers' own academic institutions. Maybe this is due to the relatively short period that the integrated and multidisciplinary approach has been tested. The present low standing of enterprise development research within our research environment can also be seen as a natural response from well-established professions and disciplines, which have not faced applying and testing the relevance of their knowledge and methods in actual situations too often. This ignorance seems to reflect a linear approach to research and the usefulness of research, where the application of research knowledge is not considered to be the researchers' responsibility, they should rather devote their time to develop theories.[3] Perhaps our

3. This linear mode of thinking also seems in clear contradiction with empiric research on factors affecting the perception of the usefulness of research knowledge. In a recent study among 85 enterprises in the

limited success with the integrated approach in traditional academic institutions so far is an indicator of how deeply these attitudes are rooted both in our surroundings and in ourselves?

Conclusion

The experiences from ED2000 has been very challenging and interesting for the participants in the Tromsø module group, even if we must admit that our integrated approach in a heterogeneous research environment has to be developed further and institutionalize itself before it can be said to shape a research practice across disciplinary and institutional borders. But does this mean that these ambitions were unrealistic or naive? Perhaps not. If integration shall succeed, we must allocate much more effort in active co-ordination and communication between the institutions and the research professions involved, otherwise the well-established individual research incentives and mechanisms will always win. Our experience so far is that this coordination both aimed at following up the interaction with the enterprises, and also focusing on team development across researchers and disciplines, requires both capabilities and a considerable effort in order to succeed long enough to produce qualified and original research and relevant knowledge, and thus demonstrate the validity of an integrated approach and a process perspective.

Norwegian seafood industry, the results indicate that cooperation *during* the process of developing the research knowledge is strongly related to the enterprises perception of its usefulness This can be regarded as a support to an interaction oriented research design advocated by the ED2000 program. It could also mean that the research institutions need to develop their own role perceptions in order to be able to provide useful and relevant knowledge to their users.

Chapter 6

Fragile coalitions

Eivind Falkum

Introduction

The Institute of Applied Social Science (Fafo) and The Norwegian School of Economics and Business Administration (NHH) applied for participation in ED 2000 separately in 1995. Fafo was originally established by LO (The National Confederation of Labor Unions) in 1982.[1] Fafo is still perceived as a work research institute with the main focus on employee interests. NHH educate MBA's, and their research is focused on business organization, management and shareholders' interests. The board of ED 2000 found it useful to merge the perspectives in the two applications, and make Fafo and NHH co-operate in the same module, a novel idea for researchers at that time. In the beginning, we openly talked about the co-operation as some kind of forced marriage, even though we had some former experience of working together.

Our shared interpretation was that unless we managed to organise a merged module, we would both be left out of the programme. We had to meet, exchange ideas and perspectives, and produce a plan that combined the separate skills and the competence within the two institutes. This process went much smoother than any of us expected in advance, probably due to the interests at stake. No conflicts emerged.

How the idea of merging the two applications emerged in the board of ED 2000 is still quite unclear. Nevertheless, one of the consequences was that the module was perceived to represent the shared interests of the social partners in Norwegian working life; NHH was supposed to represent the employers confederation and Fafo to represent the LO. Both the NHH members and Fafo members in the module have in fact written articles on management — employee relations, as well as articles on cross-company co-operation and corporate issues. The division of work between the two institutes does, in other words, not reflect the prejudiced perceptions of

1. Fafo was transformed to a foundation in 1993. LO is still the main owner, together with several business and industry corporations.

interest representation. The work in the module has been allocated according to professional perspectives and the need for specific competence in each project.

About the research institutes and the ED 2000 module

The main interest of both Fafo and NHH was to see how employee participation and external business co-operation influenced value adding processes. We wanted to explore how the implementation of modern organization concepts is influenced by union traditions and systems for collective bargaining. The opposite perspective was to see how formal co-operative bodies with management and union representatives could support business development. What would be the advantages of development driven by imported "modern" concepts, compared to development driven by traditional management-union relations?

The final application from Fafo/NHH contained the main issues of both institutes, but had also developed a shared perspective that broadened the previous scope. In addition to participation as a key element in developmental work, we included resistance to change as an opposing factor, and in addition to value added we included value waste. The most interesting elements were not the concept of resistance or value waste. This introduced the assumptions that participation may be counter-productive, and leads to value waste/loss in some cases, for instance if the union agrees to participate in processes that in the end are destructive to business. On the contrary, there may be cases where resistance is productive, and either leads to a change of direction that creates new and better solutions that increase the value of the business, or inhibits change processes that otherwise would lead to a waste of values or increased losses. In other words, we assumed that there was no significant positive correlation between participation and rise in productivity, or the other way round; significant correlation between resistance and waste of values. This perspective was the intellectual outcome of merging the two applications to the ED 2000 program.

In order to research these processes, we established partnerships with several different companies, developed our relations with both management and trade unions and took part in their various development activities. Development Coalitions was a term introduced to describe these kinds of relations between companies and research units. We had to leave the safe port of traditional social science, do other things than we used to do, and to face the methodological challenges that unavoidably occur when you become a subject in your own empirical studies. Coalitions between management, trade unions and researchers may be highly productive and can even enforce creativity, but they are also very fragile. This chapter is about our work in development coalitions, the few coalitions that still last, and about all those that broke, either by chance, or by any other good reason.

Establishing development coalitions

Most of the participating research units in ED 2000 had established development coalitions with companies, while we had to start from scratch. Participation in ED 2000 demanded action research and direct involvement in enterprise development. The program was not supposed to support traditional social science research. Researchers had to develop issues for business development and work together with the involved companies, take part in development processes, and thereafter describe and analyze both processes and results. Fafo and NHH had relations with enterprises, but none of these were familiar with action research. On the other hand, they had all used external business consultants. In our view, consultants usually introduce ready-made solutions and methods, while researchers develop knowledge about problems, and ways to handle them uniquely. The ED 2000 approach produced confused expectations among the enterprises, regarding whether we were consultants or just appeared in a slightly different shape. Another demand from the ED 2000 program was to focus on employee participation in enterprise development. In order to comply with this demand, we expressed the wish that shop floor stewards or other union representatives should take part in the meetings with each company we tried to enroll in the program from the very beginning. Usually union representatives participated in the first meetings, but in some of the enterprises this was regarded as irrelevant, or not common according to tradition.

During the fall of 1995 and most of 1996, our attention was focused on establishing development coalitions with enterprises. We had many meetings and discussions with enterprises. Some failed and some gave results. The processes can be described in three steps. First, we contacted and set up a meeting with the top management and top unionists from each company. We presented the ideas of ED 2000 and our own perspectives, theories and methods. Then we discussed enterprise problems that would suit the presented scopes. With no exceptions, the managers and unionists expressed interest in the program and wished to participate, but gave no commitments across the table. They all concluded that we had to develop the projects with subsidiaries, divisions or certain departments where the actual development processes could take place, and then we created the necessary contacts to proceed in that direction. The second step was the meetings with managers and unionists from lower echelons in the corporate structures. The specific problems and our contribution were discussed. In some cases we got immediate positive response, and agreements were reached to start research. However, in other companies, the managers and unionists expressed interest, but needed more information. New meetings were held, which eventually proved to be a series of very long "goodbyes". The third step was to make detailed plans for what to do in each of the participating companies. Our task at this stage was to capture the nature of the problems presented, and to argue for our response and proposals on what to do about them. Agreements were normally reached quite soon, and the implementation could start. Eventually we set up development coalitions with five large corporations that either Fafo or NHH had relations with from previous projects. All together they represent more than ten thousand employees in plants or offices scattered around the world. One of the corporations was involved in chemicals, one in electric and electronic devices and installations, one in forestry and paper production, one in mechanic devices and one is a typical conglomerate. In addition, we were involved in temporary development projects in small and medium range companies during the period covered by ED 2000.

We still wonder why the five corporations chose to participate in the program. In some cases, relations on institutional or personal levels between the researchers and companies seemed to produce mutual commitment. A genuine curiosity about the potential contribution from social science to business was expressed from time to time. Unfamiliar ways of thinking seemed to trigger their curiosity. In addition, ED 2000 covered nearly all the costs of the researchers and so compared to consultant fees, the program could be perceived to offer business development for free. However, three of the five corporations emphasised honest and genuine interests in the basic ideas of employee involvement as the most important reason to participate.

Models of business and research cooperation

Each development coalition got a boarding committee. The chairmen in these committees were managers of human resources or managers of internal education. Members were managers and shop floor stewards from different business units in the corporations. The committee in the chemical corporation was chaired by the manager of strategic issues, and had no employee representatives. The argument for not including unions was that the area to be developed was communication and co-operation between subsidiaries in different countries, and that this was primarily the responsibility of the management.

In two of the corporations we developed projects in some of the largest business units, and these projects got their own steering committees and reference groups. They chose to use the already established management and employee councils, like company councils or department councils (Work councils) instead of creating new units. Business development became a permanent issue on the agendas of co-operative bodies within the enterprise. Conflicts arising from discussions of development issues were taken to the special council of collective bargaining established according to the main agreement between the social partners in work life in Norway. In both of the cases, the chairing of the committee shifted on a yearly basis between labor and management. This way of sharing authority in the coalitions contributed to the development of mutual trust, interpretations, and interests between management and employees.

The researchers were full members of the committees, and at the same time strangers, giving unfamiliar information and presenting "peculiar" perspectives. The greatest challenge was to balance our viewpoints and presentations to the two social partners. Neither employees nor managers should perceive us as servants of their own or of the counterpart's interests. This was crucial, not only for the trust in research, but also for the climate for mutual trust between the social partners in the enterprise. This left us with the roles of mediators, analysts, advisors and sometimes judges on what was going on. The latter was a role we avoided strictly, unless we had scientific findings that supported one or the other party.

Problems to be solved and development processes to take place was identified, decided on and planned in the committees. The members of the committees then had to inform and mobilize the rest of the enterprise for implementation. Representatives of unions and other occupational groups informed and discussed the plans with their members, while management representatives informed their colleagues. Responsibility for different actions was allocated and supervised by the committees. The researchers made the investigations and empirical studies required either to plan action or change, or to support ongoing processes with crucial information for further steps. Results and findings were delivered to the committees, or in plenary sessions where most of the employees and managers were present.

The researchers were involved in development processes through taking part in planning, decision-making and implementation as committee members. Our partners in the enterprises were involved in the research processes by identifying issues to be explored or studied, defining samples for surveys, making appointments for interviews and supporting the gathering of data. Analyses of data and information were in most cases a joint process. Researchers systemized data and presented them for committees or other groups of relevance for interpretations and discussion of the findings. In other words, those who produced new information and knowledge were involved in using it, and those who were to use the new information were involved in producing it. In that way science and business development was integrated in one and the same process.

Sometimes development processes came to a full stop due to other issues than those of the development agenda. Sometimes the research findings were obviously surprising, and even unpleasant to one of the social partners. Instances like that would easily slow down development and maybe break the coalitions. What were the splitting forces?

Coalitions breaking apart

At the end of the ED 2000 program we were left with two development coalitions, one with the forestry and paper corporation and one with the electricity and electronic devices corporations. The others broke down during the program.

Lost attention
Knowledge development was in focus in the corporation producing mechanical devices such as locks and key systems. The union representatives and human resource managers were the driving forces in the coalition. They wanted an evaluation of an administrative system that rewarded knowledge development and education of employees. A researcher studied the system and concluded that raising status esteem from colleagues was more important than individual economic rewards. The findings were used for rearrangements and development of the internal vocational training system. A follow up study in the factory plants was planned, but never realized. The corporation was heavily engaged in buying other companies, mergers and outsourcing in the period from 1996 to1998. Attention to ED 2000 had to compete with the frequent changes in the corporate structure. The corporate workforce was more than doubled, and the name of the corporation changed three times during that period. Take-overs and mergers brought in new products and new competence. Established positions both for union representatives and managers were challenged by the new structures. Attention to the ED 2000 coalition vanished in the battlefield of corporate restructuring. However, the coalition was not broken; it more or less faded away without any noise, disagreements or any kind of trouble.

Sudden death

The story of the coalition with the chemical corporation is quite different from the one above. The coalition identified communication between subsidiaries, and between subsidiaries and the corporate headquarter as crucial to business improvement. Research groups went to three different subsidiaries abroad to explore communication problems. Managers and staff members were interviewed in 1997. Three different reports were delivered to the project committee. The reports contained analysis of the corporate communication structures and processes, and the researchers' recommendations for actions to be taken. In retrospect, two events are worth describing as crucial in the coalition.

In one of the subsidiaries the following happened. The managing director showed up about 45 minutes late for an appointed interview, letting the two of us, both from Fafo, wait in the reception. When finally showing up, he started to ask all kinds of questions about us, who we were, why we visited him, who sent us and so on, despite a detailed letter sent to him two weeks earlier by the manager of corporate strategies. He obviously thought of the interview as some kind of supervision or control from headquarters, imagining us in the role of under cover agents. Eventually we were allowed to conduct the interview. He answered all our questions, even those that covered troublesome matters between subsidiaries. Three weeks later we presented a report on the relations between the European subsidiaries and the corporate headquarter at a meeting in the project committee. The members were pleased with the results and expressed gratitude for the usefulness of our work so far. At the end of the meeting however, the chairman of the committee pulled out a letter addressed to him from our anxious interviewee, saying that he had a visit from two Norwegians and that….." the two researchers from Fafo had no knowledge about chemical manufacturing, marketing or business whatsoever. Any conclusions or recommendations from the two researchers should be considered worthless and of no relevance for the corporate strategies or development of relations between subsidiaries….". The chairman of the committee read this aloud to us, and then stared at the Fafo representative in the committee, asking

> – "What is your comment to this?"
> – "Oh, Thank you Very Much!!" the Fafo representative replied
> There was a big laugh
> – "What is he so afraid of?" the Fafo representative continued.
> – "Whatever he is afraid of, this letter shows that our focus on subsidiary relations is highly relevant" the chairman replied.

Again, perspectives of social sciences may either trigger new ideas or be perceived as threatening to traditional business perspectives. To build development coalitions from the top may create uncertainty on lower echelons, and it takes a lot of time and effort to make the whole hierarchy familiar with the ideas and methods presented.

The second event took place as the company experienced a tremendous drop in stock value, due to the introduction of a competing product. The value of the corporation dropped about 100 million dollars on the New York stock exchange during one summer day. A cost reduction program was planned to repair the damage, aiming at saving costs of about 100 million dollars a year, without reduction in productivity. This meant that the organizational slack in the corporate structure must have been at least at that level of value, despite solid profits each year. At that stage the chairman of the coalition committee introduced recommendations for rearranging the corporate structure to the top management, involving a reallocation of authority and subordination between the European subsidiaries. His recommendations aimed at increasing subsidiary synergies, and his memo was partly based on our research. The top management approved of his ideas, but they hesitated to make that leap. The final program decided upon by the top management contained cost reductions and some downsizing in some subsidiaries abroad, but did not include structural changes of a significant scale. Our chairman, however, was so convinced that his recommendations were right that he put his position at stake. When the final decision was made, he consequently left the corporation. Shortly after the top management closed down the development coalition, arguing that the cost reduction program would leave no attention to other development issues the following years, and that they brought in management consultants to help them through the necessary processes. The development coalition did not score in the top management, and met sudden death as a price of the game.

Reduced to a project

The multi product corporation wanted development coalitions in two different divisions. The first was supposed to concentrate on relations between subsidiaries in different countries. The second was supposed to focus on change management. The first one was dropped after a pilot study in Sweden. The argument was that they already had assigned a business consultant company to work on task flow, and on structural rearrangements between subsidiaries. The structural change was quickly reduced to a project on change management conducted by a doctoral student. This project was finished in 1999, and the research and business development relations were terminated.

Viable coalitions

The previous part described coalitions that broke. This part is about the viable ones. In the forestry and paper corporation, and in the electronics and electric devices corporation (El.corp) we developed projects in a few of the largest business units. These projects got their own steering committees and reference groups. They chose to use the already established management and employee councils, like company councils or department councils (work councils in Norwegian) instead of creating new settings. Business development became a permanent issue on the agendas of cooperative bodies within the enterprise. Conflicts arising from development issues were taken to the special council of collective bargaining, established according to the main agreement between the working life parties in Norway. In both cases the chairing and secretary functions of the committee was shared by the managing director and the head of the local union on a yearly basis This way of sharing authority in the coalitions contributed to the development of mutual trust, understanding, and interest between management and employees. The researchers were full members of the committees. Problems to be solved and development processes to take place were identified, decided on and planned in the committees. The members of the committees then had to inform and mobilize the rest of the enterprise for the implementation of planned actions and change. Representatives of unions and other occupational groups informed and discussed the plans with their members, while management representatives informed their colleagues at that level. Responsibility for different actions was allocated and supervised by the committees. The researchers made the investigations and empirical studies required either to plan action or change, or to support ongoing processes with crucial information for further steps. Results and findings were delivered to the committees, and sometimes to plenary sessions including most employees and managers.

The researchers were involved in development processes by taking part in planning, decision-making and implementation from the position as committee members. Our partners in the enterprises were involved in the research processes by identifying issues to be explored or studied, defining samples for surveys, making appointments for interviews and supporting the gathering of data. The analyses of data and information were in most cases a shared process. Researchers systematised the data, and presented them for committees or other groups of relevance for interpretations and discussions of the findings. In other words, those who produced new information and knowledge were involved in using it, and those who were to use the new information were involved in producing it. In that way science and business development was integrated in one and the same process.

El-Corp

The development coalition in the electricity and electronic corporation (the el-corporation) was the first to be established. Top management who were eager to improve employee involvement in enterprise development, expressed a strong belief in human resource management traditions and the concept of empowerment. In some parts of the corporation union — management relations were rather poor, and disagreements and conflicts on wage issues made co-operation on other issues quite difficult. Almost any kind of change became an issue for bargaining.

The corporate management wanted to include research activities in development processes, and the coalition became a part of the already established work council on the corporate level. However, the work council was considered to be too high level to deal with real problems in the different business units. The first task of the coalition was to support the creation of local work councils in all divisions, and to start and give most attention to the division with the troublesome management — employee relations. Quite soon the manager and the head of the local union of that division established their own work council. The researchers were included in this council, and this made it function much like a local development coalition.

The manager of the division proclaimed that they all had to face reality, and admit that the first year simply had to be a year of training in communication and cooperation. In addition to the local work council, there was also an existing local bargaining council. This unit was shaped according to the main agreement between the social partners in Norwegian working life.

Researchers attended all meetings in both the local councils for two years. The local work council made a plan for development activities. One of the first tasks was to conduct a survey among all leaders and employees, in order to sort out main problems to be handled. The survey was developed and conducted by the local development coalition. The researchers made the technical running creating tables of comprehensible data, but all the participants in the local coalition analyzed the results. The results were also presented to and discussed in a plenary session with about 200 participants. Consensus about what to develop, and in what order, was derived from these discussions. Then the coalition made a development plan and implemented it over the following years.

During these processes certain conflicts on wages and economic outcome emerged several times, each time seemingly out of the blue, as if they were an unwritten part of the agenda, no matter what issue that was in focus. Unsolved disagreements can be like ghosts haunting and disturbing rationality and any good will. Finally, the local coalition found a solution to these matters that constantly disturbed the development processes. Conflicts that occurred during the meetings in the local work council should be described properly and then handled by the local bargaining council. The bargaining council protected the positive spirit of the local work council from issues disturbing development. Two years later, management and employee relations had begun to improve. Communication was open, mutual trust seemed to develop, and operating business seemed to benefit from this.

The development coalition in el-corporation was encouraged by the results from the first division. Researchers had followed most of the different local work councils during the first year, describing the variations in form and content. It was decided to try to conduct the survey commissioned by the local work councils in all business units in order to sort out the main development issues for the whole corporation. After some time, using surveys became a tool in implementing the EFQM-model[2] in the corporation. Research was included in the general and mainstream development efforts in the corporation. A few business units refused to take part in the survey, and were sceptical toward the development coalition, the ideas of ED 2000, and the establishment of local work councils. These were seldom proclaimed as firm viewpoints. The arguments for withdrawal always came from

2. EFQM means European Foundation for Quality Management as well as the name of a specific TQM model that includes measurement of employees' work place satisfaction.

the management, never from employee representatives, and they always focused on lack of resources, close deadlines in the operating business and so on. It was in other words a kind of resistance in disguise. It would have been strange though, if no one within a large corporation expressed scepticism to either the researchers, social science or the concept of Participatory Company Development. To "win them all" is a scarce event in business development as well.

The development factory

Our collaboration with the forestry and paper corporation started in one of the paper mills. The purpose was to explore and develop co-operation between management and employees. The project and the coalition were launched at a seminar bringing management, shop floor stewards and employee representatives together in spring 1996. A description of characteristics and differences in management and employee relation was the first task of the researchers. The results were presented and discussed at a new seminar. The report was used to identify development issues. A committee was set up to run the coalition. The committee was headed by the managing director and had representatives from other managerial areas and three leaders from the union. The factory work council was used as the core for the development coalition, and the development organization. Seven departmental work councils were implementing decisions on development activities.

In spring 1997 both the managing director and the human resource manager retired. Later on that year, the board of the corporation put heavy demands on productivity and profit from the plant. The paper mill had to show sustainability by reducing costs with 18 percent within the next three years. This message was more or less conceived as a crisis jeopardizing the future of the plant. The level of activity in the development coalition rose dramatically. The committee of the coalition and the work council rapidly made a development plan aiming at a 15 percent staff reduction, but without any dismissals. Three activities should result in downsizing within three years; (1) voluntary early retirements according to the main agreements between the social partners, (2) voluntary job seeking and (3) participation in an internal education program. At the same time productivity should be increased by reorganization and improved skills. The development plan aimed at raising the proportion of employees with vocational training from 40 to 90 percent within the same period. Sick leave should be reduced from a sky high 18 percent to about 5 percent. All these elements were defined in a formal agreement, committing the management and the unions to take part in the process according to a specification of tasks and timetable. The agreement was the only written document to be followed in the development process.

The research group was consulted several times during this process, and was asked to find out how the employees would react to the defined crisis. A survey was developed together with the committee and conducted very fast. The results showed that voluntary early retirements and normal job seeking would produce the wanted downsizing, given that vacancies were not replaced. The education program would not be necessary for downsizing purposes. The coalition, management and work council should focus on how to keep up production with a reduced staff, rather than on how to handle the downsizing.

Half a year later, the production had increased with 8000 tons of paper in the period the downsizing was accomplished, sick leave was still high, and the reorganizing process went too slowly. The development plan had obviously been too effective. When coming from outside, the development activities could easily be interpreted as the main purpose of the plant during this period. The future was at stake, and the response was a tremendous collective effort to hang in with business.

There were disagreements of course. The development plan was presented as a mutual commitment between management and unions that was the result of tough negotiations. Management could insist on something like 100 dismissals. The unions could refuse to participate unless certain demands were agreed upon. The dialogue in the committee and in the work council was open and honest, sometimes very high tempered, and even close to breakdown several times. There were disagreements within the unions, and within the management as well. In the end, however, the conclusion was reached through arguments from both parties, based on mutual respect for each other.

Preconditions for development coalitions

To make social science research work in enterprise development demands an ability to communicate with other professional groups. Most industrial leaders in Norway are either engineers or economists. Employees are mostly educated or specialized through work. Their perspectives, skills and social identifications differ from those you will find among social scientists. The challenge is to catch their perspectives, and try to interpret reality in their way, in order to sort out what the research issues might be. An empathetic attitude is necessary.

Research and development coalitions have to compete for corporate attention. The three coalitions that broke apart show how external factors attract attention. Mergers, take-overs and stock exchange fluctuations demand new strategies that may reduce the relevance of any on-going development activity. It was only in the chemical corporation that the coalition was closed down by a managerial decision, disapproving of the recommendations of the development committee. Coalitions in the multi product corporation and the mechanic corporation were closed down for capacity reasons. Other change processes demanded resources that left no room for the business-research activities. In addition, our approaches could intervene on other activities and processes. We lost the competition for development attention. Our perspectives may have been perceived as less relevant, and our legitimacy may have been less than that of the business development consultants.

Internal forces may also be crucial to the existence of business-research coalitions. When corporate structures are rearranged, as in mergers and take-overs, lots of influencing activities take place. Positions are changed, corporate power is reallocated and there is a competition on authority taking place. Research and development coalitions may all of a sudden become a part in the on-going battle, either by being held to support certain viewpoints, or perceived as a threat to management.

The development coalitions that broke apart were probably too new, too unknown and too unpredictable to the corporate management to be included in operations crucial to bottom line results. This assumption points to the fact that development coalitions demand trust, legitimacy, lots of time and open dialogues between the parties involved. Senior research skills have to be offered from the very beginning.

There are certain similarities between the two viable coalitions. Employee representatives and unions were included from the very beginning. The parties developed mutual understanding, exchanged viewpoints, argued heavily and were decisive together. The researchers were neutral to both parties, and the research tasks were defined by the coalitions, not by the researchers alone. It seems to be important; (1) that the employees are organized and that these organizations are actively engaged in enterprise problems; (2) that there are arenas for management and employee cooperation, communication and coordination; (3) that management and employee organizations develop mutual respect for each other and their respective viewpoints; (4) that the management valuate the involvement of employee organizations in enterprise development; (5) that researchers and employees develop a shared understanding and interpretation of different terminology, perspectives and skills; and (6) that time and resources allow for slack and adaptation to new situations on all sides.

Research challenges

Researchers meet the challenges of different role expectations from the parties in the enterprise. Each party will try to convince the researcher of his or her perspectives and viewpoints. Researchers are expected to tell the objective truth about events and situations, and to guide the enterprise through the problems at hand. This expert role is only to be fulfilled when research methods create answers to specific problems defined by the parties. Then it is science that gives the answers, not the researcher as a person.

As member of a development coalition, the researcher will influence the situations or processes to be explored or explained. You become your own empirical subject. This is one of the reasons why action research is often criticized for being biased and unreliable. The problem is mental distance on the one hand, and methodological skills on the other. To follow methodological rules, and apply all known control routines will certainly help to avoid the most obvious traps. The presence of coalition parties with different perspectives, angels and expectations to the research demands neutral researchers. The demand of neutrality towards the parties helps to report nothing but the actual findings and to avoid biased interpretations of data.

In setting up a development coalition you will have to involve and include the social partners in the development of specific methods, tools and analytical processes. The purpose is to use the analysis in directing the enterprise. This is much more likely to happen if the implementers of enterprise development take part in the analysis and thereby make the conclusions for themselves. Only actors in the enterprise are able to develop new capacities, processes or structures.

Enterprise research participation

The management is responsible for strategic development. The establishment of a development coalition changes this position. Identification of development issues has to be discussed, outlined and agreed upon by all members of the coalition. Negotiations, bargaining, agreement and consensus are words that describe decisions on what to develop and in what way. The researchers could propose certain issues to be explored or investigated, but the enterprise parties would either approve or disapprove of these proposals. The development issues identified by the parties defined the research tasks.

The employees took part in the analysis of data provided by the researchers. This was useful in several ways. In some cases the researchers could prevent misinterpretations. On the other hand participants from the enterprise knew much more about the local reality than the researchers, so they were much more capable of explaining findings. This helped the analysis a lot in most cases. The co-operation between managers, employees and researchers seemed to improve relevance, usefulness and the quality of the research. Both managers and union representatives were surprised by some of the research findings. Both groups held the findings to support their point of view, and the researchers had to explain what the data actually meant. The best way was to include them in the research processes, and thereby make perspectives, assumptions and methods familiar to them.

Fragile coalitions and the role of research

Development coalitions in corporations encounter some special problems. Firstly, there is the problem of size. Researchers cannot get involved with all employees. Contacts are limited to certain representatives, steering committees, and members of coalitions, the board of the corporation, and the boards of the unions. In order to access the viewpoints and interpretations from all employees we were left with quantitative methods like surveys and questionnaires.

The coalitions were established and organized from the top of the corporate hierarchies. The development coalition was perceived as belonging to the headquarters, and any confusion between corporate headquarters and subsidiaries would affect the research processes in the subsidiaries. Some subsidiaries would do anything they could to please the headquarters, and they would support any research request in order to do so. Others would try to inhibit research in order to preserve their autonomous position.

When the development agenda is launched or changes are implemented, many different interests are at stake. Reorganization like mergers, takeovers, outsourcing or other kinds of restructuring are often central business activities. Such activities may reduce the relevance of the ongoing development coalition and close it down. Restructuring opens up the arena for competition on new managerial positions, and that will normally not help ongoing development processes.

Development coalitions have been effective in enterprise development. But are they reasonable tools for research in the private sector? They obviously give access to problems, enterprise perspectives, new research issues and data that otherwise would be difficult to attain. On the other hand, there is the problem of narrow scope. Each coalition defines problems of relevance for the enterprises. The results may be very relevant and useful to the actual enterprise, but almost worthless for generalizations. One strategy for attaining generalized knowledge would be to include several enterprises and networks of enterprises in one coalition. Such coalitions could aim at developing groups of enterprises more than one by one, and thereby reach certain levels of generalized analysis.

Coalitions are vulnerable to internal rivalry as well as to environmental turbulence. Any coalition is an attempt to merge different interests, and try to reach consensus on certain issues. The interests of the coalition as such will always be less than the interests of any internal actor. That makes them fragile.

Chapter 7

Networking industrial development

Tor Claussen and Henrik Kvadsheim

Introduction

Action research at Rogaland Research (RF) involved many different participants in development and research activities. An important implication of this action research profile was strong collaboration between research, enterprises and networks. In addition, several different funding agencies expressing different guidelines and obligations related to our research were involved. The complexity and variety of obligations and demands represented *new challenges.* These challenges raised two important questions:

- How would it be possible to co-ordinate the different interests, expectations and competencies in order to make them collaborate in this kind of action-research project?
- Would the collaboration and interaction between the participants result in conflicts and destructive practices in the module, or would the interaction and collaboration result in the initiation of new kinds of learning processes between the participants?

These different obligations and demands also challenged organisational aspects of the research activities. For our research and developmental activities these challenges required *commitment and trust* among different participants and actors. Differences of interests and opinions had to be balanced and utilised constructively in order to make use of the different contributions. Commitment and trust were prerequisites for the implementation of research and development activities. On the other hand, different interests and opinions contributed to the development of the module as a joint initiative of the different partners.

In this chapter we emphasise (1) the challenges regarding commitment and trust that we as researchers were faced with in order to fulfil the different obligations and demands, and (2) what consequences the interaction and collaboration between the different participants had for the work in the module. Adding on to this, we sketch different solutions and moves we made in order to face these challenges, with lessons learned from our experiences. Creating commitment and trust without downgrading differences of interests and contributions will function as a point of reference in the stories we present about our module.

The Rogaland Research Module

The module was jointly financed by the Research Council of Norway (NFR), the Confederation of Norwegian Business and Industry (NHO) and the Norwegian Federation of Trade Unions (LO). Financial support from several sources was one reason for the size of the RF-module, which had a substantially higher budget and level of activity than the other modules. The RF module was organised in four projects, each directed by its own project manager. Three of the projects were directly linked to three different networks:

- SYNERGI (Co-operation between offshore-related companies concerning the use of data on safety-management)
- TESA (Technological Co-operation between companies in the Jaeren Region)
- IfS (The Industrial Network for the region of Sunnhordland)

Each of the networks consisted of several independent enterprises. The main function of each network project was to fulfil the obligations to the collaborating enterprises. The fourth project, however, consisted of joint activities across the three networks. Our module leader had the main responsibility for this fourth project. The module leader was also responsible for the integration and presentation of the total module activities, including publishing, seminars, theory and model development, doctoral thesis, etc. A total number of 30–35 enterprises participated in the module. Ten of these enterprises were involved on a long-term basis. The research group consisted of as many as 20 researchers, 8 of them forming the core-group, including three doctoral students.

The participating enterprises and networks exposed a variety of expectations in the initial phases of the work. The different funding agencies required emphasis on specific initiatives in the research conducted. Enterprise development as well as specific work environment conditions were to be improved. Internally, ED2000 represented the biggest program we had ever taken on. Organising such a large program posed formidable internal challenges.

Collaborating consultants and social science researchers

Getting "traditional" researchers and consultants to work creatively and constructively together was the greatest initial challenge. Our institute was organised in different departments, with separate economic targets. The design and implementation of the Rogaland Research (RF) module was based on co-operation between two research departments. These departments represented different cultures and research practices. The Department of Business Development consisted mainly of engineers and business consultants. The department had lots of experiences from conducting project-work for private enterprises. Their strengths were mainly in solving practical company related problems based on public financed R&D programmes. The results of their work were seldom accessible to others as the researchers seldom published for the research community. Recruitment to the department was based on experience from business life. These researchers represented the role of consultants in the RF-module.

The Department of Social Science recruited researchers with a university degree in different social science disciplines like sociology, organisation theory, economics etc. These researchers were mainly funded by national research programs. For this group, publishing for the scientific community had a high value. These researchers represented the traditional role of researchers in the ED-programme.

Traditionally there had been little co-operation between these two departments. They differed in professional positions and understandings of 'the right way' to conduct business-related research. ED-2000 challenged the two research units as they had to co-operate closely for many years working in different enterprises and enterprise-networks.

By the time ED2000 started, there was a great deal of suspicion and distrust among researchers from the two departments, even though the researchers from both departments participated in writing the proposal. The distrust between the departments was related to earlier history and stereotypical views of one another. One of the departments had the necessary close links to the enterprises and networks involved. The other department had the required background in social science research. Researchers from both departments accused each another for not being able to handle demands and obligations towards the different clients. The business department would not have radical social researchers, who were not properly dressed and did not conduct themselves in a proper manner in their teams, facing managers and important participants from enterprises and networks. Researchers from the "social science department" would not perform what they termed "dishonest" commissioned work executed by consultants. The different images and opinions between the two departments were openly articulated when ED2000 was to be organised at the institute. Differences in professional positions, as well as interests related to economic performance, were some of the underlying motives related to the evolving conflicts. The conflicts and differences had to be sorted out before ED2000 could be initiated.

The presence of these differences and diversities had already been utilised constructively in the process of forming the initial proposal. In the proposal we sketched the main challenge related to some of the topics involved in the conflicting images prevailing in the two departments. The management directed business and engineering research represented challenges towards traditional social science research and vice versa. Converting these challenges into constructive and complementary contributions would enhance the whole ED2000 initiative at our institute. Aiming at utilising this possibility became the main target initially. This also became the point of departure in the formulation of the overall research objectives.

Formulating the *overall objectives* became an important task when we started working with ED2000. These overall objectives were related to the question of how international management concepts might be integrated in Scandinavian work life traditions. International management concepts were seen as the product of engineers and business economists, while the Scandinavian work life tradition was associated more with social science approaches. Special attention was given to ways that these different and sometimes conflicting traditions could contribute to the further development of enterprise democracy and work environment. The development of industrial democracy and good work environment was expected to increase competitiveness and job security for the participating enterprises.

For different purposes, we had to specify the overall objectives in order to develop the specific research and developmental targets:

- Initiating developmental processes in the participating enterprises based on both direct and indirect participation. A variety of improvement projects were initiated.
- Building of co-operative structures in and between different networks (IfS, TESA and SYNERGI). We tried to establish new arenas for co-operation between enterprises and social partners, built on the experiences from the developmental processes initiated at the enterprise level.
- Relating structural preconditions (market, government, etc.) to the research and development of the networks and the different enterprises. At an early stage of our research we discovered that structural preconditions had to be downgraded in order to fulfil the obligations related to the other research objectives.

Collaborating enterprises and networks

The collaborating networks in our module had some distinct characteristics as they were organised as quasi enterprises with a joint-stock ownership structure. This ownership structure gave the networks a more solid structure than networks based merely on joint market relationships, or other looser forms of collaborations between independent enterprises. On the other hand, each participant acted as a separate company without giving up any kind of independence characterising individual companies in a regular market economy. Two networks (IfS and TESA) had established an organisational structure consolidating the network collaboration. Each activity was organised into separate units. These units focused on issues like market, economy, organisations, and productions. This internal structure reflected much of the functional division of the separate departments in the enterprise itself. This was another reason why the network structure was characterised as a quasi enterprise, something in between market collaborations and a hierarchical company structure.

Our co-operation with the different networks had been established prior to ED2000. Researchers in our team had a long history of involvement in research and developmental activities. Our research institute had a long tradition of co-operation with the TESA network. This is the oldest industrial network of its kind in Norway. Our intended research collaboration with the three networks was introduced through the developmental activities previously established. Each researcher utilised their key role in the networks to introduce the basic ideas of ED2000. These arguments were prepared in advance. The introduction was done stepwise, to obtain the necessary involvement by the networks and enterprises.

A presentation of the participating networks

The IfS-network is located along the Western coast of Norway. It represents around 10,000 employees and a total sales of several billion NOK. Altogether there are 14 companies in the IfS network. Seven of these were core enterprises in the ED2000 project at RF. They were identified as core enterprises because they committed themselves to establish TQM-processes in close co-operation with the network organisation and RF. The rest participated in less committed ways. The offshore oil activity dominates the Norwegian economy, and has a tremendous impact on the development of the West Coast. A few national suppliers dominate the Norwegian offshore market. They are called "super suppliers" because they have received increased responsibility for offshore projects through new forms of contractual agreements The "super supplier" in the IfS network played a major role in the industrial and economical development of the region. This company had an important role as an industrial locomotive for the regional SME industry.

The TESA-network is the oldest known formal enterprise network in Norway. It is located along the West Coast of Norway, south of the IfS network. There are 13 members in the network. Seven of these members had close collaborations with the ED2000. Members of the network cover producers of relatively conventional mechanical products to high tech products, including producers of communications technology as well as flexible automation systems. TESA is about *half* the size of IfS both in sales and number of employees. Among the most significant differences between these two networks were a lack of commitment and involvement in TESA compared to IfS. This was especially the case in the initial stages of ED2000. One of the reasons could be a stronger corporate network linking TESA enterprises to obligations outside the network structure.

The SYNERGI network consisted of five of the largest enterprises in Norway. They are mainly related to the offshore market. These enterprises had no specific regional location, their activities are scattered all over Norway as well as globally. They employed a total of almost 90 000 employees and have a total sales of more than NOK 100 billion. In the *SYNERGI-network*, safety management was the main focus. Safety information and other health and safety data were collected in company specific databases. These data were then made anonymous and transferred to a central database where they are processed, so that company specific data and analyses can be compared with data from all participating companies. A basic assumption in safety management is that accidents are preventable through effective feedback control; i.e. through mechanisms by which information about accidents and near misses is employed as a basis for actions to increase the level of safety. The purpose of the SYNERGI-network is to support development of safety considerations, safety management, and safety control and accident prevention. The latter is of special significance and importance for ED2000. Although the SYNERGI network made important contributions to the research activities in the ED2000 module at RF, we will concentrate on the stories of IfS and TESA.

The story of the work

The network activities were organised as separate projects with their own project leader. This was partly due to the differences between the networks as well as the kind of research and developmental activities that took place in each network. The autonomy of the network projects was a great challenge related to the integrity of the module as a whole. Adding to this was the internal tension between researchers committed to social science research and researcher with a more consultant type of profile in their work. Researchers with a more consultant type of profile were the project leaders for the network projects.

Despite the internal efforts to establish a shared research design in the different network projects as well as the overall activities of the module, each network can be viewed as a separate initiative. It also became apparent that the independence of each network project created obligations and commitment of researchers and consultants towards *their* network project. This was both an advantage stimulating the researchers and consultants engagement in the network activities as well as an obstacle creating less commitment to the overall module obligations.

The IfS network

One major actor played a significant role in the organisation of this network as well as in the different developmental activities that took place. This company established a close relationship with our research institute. The ideas of Total Quality Management (TQM) promoted by this company were highly congruent with the basic research ideas in ED2000. As a starting point, the company had experience from working with an international concept like TQM and had already adjusted this concept to the Norwegian work life traditions. It was agreed to start continuous improvement based on TQM in a number of core enterprises that independently decided to join ED2000.

Although there was no obvious pressure experienced by the enterprises in the network to join ED2000, the fact that this major company strongly recommended the project, was a driving force. For many of the companies joining ED2000 could be a way to become a supplier to this dominating company in the region. Becoming a supplier to this company would also require the implementation of TQM. This was probably a driving force in the commitment to ED2000 from these smaller companies. At a later stage, ED2000 proved to be a useful enterprise development program, regardless of the specific ambitions to become suppliers to the "super supplier". This encouraged continued participation and expanded interest in the program among the committed enterprises.

An *opening conference* involving the working life parties and the dominating company, initiated the collaboration with the network. Establishing commitment and developing trust towards the project's overall objectives was a major focus at the conference. It turned out to be a sort of happening, a major success that gave us a flying start in the collaboration with the network. We felt that we had to know the different enterprises more thoroughly. We decided therefore to map each company in detail. After this *survey* we started to analyse the material and worked out reports to the participating companies.

This was probably the most critical stage of the whole project. The participating companies were eager to start the actual work, and we almost lost all the trust we had established in the beginning of the project. Conducting interviews and then successively withdrawing without any more signs of existence, fulfilled all the prejudice and mistrust that the industry formerly had developed towards research. We hastily had to present ourselves as dynamic consultants eager to produce tangible results. On the other hand, we were appreciated for our trustworthy professional neutrality. We were trusted because we did not have a dedicated solution, which we wanted to sell at any price. This was a conflict between acting as a "neutral" scientist or as an active, dynamic and dedicated consultant. We had to cope with such conflicts that are a characteristic feature of action research.

After the opening conference, we arranged meetings with its participating members to discuss the scope of work separately. In co-operation with the companies, we decided to start with a separate conference in each enterprise. This was coined the *enterprise conference*. Each employee participated on equal foot regardless of his or her position in the company. If the companies employed more than 50, we suggested that a representative group of around 30–40 people were selected to participate. In the enterprise conference, a number of specific tasks and challenges were suggested by the participants and given priority in accordance to specific guidelines. We advised the companies to give the highest priority to improvements that could create immediate results. After each conference, feedback was forwarded through separate meetings with a group consisting of the company's management, shop steward, and safety personnel.

Each company was invited twice a year to join a *network conference*. These network conferences worked out some of the same priorities regarding tasks and challenges that were listed in the enterprise conferences. At the conference, shared challenges and tasks for the participating companies were identified. It was decided that these common task and challenges should be given special attention in future network conferences as well as in special seminars. At the different conferences and meetings, both representatives from the working life parties as well as from the major actor in the network took and active part alongside the researchers/consultants. On an equal footing, we engaged with the individual enterprises in the different tasks. The dedication to a joint effort in research and development both on enterprise and network level, was of major importance for making the IfS network a success.

The network conferences encouraged trust and commitment. Each company committed themselves to follow up on specific improvements according to their own priorities and present them at the next conference. This commitment was a driving force in fulfilling their internal improvement obligations. For each participating member the network conference gave an opportunity and obligation to present their own company and the specific achievements accomplished. The presentation of the company was made regardless of the hierarchical position. For shop stewards and safety personnel this was a good but sometimes painful opportunity. On the other hand it meant acquiring important skills in discussing and reflecting on their own company as well as on specific working conditions.

The TESA network

The intensity of the network collaboration has fluctuated quite a bit. Recently a majority of the participating companies have merged with an international corporate company. As a consequence, these corporate relations started to compete with the TESA network relations. Something had to be done in order to attract attention to the network. Our close collaboration with the TESA enterprises made us aware of this situation. We saw the ED2000 as a possibility to renew the vitality of the network. Utilizing this possibility, though, was something quite different from the easy match we initially thought it would be.

The previous experience with TESA had created tension as well as mutual trust and respect. The attitude of the enterprises towards research varied and represented a great challenge. We had to cope with some of the same scepticism as we experienced among companies in the IfS network. This was dealt with quite differently in relation to TESA. In the TESA case, we choose to link our research closely to management and strategic challenges facing the leaders in the different companies. This strategy was followed despite the overall philosophy of ED2000 placing decisive emphasis on both employees and employers in equal participation in the project. We figured that this strategy was necessary to create essential trust that could be the basis for later employee's commitment. Involvement and commitment related to ED2000 was a cumbersome process for the TESA enterprises. We experienced that a gathering of the top leaders briefly touching ED2000 had a greater success in the beginning than the specific improvement projects we tried to introduce.

The TESA network lacked a "locomotive" company. It therefore seemed impossible to get a unified committed process started in the TESA network. Tense relations also made it difficult to get acceptance for the involvement of trade unions. This was a crucial factor in the IfS case.

TESA was in many respects markedly different from what happened in IfS. These differences can be summed up as follows:

- In the IfS-network, the researchers took advantage of an internal mobilisation process. In TESA they had to be part of a renewal-process.
- A great deal of tension was present in the TESA network
- In the TESA network, no dominant actor had the power to define basic premises, as was the case with the IfS network.
- There was no significant overlap between the basic research objectives in ED2000 and similar focuses in the TESA enterprises.

- The research framework in the TESA network was not based on a common framework like the TQM-concept in the IfS-network. This made it more difficult to establish development — and reflection processes between the network members based on a common practice.

The results and engagement from the IfS network attracted attention through the exchange of information that took place in the reference group organised for the whole module. Participants from the networks, the working life parties, and the funding agencies were represented. The awareness of what was going on in IfS, together with the success of some of the projects, stimulated an increasing interest in ED2000 among the TESA members. We became more competent in handling the specific challenges of the TESA network, along with the development of closer personal relations. Later on, the secretariat of TESA was located at our research institute. This enhanced the collaboration and the interest in ED2000 significantly.

The interest and engagement in the TESA network grew tremendously. Many of the experiences and results from IfS have been implemented in TESA and vice versa. These networks have started collaborative efforts.

The differences between the networks, the projects and the preconditions related to the collaboration with our research team in ED2000 varied significantly. This accounts for some of the reasons for the difficulties we experienced in establishing a common framework for our research module.

Coping with heterogeneity and new forms of collaboration

In this section we reflect on some lessons learned from dealing with action research related to the importance of facilitating trust-building, commitment, and reflection processes among the involved participants. The main objective is to emphasise that when enhancing internal collaboration and reflection processes it is necessary to cope with heterogeneity.

During the initial phases of the module work, co-operation between the management consultants and the social science researchers was characterised by scepticism. The initial design of the RF-module represented a challenge for the researchers in how to understand the aims and means of action-research and how to carry it out. A continuous discussion between the ten RF-researchers participating in the module-work dealt with matters of how the researchers should intervene and influence the developing processes in the participating enterprises. For the IfS-network the overall objective was related to the implementation of a common concept of development based on Total Quality Management (TQM) in the participating enterprises.

The "consultants" wanted to go for a research practice which mainly focused on TQM-techniques and expert advise to the companies. This practice would lead to close relations, characterised by usefulness and confidence between RF and the enterprises. The social science researchers highlighted the problems of combining "the advisor role" with the critical research. For them "the advisor role" in the enterprises would make them committed and responsible for the development in these enterprises, and thereby make it difficult to evaluate the actual outcomes.

In order to visit the enterprises, the researchers had to travel several hours with cars and ferries. Discussions were carried out on these ferry-trips concerning how the researchers ought to carry out their researcher role in the enterprises. The mainstream opinion came to be that the researchers should keep some distance from the decision and implementation processes in the enterprises. Their role should be that of "the facilitator".

This interpretation of the action-researcher role became the mainstream opinion, even though there were many differences regarding the researchers´ practice. More interesting was the composition of research-teams in the enterprises as they included both consultants and researchers. This composition made it possible to play the role of an advisor and of a critical researcher. The continuous discussions between the researchers within each enterprise research group contributed to critical reflections and made it possible to reflect on and learn from their own practice. The consultants learned about scientific practice, and the social science researchers learned about obtaining relationships with enterprises based on usefulness and trust. Presentations, publishing, joint seminars and conferences were frequently arranged and became more and more important as the project evolved. These common activities were of major importance in relation to our main financial supporters.

Halfway through the ED-2000, the two departments were partly merged. The scepticism between the researchers in the two departments was replaced by respect for the different roles researchers and consultants play in action research. The researchers have on their side acknowledged the advantage of carrying out action research, not as individuals, but as a divergent team.

Coping with obligations to our funding agencies — Proving our usefulness

We were anxious to prove the usefulness of our different module activities. One important reason behind our anxiety was the combination of research and development, as well as the action research approach. Both of these aspects emphasised collaboration with "customers" to achieve identifiable results. We felt obligations towards our funding agencies, and the stress that they had put on the importance of results enhancing competitiveness and job security. These obligations were central issues in the program objectives. In short, the program and different module activities always had to prove its usefulness towards the funding agencies, as well as important actors in the scientific community, in addition to politicians, government officials, and employee/employer organizations. We felt that these obligations were continuously communicated to the participating researchers as an important aspect of the overall program's legitimisation.

In the RF-module, these challenges have been dealt with in several ways. In the initial stage of the program period, a large mapping of all the participating enterprises in both TESA and IfS took place. The aim was to collect both quantitative and qualitative data, which would make it possible for the researchers to picture the state of affairs in each enterprise and network. In this process, the term "benchmarking the Scandinavian way" was suggested. It illustrated the incorporation of indicators such as degree of work place democracy, direct participation, work environment, degree and use of network relation, as factors contributing to the overall efficiency of a company. The process of designing the mapping — questionnaires was in itself a challenge. The researchers represented different disciplines and interests of different subjects like management-theory, production, work democracy and work environment. They now had to work together on developing common questionnaires, which they afterwards had to use as a common reference for their mapping activities and interviews of different actors in the enterprises. Three years later, they had to do the same mapping and comparing the state of affairs in each enterprise and network. The reflection on different indicators in this mapping process represented an important contribution to crossing the borders of different subjects and disciplines, and made it possible for us to see new connections and overlaps between different subjects such as management-theory and work environment. Today our research institute has developed new kinds of projects, integrating enterprise development and the development of the work environment. The Norwegian Research Council has recognised this integration by sponsoring our institute with strategic program funds for further developing this kind of integrating strategies and knowledge.

Coping with enterprise heterogenity — Enhancing external collaboration and reflection processes

Enterprise development through network co-operation can be a way for companies to enhance their knowledge of how efforts to improve are fulfilled among competitors, customers and other enterprises. Knowledge from and comparisons with other companies can contribute to a better understanding of how to change. Enterprise development in networks may increase the demand of viewing and comparing oneself by taking the "other point of view". In this way, enterprise development can make contributions to company awareness.

These possible gains seem however to be based on some preconditions. Initially, the build-up of trust between participants and researchers was regarded as a prerequisite for co-operation. On the other hand, trust would preferably also be a product of different forms of collaboration. In our networks it was (1) the relationship between the companies and the researchers, and (2) the relationship between the companies themselves that was of special importance.

Let us first look at the growth of trust between the enterprises in the network. At the first network meetings in IfS network, we realised that a number of the companies were very cautious about describing their own situation. These reservations can be explained by the fact that the companies to some extent competed, and they therefore did not wish to reveal their own weaknesses to the others. A number of them also had a customer-supplier relationship. The detached attitude during the initial stages was reflected in the fact that the participants were unwilling to talk about the internal matters except for the factual improvement areas they had selected. In the course of the process, however, this changed. The enterprises became more and more open in their presentations. After some time, the network meetings changed to a forum where they could get useful input from the other companies on internal problems.

Network presume the trust of the other participants, regardless of whether they are competitors, customers or suppliers. In this context, trust means relying on the other companies not using sensitive information for competitive purposes or in negotiating situations. When such trust has been established, it can form the basis for a type of communication where solutions to problems are channelled across the companies.

What about the companies "trust" in the researchers? Initially the companies expressed scepticism against the researchers. The initial mapping of the companies confirmed their expectations of the researchers as persons mainly interested in extracting information from the companies without giving anything back. Later, a survey showed that the companies regarded the role and presence of the researchers in the project as both useful and constructive. The reason for this change in attitude may partly be attributed the role of the researchers, committing themselves to the enterprises as process-facilitators and advisors. Twice a year the researchers had to visit the participating enterprises as discussion partners and advisors on the development process. In addition, the researchers met regularly in the network-meetings. The lack of trust, which colored the first stages of the project, was to a large degree replaced by close relationships of trust. This development has provided fertile soil for growth in the creation of new joint activities between RF and the IfS network.

One of the reasons for having the companies meet regularly in network forums was to establish a meta-organisational arena that would commit and motivate the companies in their development work. The participation of the major company in

IfS worked as a magnet in the development project. The network meetings were regarded by some of the enterprises as opportunities to establish contacts with the major company, an important customer and mentor, and at the same time they represented opportunities for the enterprises to promote themselves. However, later on in the process, the role of the major company lost some of its significance.

Having to stand up in the network forums and give a progress report on improvements was an inducement to the companies, almost like tying oneself to the mast. The network gatherings were also an important source of inspiration and helped to motivate the participants to continue their improvement work.

The positive and supportive attitude of the employee representatives to the development processes in the company must be seen in the light of the fact that they were brought into the development project at an early stage. They also had the opportunity to discuss their experiences in the regular meetings of employee representatives. The middle managers and first line managers were not involved in the network collaboration at the initial stage. The impression is that the middle management do not identify themselves with development processes. This shows how various network forums can give collaboration more depth by including various key participants, and how these forums can create support in generating mutual commitment, enthusiasm, and motivation in the follow-up process.

One of the main objects of network collaboration was to give the companies a chance to exchange experiences and learn from each other. It was expected that using the same basic TQM concept would establish a common foundation for the exchange of experience and learning. There is no doubt that common challenges in the process formed a significant and unifying prerequisite for the exchange of experiences. As time passes, mutual trust provided the basis for a more open exchange of experiences, which in turn gave a greater return in the form of learning. However, the common frame of reference for the exchange of experiences played an important part in ensuring that the exchange of experiences and the learning processes between the enterprises were felt to be relevant, useful, and recognized by the different participants.

The network meetings also created opportunities for the participants to raise *new kinds of questions* concerning the development practice in each enterprise. These were questions related to the substance and objectives of the development processes in each enterprise. Initially the ED-2000 was a program related to enterprise development. Thus in the IfS-network meetings the researchers early emphasised the importance of integrating worklife issues into the enterprise development issues. Framing these issues was partly done because the Working Life Fund in the Confederation of Norwegian Business and Industry (NHO) was one of the modules main funding agencies. By framing this kind of issues through the network arrangement, as well as inviting occupational health and safety persons

(HS) to the network meetings, we created an common opportunity for discussion and reflections on worklife issues in an enterprise development context involving enterprise leaders, shop stewards, and specific HS-personnel. By questioning traditional ways of perceiving enterprise development, we may characterize this process as an example of "double-loop learning".

The network meetings were not established in the TESA-network. Hence, we did not get the common opportunity to introduce worklife issues as an integrated part of enterprise development. As a result, the TESA enterprises emphasised worklife issues to a much lower degree in their enterprise improvement projects compared to the IfS enterprises. This illustrates that network-arrangements may play an important role in the process of introducing questions and issues into development processes for reflection, understanding and legitimatisation, both within and between enterprises.

Conclusions

We specifically draw the attention to the possibilities of employing internal and external heterogeneity in critical and reflective learning processes. The different interests, opinions and obligations were a great challenge to our module and the specific action research conducted. External funding agencies forwarded different demands and emphasised several and sometimes conflicting requirements. Among the researchers in our team, there were several differences in approaches and ways of doing research. The participating companies had different interests and also expressed internal cleavages. Forming a common ground for action research in this manifold of interest and obligations was a challenge. On the other hand, this multitude of interests and opinions represented new possibilities for critical reflection and learning processes. We have tried to illuminate this in the storytelling about our work.

These new possibilities for critical reflection and learning processes can be listed as follows:

- Internal heterogeneity expressed as researcher vs. consultant, contributed to an internal reflection process on the role of action research. In addition, these internal critical reflections involved different approaches and ways of conducting research. Collaborating in action research contributed to a new understanding of the different roles researchers and consultants may play in an action research context.
- The network-based development processes contributed to commitment and motivation among the participants, as well as self-critical reflection processes. The network arenas forced enterprises to present results from improvements

they had committed themselves to accomplish and "mirror" their performance in relation to others. They highlight this aspect of enterprise development and the utilization of the network setting in encouraging specific company performance. The networks served as arenas both to facilitate more traditional learning and exchange of information, as well as for benchmarking the companies themselves. Also, the network arenas served as driving forces in the actual performance of the developmental activities encouraging promised improvements to give promised results.
- The first and second point attract attention to the specific possibilities given for critical in depth reflections on action research regarding our own actions in the enterprises and networks. An important element in these critical reflections was the different approaches and guiding opinions that were present at the outset. These different and sometimes conflicting approaches and opinions presented themselves as great challenges. At later stages, they were important resources in the critical reflection processes for the researchers. The critical reflection processes among the researchers formed a baseline for preliminary, self-critical learning processes within the enterprises and among the enterprises. Through self-critical reflection processes, a number of the enterprises managed to form new ways of handling challenges facing improvements and change processes.

Due to the differences in the three networks, the establishment or furtherance of a development organisation in the participating companies has been fulfilled to a varying degree. In the IfS and the TESA network, each participating enterprise went through several stages in implementing a development organisation. Some of them succeeded quite well.

With respect to the establishment or furtherance of a network collaboration for development work the RF module has been quite successful. We initiated, together with the participating companies, three network projects. Two of the networks have been further developed as a facilitator for common activities.

The main focus in the RF-module has been the question of how international management concepts may be integrated with the Scandinavian working life tradition. That question governs our research activities. In our projects we have been able to establish concepts and frameworks useful in improvements and enterprise development projects. These efforts have been guided by ways of integrating and utilizing the differences and similarities between Scandinavian working life traditions and international TQM management concept.

We experienced that trust and commitment were basic building blocks in enterprise development and action research approach. Through commitment and trust we were able to engage a number of participants within and outside the companies and the research team in the developmental efforts. These efforts were small steps in the necessary changes through which the participant could gain enhanced competitive advantages. What we did not achieve was more significant structural and innovative changes. The need for more fundamental changes will emerge in many of the co-operating industries as an effect the down turns of the oil industry. Our research has been aimed at giving a unified homogenous commitment to common expectations, interests and tasks. The creativity and innovative capacity related to differences of opinions and interests was clearly present, but it has not yet been fully utilized to achieve the necessary innovative and creative developmental processes required in the future. This is the main target in our future research ambitions.

Chapter 8

The action learning processes of the Nordvest Forum coalition

Jon Hanssen-Bauer and Håkon Raabe

Introduction

Nordvest Forum is a multi-firm, regional learning network centered around the city of Ålesund in the northern part of the West Coast of Norway. The network was established in 1989, when close to 20 shareholding firms sat up Nordvest Forum Inc. to service the network and manage its activities. Its stated purpose is to improve regional competitiveness by upgrading the management capacity and leadership capabilities of the shareholding companies and other firms in the region. The number of shareholders has increased over the years to 50, and the number of companies involved in the network activities is approaching 150.

The Board of Directors of NVF decided to apply for funding for a module in the ED2000 program, on behalf of all the companies it represented, as it recognized the general need in the region for building and strengthening relations with research institutions, to obtain the support required in coping with organizational challenges. As NVF was not engaged in research itself, NVF planned to commission the research component of its module from various research institutions with which the network wanted to co-operate, to upgrade the competence related to enterprise development among the network participants.

Our purpose in this chapter is to review the design and the experience of this module, with a particular focus on the learning processes established for and among the researchers that were invited to participate. The module was planned with an action research design. It intended to nurture co-generative learning among researchers and practitioners, as well as between researchers from various institutes and disciplines, as they co-operated to help improve organizational performance within the participating firms, and to upgrade the competence of managers and employees in enterprise development issues in the region.

Learning implies deconstructing one's previous view of the world, in order to reconstruct the patterns in a new order that gives new meaning. The module design therefore consisted of a set of arenas and processes that we thought could enhance such a deconstruction and reconstruction of meaning on various levels: personal interaction with the field in enterprises, the sharing of experience among regional actors on the network level, as well as the comparing of notes and interpretations among involved researchers.

The chapter focuses on the assumptions and intentions that influenced the module design, with a view to taking stock of its effectiveness in enhancing learning and research. In doing so, it is inevitable to also comment on the outcomes in terms of development of the enterprise organizations, and the particular research and learning environment, or infrastructure, established and operated by the ED2000 program.

In the following we present the NVF as a network construction, and the more general research interest that influenced the design of the module. We then describe how the module was designed in terms of actors, arenas and processes that were intended to address the various learning issues. In the third part of the chapter we describe the outcome at the most immediate level, i.e. within participating firms and in the regional learning network. Finally, we describe the outcome and effectiveness of the learning among the researchers.

The Nordvest Forum network construct

Nordvest Forum has previously been described as a regional learning network organization that was developed in response to regional firms' increased exposure to competitive environments on a global market.[1] The Northwestern coast of Norway has for centuries been an externally oriented part of Norway where the area's links to the sea traditionally have made access to the international markets easy. Fish processors, ship builders, and furniture manufacturers in the region are highly export oriented, and the region is recognized throughout Norway for its industrious, entrepreneurial, business-minded people. Companies are typically small by international standards, even when they are part of large Norwegian corporations, and the family-owned firm has traditionally been — and to a certain extent still is — a prominent feature of the area.

A successful response to increasing competition on the world market requires great organizational flexibility and adaptability, which are generated by the ability to develop and apply new knowledge quickly and consistently. This fact has urged many scientists to focus on how to create such an ability in competitive firms. Their

1. See Hanssen-Bauer, J. and C.C. Snow (1996), "Responding to Hypercompetition: The Structure and Processes of a Regional Learning Network Organization", *Organization Science*, Vol. 7(4): 413–427.

focus has often been on large companies and on how former "giants learn to dance", or on how an organization's wide repertoire of knowledge can be integrated in a flexible and effective way. The resulting literature on organizational learning is voluminous, and it presents to the reader several models of learning processes, and of how to organize in order to promote such internal processes.

The Nordvest Forum case presents a different set of related research problems than that of learning processes within firms. As market challenges and changes in the business environment for the small companies call for improving organizational performance, these small companies are exposed to many of the same challenges as bigger enterprises. However, they find themselves in a situation where it is difficult to identify themselves with the descriptions and solutions suggested in the current literature. Suggested concepts for organizational development are designed for large organizations, and experience from development processes is typically reported from world class, global corporations. Both experience and concepts, therefore, need translation and interpretation, in order to become relevant for the small firms on the northwestern coast of Norway. In addition, these small companies often lack fundamental resources, both internally and in the region, for organizing their own learning.

The owners of Nordvest Forum created the network as a response to this problem. The network would compensate for the small size and the ensuing scarcity of internal resources in each individual company. By banding together, they also felt they would become a more interesting partner for research and development institutions. They could compete more successfully with larger corporations for these centers' resources and know-how in organizational development, than each company could on its own.

Hence, Nordvest Forum contributes to solving a problem of critical mass and resources, by creating learning processes across firms in the framework of a network. Its challenge, then, consists of finding the best way of mobilizing the network to promote such inter-organizational learning within the whole network, *and* thereby strengthen organizational change processes in the individual firms. The literature is less abundant on these topics. As we have described elsewhere,[2] the Nordvest Forum development module is an experiment in optimizing the *learning cycle of a regional learning network* with this dual perspective, through building relations to social science research institutions.

---

2. A description of the action research approach and how it was adapted to the NVF module can be found in Hanssen-Bauer, J. (1998). "Networking to Learn in Nordvest Forum: Optimizing the Learning Cycle of a Regional Learning Network through Action Research". In Gustavsen, B., T. Colbjørnsen and Ø. Pålshaugen (eds.), *Research and Development Coalitions*. Amsterdam: John Benjamins Publishing Company.

Researching the challenge of network renewal

The first steps leading to the creation of the NVF module were made in 1992. During the first years of its existence the network obtained funding to build up its activities, management training and a forum for top executives being the two most central ones, from a national program for business development supported by the Norwegian state and the labor market parties (the Norwegian Work Life Center, SBA). The support from SBA consisted of both financial resources and advice,[3] and as SBA also worked with other similar networks and tried to establish similar initiatives in other regions, an effort was made by SBA to understand the potential of networks in the context of organizational change, as well as to understand how such networks can be constructed and supported "from the outside". In Norway at that time, a rather reductionist view on networks dominated thinking,[4] making it necessary to rethink the concept in order to use it to create arenas and instruments for learning and change. In order to help develop a strategy of supporting network creations, it became interesting to identify the critical design elements for such learning networks in terms of structure, system set-up, processes and functions. The SBA presented a set of preliminary assumptions and ideas that were influenced by various reports and studies from other countries. In 1992, SBA evaluated the NVF network three years after its inception and summed up what seemed to be the main challenges for the long-term survival of the network.

The SBA lessons seemed to indicate that the success of learning networks is inversely proportional to outside input and dominance: The crucial factors for survival are to have a learning agenda controlled and driven by the needs of the participating firms, which themselves experience pressure from the global market for development, and a support structure that can provide adequate and timely responses to these needs. The more the network is constructed "from outside", e.g. by a research oriented institution, the bigger is the challenge to establish viability over time. For NVF, this lesson implied that the crucial challenge in 1992, after successfully establishing basic structures and activities, would be continuous renewal of the learning process, by expanding the support structure which provides competence in various areas to the network, at a pace matching the developing needs of the most advanced participating firms. A second lesson emerging at that time was a need for more focused and systematic collection of local experience from practical enterprise development work. The answer to these challenges

3. One of the authors, Hanssen-Bauer, was at the time employed by SBA and had the responsibility for the follow-up of the NVF network.

4. The dominant view saw no difference between business partnerships and networks, and basically portrayed the network as a substitute for the value chain.

seemed to be to increase the capacity of NVF Inc. in ways that also strengthened its links to research.

The board of NVF decided to hire two doctoral students who could help remold the relationship to the Norwegian University of Science and Technology (NTNU) and to academia. The board also made the network a business associate with the internationally renowned Institute for Management Development (IMD) in Lausanne, Switzerland. The significance of these two moves was that the network would improve its ability to take in new ideas and stimuli, and at the same time increase its "in-house" capacity to reinterpret such ideas in the context of regional businesses. The students were supposed to be reflection partners. They were to introduce problems from regional businesses into teaching at NTNU, and bring ideas and theoretical reflections back. Because they would be part of regional business life, as they were employed by NVF, they would be students of the network, and therefore in a better position to become "significant others" in the reflection processes within and across the enterprises than other researchers or academics. As both NVF and NTNU would have responsibility for their student careers, a common link and interest in teaching at NTNU would be created. As the students would work with and research on concrete and real problems of their host enterprises, another shared responsibility would evolve, i.e. a responsibility for supporting these enterprises in finding ways to handle their development challenges. The result should become, in our view and analysis, a learning loop designed to stimulate second order learning (learn to learn).

To learn and to change: An action research design

The positive experience gained from having two doctoral students at work in the network made it interesting for NVF to become a module in the ED2000 program. The objectives can be summed up in two main points, one related to the learning effectiveness of Nordvest Forum, and one to more academic interest in testing empirically how it all works:

1. To improve the structural relationship between academia and the real life of business, in order to make academia more sensitive to business life and more apt to be a real partner in development, on the one hand, and to demonstrate to local businesses in the region that input from social sciences can be of use in learning faster and managing change more efficiently; on the other hand.
2. To test the general model of inter-enterprise learning in networks, that was partly developed earlier, in order to create better network designs.

NVF wanted to use the program to increase co-operation between business in its region and research institutions in Norway and internationally, and it was particularly interested in hiring more doctoral students.[5] The core research and development question consisted of developing a more comprehensive model of how a network learning cycle can be designed, in order to enhance productivity in the region. Such a question can best be answered through action research, i.e. a type of research where researchers and practitioners engage in a joint process to study a given problem. The objective is both to identify workable solutions to the problem — based on a merger of local knowledge and experience on the one hand, and, on the other, general assumptions and guidelines derived from theoretical knowledge — and to create new learning and knowledge during the process. At the core of the ensuing coalition between the researchers and the practitioners, therefore, is a particular social contract or relation that is both symmetrical and responsible, as opposed to expert intervention and the non-intervening, observing researcher.

The module aimed at intervening at two levels of the regional learning network. First, the level of the regional learning network itself, where the module embarked on several projects focusing on the efficiency of its learning. Second, five clusters of companies engaged in development projects banded together to host a doctoral student who was to take part in their development work and use the experience as input to doctoral studies in disciplines of relevance for organizational change.

The design of the module thus incorporated the need for bringing research based experience into cases of business development, and at the same time exploring current practices and local knowledge guiding enterprise development, as well as obtaining experience, for further learning and dissemination. Learning is best understood in the context of organizations as innovative processes, in which the organization creates and defines problems, and then actively develops new knowledge to solve them. To study such learning processes requires being part of the processes, and at the same time being able to "step out" of the participant role and reflect on the learning from a distance. Therefore, the core actors in the model were the doctoral students, who were supposed to take part in development work in the organizations as reflection partners to the company practitioners, as explained above, and various mechanisms were established to create sufficient distance to facilitate research.

Another level of reflection arenas and mechanisms had to be developed as part of the module. Firstly, the students were linked to mentors or supervisors at the universities. The module engaged these scholars as senior researchers and asked them to develop their own research using the regional firms and the NVF network as empirical input. The seniors were mobilized as resources both for the network

5. The companies behind NVF are concerned about the lack of professionals in the region. To offer positions as doctoral students was considered a way to attract talented, young people to the region and train them both in servicing the region's firms and within interesting disciplines that are in short supply at the moment.

activities (e.g. as lecturers at network seminars and events) and for company development projects together with their students.

Secondly, the senior researchers and doctoral students scheduled a series of workshops to discuss and reflect on progress of the module in general. The intention was to invite international scholars, and in some cases also researchers from other modules in ED2000, to some of the workshops in order to help develop our academic reflection process.

Thirdly, the Nordvest Forum network arenas were actively used for discussion among practitioners and for dissemination of learning. The "cases", or description of the development projects in the companies, were presented to management training courses, and the responsible manager for a given development project would be enrolled at the Nordvest Forum's "Management of Change Program" and use the project as his or her training project in the program. This again meant that he or she would have access to advice from a senior manager in the region acting as mentor. As we discovered that new arenas were needed, these were developed and added. By way of an example, a specific training program was developed for union representatives taking part in development projects, and a workshop focusing on manufacturing was developed from the work of one of the doctoral students, in collaboration with the Institute for Management Development in Lausanne.

In summary, the NVF module of the ED2000 program was based on a rather comprehensive and compact theoretical position. The module also developed a complex action research design for studying how a regional company network can help its members to learn how to undertake enterprise development in a global context. The module had an ambition to produce changes in the world, and the remains of this chapter is devoted to the story of what we learnt when the design met the real world.

The inherent robustness of real life

So far we have presented the module as *theory*, or as a combination of prior experience, many assumptions and complex thinking among many actors that had accumulated over years prior to the start-up of the module, and that then directed and colored the way the module was transformed into real life work. In hindsight, we see the value of such theory, and we can discern how the preparations made an impact on how the module actually performed. We also have to conclude that life is more robust than theory: The plans were overridden by real life events, and the outcome of module work did not fulfill the ambitious intentions completely.

In the following, we present how the module unfolded in practice with a focus on the outcomes and why these particular outcomes were produced. We will do so in four parts: First, we need to look at the performance in participating companies. Second, we focus on the NVF network arenas. Our third topic is the interaction between researchers and their arenas. Our final topic is an analysis of the ED2000 program as an infrastructure or context for the module research.

The immediate outcome of the module was quite good: it did help produce significant changes in the clusters of participating companies. It also impacted on how the NVF network performed, and helped ensure a generational shift among the NVF Inc. staff. In addition, it created a significantly higher acceptance for social science and its potential contribution in the regional companies. The doctoral students will all except one pass their exam (and the one who will not pass has been recruited by a company in the region). We have produced academic texts and more are under way. We think that the Nordvest Forum has become an exemplary network construction renowned far outside Norway, and it functions as a living example of a successful regional learning network. It has clearly enhanced its prospects for survival as a network, able to develop itself to serve local businesses in an effective manner.

The module has very good results in three of the five clusters of companies, while results are more uncertain for two others. We experienced a series of structural changes like take-overs, buy-outs, changes in management and others that alter the possibilities for working with these companies. All in all, the module has given a close-to-life experience where actors, structures and themes change while you are engaged in the development process. Nevertheless, we obtained results in concrete work, and the companies most often did not cease development work even while in substantial external turmoil. It has been rather taxing on our students, who have demonstrated their added value to the development work for the companies, as well as their ability to give flexible responses to different needs.

The module defined its aim as increasing knowledge about business development in the region, and about learning in networks. We did not have the ambition to change the normal flow of development work in the companies into any kind of pre-defined development structure, but to strengthen on-going activities and influence as partners in these processes. Therefore, it has not been a contractual prerequisite that a development organization is established, or that development work has to start with conferencing methods and the like.[6] We have stressed participation and involvement as the way to achieve success, and not as a prerequisite for participation in the program. We have preached the need to involve the trade unions and make them part of the development management structure, just

6. We respected the ED2000 request to only work with companies that are organized with the labor market parties, and we set up contracts to regulate the participation of these companies. The companies had to contribute financially to cover the costs of the doctoral students.

as we have lectured about the need to anchor development firmly within the management structure. In the end, we have respected company priorities, as requested by the board of NVF Inc.

This strategy may have caused less returns in terms of development successes (even though we seriously doubt it). It definitely contributed to a better grasp of how the advanced part of the regional industry engages in development work, based on the general models and ideas that the managers in the region take in from the outside and incorporate in their own strategies for doing business. We also avoided a paternalistic research approach in which we might implicitly communicate that we have the answers to the concrete questions. We feel that solutions must be reinvented locally through concrete experience. In this way, the value of the cases for the development of NVF has improved. Now the managers of the companies can relate their experience as their own in the seminars and meetings of the network — and not as witnesses of the value of "foreign" models (i.e. the ED2000 model). The companies did not engage in development work to make a statement, but to generate solutions to their challenges. As we will soon describe, all the participating companies ended up working with issues of crucial importance for their long-term survival, and even if most of them started up defining projects of a more limited scope, the objectives changed over time.

Radicals and incrementalists in furniture

Our first cluster of companies, within the first generation of development projects, was within furniture manufacturing with Ekornes and what later became the Stokke Group. The development work was initiated in Ekornes with one of the first doctoral students back in 1993, and then on a topic defined as implementing quality management systems. The project ended up in a reorganization of the value chain, with profound implications also for internal work organization.

The development of the Ekornes corporation has been highly impressive: The company, which was almost out of business in 1990, performed a radical turnaround in the early 1990s, and today it has established a very healthy situation with pre-tax profitability of 15 to 20 percent in each of the last four years, combined with steady growth of sales and no signs of slow-down. A high percentage of the sales consists of exports to competitive and global markets. In the same period, the company developed a new production philosophy that has attracted international attention. It also changed its focus from the single company view to a holistic view on the value chain, including first of all their relationships with the external customers, and internally in the group on customer-supplier relationships. The change in focus led to changes in work organization, both regarding product lines and the design of new products. The doctoral student was invited to assist with ideas and concepts in these changes as a reflection partner to top management, and also as a resource for development work. Gradually, Ekornes has shifted from a rather conventional organization of development to increased participation in development activities. This shift has had deep impact on earnings, productivity and on resulting working patterns in production, and it represents quite a successful innovation.

The Stokke Group has traditionally seen its emphasis on design, product development and innovation as its competitive edge. It pursued a strategy of becoming a product design leader, as opposed to the Ekornes strategy of being a product and production leader. Both companies have been successful in their (quite different) marketing and brand building strategies on the international market, and they are similar with regard to geographical location and a traditional ownership situation. They differ in their approaches to distribution, production, corporate organization, competence development, participation and working environment.

In the Stokke Group, development work was initiated in Møremøbler, one of the companies later to be acquired by Stokke, and it focused, as in many of the other cases, on quality systems. Later on the development work shifted, from a turnaround process to a process involving gradual and continuous improvements, that incorporated core areas for strategy such as partnerships with external furniture designers, manufacturing improvements, cooperation with suppliers, and the alignment of distribution strategy with product/market strategy. The main contact point for the student was the top executive group.

In the case of Ekornes and Stokke, the doctoral student probably had one of the best working situations among the students *in the field.* During an initial period, he could concentrate on Ekornes, and both companies are of such a size that they represent relatively stable partners, with varied, but related themes to work on. The insight gained in one of them was directly transferable to the other — either through similarities, or through contrasting ways of doing the same type of business. In addition, this also was the case where the module probably generated the broadest involvement of senior researchers and *access to research institutions,* with the IMD in Lausanne in particular. The result was that in terms of conceptual development within research and impact on the NVF network, the Ekornes-Stokke case represents innovations. The experience from Ekornes helped forge the concept of Demand Chain Management together with the IMD in Lausanne.[7] This way the co-operation also strengthened relations between NVF and IMD, and contributed

7. It was widely published by IMD researchers and the doctoral student, and Ekornes has become a reference case internationally through the descriptions in Harvard Business Review, Financial Times and in business publications in a series of countries.

to building a new NVF activity, the Manufacturing Strategy Program, where Ekornes and Stokke are the core cases and central contributors. Both examples are regularly used in the management training program of NVF as well. The Stokke Group was the first regional company to benchmark their production units internationally.[8] Later, Ekornes and other regional companies (among them Glamox Fabrikker and some of the Ulstein Group units) did the same benchmarking exercise while participating in the NVF "Manufacturing Strategy Program".

Learning participatory development from differences

The second company cluster was more varied and complex. It consisted of an air transport company (Mørefly), a hotel and conference facility in the region (Ulstein Hotel), and a manufacturer of electrical transformers (Møre Trafo). In this cluster, the second of the first generation students in the module worked, and it represents very good results locally, with quite a few, albeit more limited, innovations.

Mørefly operated helicopters, ambulances and business charter flights. The development work started out developing a system for total quality management, and went on to engage in profound transformation of the work organization into an advanced matrix organization that was definitely an innovation in the region. The development resulted in dramatically improved workers' participation and definite improvements in productivity (arguably the best productivity in the air-carrier sector in Norway at the time). However, the company was acquired and taken over by a competitor, Helikopter Service, and is nowadays only alive as an exemplary local case used in the NFV programs, and as a reference on matrix organizations by managers in the region.

Møre Trafo initiated the co-operation on issues related to total quality management systems. This was one of the cases, together with Ulstein Hotel (see below), where the development work soon turned into the traditional pattern of starting an incremental improvement processes with dialogue or search conferences. Møre Trafo has gained a position in the region as a reference case on competence development and a supportive compensation system, which is quite innovative. It has struggled with a main strategic choice, between a customer focus on tailor-made deliveries and single-unit based production, versus a focus on standardization and optimization of the manufacturing system (batch based production). This dilemma is well known in the NVF network, however, and it is subject to much

8. The benchmarking was against the "Made in Europe" and "Made in Switzerland" samples resulting from a large-scale study of manufacturing practice and performance in several European countries carried out by London Business School, IMD and IBM Europe.

productive reflection among managers in the region. It is often used to illustrate how to implement participatory development processes.

The Ulstein hotel started the co-operation by insisting on being part of an industrial cluster, as the manager claimed they had more to learn from completely different companies struggling to implement service oriented business, than from other hotels and companies similar to themselves. He wanted to change the operational concept of the hotel, as a substantial extension was going to be built. The hotel implemented serious benchmarking against other hotels, and then looked for inspiration in more industry-like organizations for developing their operational concept and their total quality management system. The hotel managed to develop new forms of worker participation, and is proud of being not only the host of NVF activities, but also one of its frequently used learning cases.

In these three companies the student played a very active role in organizing the development work.[9] The organizations were smaller than in the first cluster, and seemed to rely more heavily on external assistance. This assistance was, however, directly linked with the top executives of the organizations, and it related to issues of crucial importance for the survival of the companies — even if the initiation phase of the work had a more limited ambition level; such as developing a quality management system. The learning communicated from the cases to the network is essentially that such apparently limited objectives will lead nowhere, unless the top management takes it into the core strategy, and organizes development work as a participatory process.

Heavy dumpers and light metal: Optimizing manufacturing

The second generation of company clusters in the module is less developed, for various reasons, time being one (they were started almost three years later). One of these clusters consisted of a co-operation between a manufacturer of electrical lighting and heating fittings (Glamox Fabrikker) and a manufacturer of heavy, articulated dump trucks (Moxy Trucks). The latter had, some years before, seen one of their main Japanese competitors (Kumatsu) buy up a third of their shares and become directly involved in the development of their products. Both companies are located in the same area, and were initially founded by the same person. In both companies, the involvement of the student started with organizing dialogue

9. The experience emanating from the work with these companies is also published in a doctoral dissertation by Gaute Knutstad (Knutstad, Gaute A. (1998) *Medvirkning og innrullering av sosiale- og teknologiske aktører i endringsprosesser: En studie av hvordan medvirkning i endringsprosesser bidrar til ny organisatorisk praksis i tre bedrifter på Nordvestlandet*, Trondheim, NTNU, Inst. for industriell økonomi og teknologiledelse, dr.ing. avhandling 1998:7).

or search conferences, and then evolved into major development projects directed at optimizing manufacturing processes. Glamox Fabrikker embarked on integrating the development of products, processes and administration and control systems, to a level where it became internationally advanced in its flow-oriented production philosophy. The pilot case at a small sub-site of the company managed to reduce lead time from four weeks to one day. The new production philosophy and organization were later disseminated to other factories in the group, and Glamox Fabrikker was awarded the Work Environment Award in 1995, and is renowned for basing their development processes largely on direct participation.

After an initial search conference that resulted in a series of efforts to improve the organization of the production in Moxy Trucks, the overall success of the development work was hampered by an increasingly difficult market situation where large, global corporations dominated the scene. Komatsu provided access to new networks and competencies, especially in product development, but later pulled out as an owner, leaving Moxy Trucks with serious problems in building an effective market organization on their own — and thereby prospects of a rather dismal future.

The student managed well in the development work. He was offered the chance to work in the companies he studied, and ended his academic career without providing us with a full description of the cases. Nevertheless, both companies are often used as cases and references in the network, and the experience of having a Japanese owner involved in product development has been of large interest. Glamox is frequently used as a case and reference in NVF sessions, especially in the "Manufacturing Strategy Program".

Fish and Ships: Strategy development processes

The last two company clusters of the module have developed quite differently from the previously described ones. The Ulstein Group is a shipbuilder and producer of marine equipment, while the Domstein Group processes and trades fish and seafood. Originally, the latter was supposed to build a cluster with neighboring industries, but these had to withdraw due to opposition from their boards of directors. To these two companies were assigned students engaged in doctoral studies at the Norwegian School of Economics and Business Administration (NHH) in Bergen, hence not within engineering disciplines like the previous ones, but economics and business administration. Both students are still some time away from defending their degrees. Both were generously welcomed by their companies and invited into all internal arenas and processes, but both experienced severe problems of time management, because they had to combine their studies with presence and participation in the companies.

In the Ulstein Group, the student was invited to participate in the development of their international strategy and entry into new markets, as well as in the development of partnerships up- and downstream (vertical networks). In the Domstein Group, the co-operation centered on a long-term strategy process, with many very interesting facets. The process spanned topics like gradual divisionalization of the Group, transforming traditional fish landing to modern production of sea food, as well as changes from family ownership to a professionally managed corporation registered on the stock market. At the same time the company was central in a series of mergers, transformations and vertical integrations within the whole fishing industry in Norway.

The doctoral dissertations will provide interesting material on these processes of high importance for Norwegian business life. Meanwhile, we feel that the situation of work has been much more strenuous for these two students than for their predecessors. There are two main causes for this: First, they were linked up to academic disciplines where NVF and the module lead researchers had less previous experience, and the two were left with too little senior assistance and support within the module. Second, they had to follow a quite different and more school-like educational program in Bergen, and this made participation in the companies quite impossible for prolonged periods.[10] In addition, their supervisors did not share the basic approach to research of the module. They will probably make good scholarly performances, but the depth of our total insight into the important strategic processes in the two companies will be less than expected. Nevertheless, Ulstein[11] is regularly providing cases in the network activities, still being among the core members of the network. Domstein, however, has become somewhat more peripheral as the work of the Module, troubled as it was at times, did not help bring them closer to the core of NVF.

The academics: The art of sharing field and frames

A central part of the learning agenda of the module was the senior researcher network. In hindsight, we see that the potential of the design was good, but we did not fully realize this potential. Three major causes could be stated: First, we were inadequately resourced in financial terms to match the needs of the comprehensive

10. They had to live in Bergen and therefore also participated less in the NVF network activities, and they were seldom able to stay in the NVF offices in Ålesund. The other students had to a larger extent NVF as a base.

11. The Ulstein Group was split into two parts, the one being Rolls-Royce Commercial Marine (marine equipment) and the other, Ulstein Verft (shipbuilding), being still owned by the Ulstein family. Both continue as core members of the NVF network.

agenda and the number of researchers. Second, we clearly underestimated the time and investment needed to fully build a common research agenda among the various participating researchers. Third, the activities at the program level of ED2000 tended to disrupt the planning on the module level.

In planning, the module was anticipated to continue established relationships with the university in Trondheim and the Oslo-based Fafo as the core of the senior researcher network. In addition we planned to extend the cooperation to NHH in Bergen. There, the initial planning took place with a senior faculty member who already had experience with the NVF network, but he left the institution. Later, the project was implemented with two other researchers. The Norwegian Research Council also actively intervened to add Møre Research, a regional education and research institution, to the research network. The result was a much broader and more resourceful research network, which was able to entertain a broader research agenda than planned. At the same time the budget was reduced, leaving less resources to be stretched over twice as many researchers as originally planned.

Our main mistake in this situation was to not fully realize the increased gap between needs and resources. We still thought that a combination of the forces from the field with a sharing of frames in workshops would help the researchers, each with their own interest and tradition, engage in cross-feeding and collaboration which would enable fruitful new insights to emerge. We did not see the imbalance between the long-term thinking of designers of the module — a few of the senior researchers — and the much poorer preparation of several newcomers. Still, these newcomers were invited to take responsibility for important parts of the work. We underestimated the disciplinary variation, and did not really face the challenge of sharing our different frames and positions in order to develop a common approach to the joint work. The resources were too thin, in terms of time and money, to engage in broad co-operation in the field and in seminars. The researchers were given budgets that did not allow them to take up the expected roles in the field, and the "veterans" were so busy administering within their own stretched budgets that they tended to forget their previous lessons: The researchers and students must spend time together in the field.

The research network organized seminars and workshops to engage in discussions on topics from the field, and invited international scholars. The meetings were rewarding, but not sufficient for forging a joint research agenda. Therefore, the various senior projects are more parallel endeavors than really complementary or cross-disciplinary studies of the same field. We do most likely not share the same basic research values and orientation, and we did not solve the issues that emerged over such topics as the value of case design studies and qualitative method, not to mention the value of action research.

Another challenge was to cope with activities on the ED2000 Program level. On that level, the program board seemed to focus on integration *across* modules as more of a concern than integration *within* the modules. While we were busy building a regional coalition, they seemed to measure our success in terms of the effects on the national infrastructure. We felt that our work was disrupted and unduly overtaken by a series of requests from the program board. Although we do understand the need for such program level activities, they ended up competing for our very thin resources. With more robustness on the module level, the same activities would have been enriching, not disturbing.

In spite of these shortcomings, the network is producing a series of academic publications, the region and its business life have definitely been put on the teaching agenda of the academic institutions, and the participating institutions have all gained both respect and legitimacy within the region's business community — and they are used more by the NVF network.

Conclusions

To sum up the lessons we have learned from the Nordvest Forum module: In our view, we had a beautiful albeit complex design. We went quite some way in implementing the design, and we produced good results, but we did not fully reach our goal. We ran into challenges that we were not able to meet with the resources at our disposal. The learning processes were effective because they integrated theory and learning from the field.

The module's research activities were marked by multiple, or rather, shifting roles. The students started out as 'students' and observers. Over time, they became participants with more focused contributions, as a result of building their understanding of the field and of gaining theoretical insights. In the best cases, we managed to create parallel processes of theoretical training and need for competence in the field, where they both impacted positively on each other. It was particularly important to visit a foreign research institution (3–6 months). The "break" helped gain professional "weight" and visions.

The participation of students in the development work in the companies was a good investment for the overall learning of the members of the network. The end result has been "thicker" and more comprehensive cases to be presented in the various network arenas, as well as the creation of new arenas, mainly through the practitioners themselves, but also by the students. The Nordvest Forum sent them to other organizations to lecture and provide input for seminars, and this way they contributed to disseminating both theory and lessons, and, not least, information about who had done what with which result. At a decisive moment in the network's life, NVF Inc. recruited one of the students as assistant director with the responsibility for developing the learning activities. This both helped NVF Inc. through the first change in management, and the network in broadening its learning agenda and institutional network.

One lesson is that while we have developed respect for the time needed in the direct work with the companies, we have yet to understand fully that research, and particularly cross-disciplinary research, is time-consuming before it can yield results. A strategy to produce cross-fertilization between different research institutions has to have a long-term perspective, and be based on comprehensive experience from joint projects. This is a major topic to discuss further, as our ability to properly respond to the various needs of the business community on *substance and content* is dependent on such cross-disciplinary activities.

Another lesson is that modern educational institutions will have to revise their own teaching, curricula and other systems, if they want to respond to the rapidly developing needs of the business community. The tradition is to prefer keeping students as students, and to train them to see business life as a passive field of research, and not an active partner in research, until at least the students are properly certified through final exams. This tradition threatens to make these institutions into slow learners and irrelevant partners for the business community.

A final lesson is that the processes we engage in are both volatile and robust: Persons and companies are in a constant flux of change, but to *help* change them usually necessitates a long-term perspective.

Chapter 9

Integrating the disintegrated

Morten Levin, Ida Munkeby and Johan E. Ravn

The inspiring landscape

A first meeting in the mountains: engineers, economists and social scientists are gathered on the footsteps of the North central mountain plateau in Norway. The researchers were invited for a two-day meeting to discuss the potential of collaborative research in business development. The discussions were positive, supportive, and had the character of an open inquiry process. A beautiful lake, great mountains and flying clouds staged a relaxed atmosphere. The meeting ended with a general agreement among the researchers, all working in Trondheim, either in university positions (NTNU) or as researchers in the affiliated research organization (SINTEF).[1] The meeting concluded with expressions of positive attitudes towards creating research across professional boundaries. These were the initial steps on a long hike that gradually shaped the Trondheim module of ED2000.

After this meeting, the work did not really take off. Many discussions took place, involving members of this same group. Local perspectives were created, a plan for company involvement emerged, and the research council was approached in order to get the plans approved. That negotiation soon became a stumbling block. The research council was not satisfied with the perspectives written into the proposal. We never got a clear understanding why we did not fill the expectations of the research council. Part of the communication was on lack of documentation of relationships with participating companies, partly it was related to the substance of the research proposal, and in addition it was probably not clear how we intended to pursue the work in the different companies. Finally we learned that the board of ED2000 did not have any funds left. That blew our minds. Some of the researchers in the group advocated to give up on creating a research module linked up to ED2000. It was strongly felt that the whole negotiating process was a waste of time.

---

1. NTNU; The Norwegian University of Science and Technology, SINTEF; The Research organization affiliated with NTNU, comprising both engineering, economic and social researchers.

Sleeping on the issues for a couple of nights, and rethinking our strategy, resulted in a continued effort to become a partner in the research activity.

The creation of research activities

The first module leader took the inputs from the mountain meeting and transformed them into a perspective where the relationships between employers, trade unions and researchers took a form that was well proven in the Norwegian context. This did not leave much room for breaking borders between engineers, economists and social scientists. The initial construction of the module was deeply rooted in the "Scandinavian" model of labor relations, where the parties on the labor market (employers and trade unions) were expected to have an equal opportunity in enterprise development. In this respect, the major conceptualization was to work with the two dominant actors on the labor market, and not dwell on the non-homogeneity among these stakeholders. There was a full acceptance of bringing in other researchers than social scientists, but it was not very clear how this should be done. Good will and idealistic intentions were in abundance, but the selection of companies to work with, and how to approach the multi-professional work, was not clarified. We were on a positive track, but the whole activity did not get off the ground. A focal reason for this was the continuing negotiating process with the board. They were not satisfied with the development of the Trondheim module, and it was not clear to us whether that was based on the potential participating companies, or on the local organization of the research process. A sort of final blow came when the board had partitioned its entire fund to the five other modules, leaving no money for the Trondheim module. Our interpretation was that we were either discarded from ED2000, or we could be used as leverage in internal bargaining in the research council to obtain more funding for the whole program. The latter was probably the case, but this was never confirmed. In any case, the result was an endless process of negotiating, waiting, arguing, and receiving not too well structured information. After many frustrating months we were at last able to start our work, and we did that without having any formal contract in our hands.

Shortly after the module initiated the research and developmental activity, the module leader was offered the position as the administrative manager for the whole program. After some hesitation, he accepted the offer, and he left the position as the module leader. The second leader then took over. He followed in the footsteps of the original perspectives, as he had been an active member of the research team from the beginning. A dimension of regional development was to be introduced. The researchers in the module wanted to create a relationship with a number of small businesses in a rural setting (the town of Leksvik) some 70 km north-west of Trondheim. This community had for years been industrialized, and several of the companies were successful in the international marketplace. We considered the township to be a very interesting "case" of regional development, as this small community of 300 people had created a dozen small companies (ranging from 5–100 employees) able to compete globally. This proposal was not either well received by the board of ED2000. The second module leader resigned, when he took over as a director of the Institute for Social Research in Industry. Most of the social scientists in the group came from this institute, so the important change was the loss of an experienced researcher.

The third module leader followed basically the same tracks, but left out the strong focus on regional networks. Instead a stronger focus, on a multi-professional perspective integrating technology and organization, was launched. Internally we discussed and planned to integrate economists in addition to engineers in the module, but that idea never materialized. This was a natural move in light of being located within the dominating engineering school in Norway. The third change that the group embarked on was a decision to engage in a very limited number of companies. The major concern was the ability to work in depth and on issues that really mattered for the enterprises. The strategy was to seek engagement in change processes that were considered vital for the company in question. The initial research group had invited engineers with a fairly wide range of experiences to participate in the creation of a program. Perspectives brought to the table were production engineering, health and safety. This added to the social science perspective held by the initial core group of researchers. In discussions, we had tried to create a ground for collaboration, but we also realized that we had limited options for in-depth engagement until we could start the work at company level. These talks had a good atmosphere, and the group enthusiastically embarked on the initiation of the research. The Trondheim module was up and running by late fall 1995.

The module leader held a position as a professor at NTNU, and thus it was evident that it was necessary to construct a leadership team to enable the sharing of the leadership possibilities, obligations and administrative tasks. In the first phase, this was a team of two, but that changed when the SINTEF researcher left to take on a public duty as a political advisor for the Minister of Industry. The next leadership team was made up of two SINTEF researchers and the NTNU professor. This team developed a way of sharing the work that was quite dynamic, and as we got more experienced with working together, it turned out to be very easy to divide the work according to capacity and capability. It was probably a good sign of the team's ability to co-operate that we did not develop a permanent division of labor, but it shifted according to contingency factors. The leadership troika found great satisfaction in this mutual effort to lead the Trondheim module.

The research perspective of the module evolved as the research group gained experience from the ongoing projects. Our stated interest was to work with companies that were heavily engaged in change efforts. We did not want to work on change projects that were not at the core of the company's interest. It was an early decision not to establish co-operation with an enterprise unless the company was willing to fund part of the research activity. The concept of a development organization was far away from our thinking. Our understanding was that the core problem of development organizations was that the change activity easily could become marginal. It was easy to see how this development organization activity potentially would become an activity that was nice to have, but of no vital importance. Change activity is more demanding than what can be achieved through a development organization.

We wanted to prioritize working in depth with few companies, rather than working with a large group in a network-based approach. This position was argued to the board of ED2000, and after a fairly long process of negotiation we finally received an acceptance for engaging in-depth with five companies. Fairly soon one of the companies backed out. This was due to corporate redesign of the entire production and development structure in Ericsson. The production facility was sold to a Norwegian electronic company, and the corporate tried to move the engineering division to the Norwegian capital Oslo. A major local political action was launched, and Ericsson gave in and kept the engineering activity in the local community. The turmoil created by this major restructuring activity also brought an end to our engagement, which lasted less than a year.

The second company (Norsk Jet) never passed beyond the initial assessment phase. When it came to implement the plans agreed upon, they were not able to make a decision. We never managed to get this issue straight, but the company was not able to move ahead and make a decision as to what should be the focus of their organizational change. After several attempts to cut through this Gordian knot, we decided that it was not worth the effort to come to an agreement with the company. In fact, we never even started the work in Norsk Jet. The number of companies was now down to three. Seen from our point of view, this was not problematic at all. Our intention was to engage in-depth on the local change activities.

The three core companies

Out of the initial five participating companies we ended up working in depth with three of them. *Aker Maritime Verdal* (AMV) was an offshore yard specializing in jackets and production modules. The yard is located some 100 km north of Trondheim. The yard employs a little bit more than 1, 000 persons. The research team at AMV consisted of two social scientists (and in some periods three) and two engineers, working on issues and projects that spanned very different local development activities. *HAG* is a chair factory located in the small mountain town Røros some 150 km south-east of Trondheim. It has some 250 employees, and produces office chairs. Their trademark is excellency in design. The research team at HAG has varied over time. First it consisted of a social scientist and an engineer working on production planning and control. The next period included two social scientists working on issues related to Quality of Work Life issues. In the third period, one researcher was running a training program for middle management. Over the whole period the company had been deeply engaged in engineering research, aimed at developing the next generation of office chairs. The third company is *Norsk Hydro Sunndal* (HAS). The aluminum smelter is located some 200 km southwest of Trondheim. It employed 850 persons, and the research community in Trondheim has had a long standing relationship with this company.

The Aker Maritime Verdal Offshore Yard

When we first visited the yard in the summer of 1996, we were impressed by the huge red buildings, the tall cranes and the enormous steel constructions. Employees rode a bicycle or drove between the production halls or to the administration building. Furthermore, the company has its own quay structure, and the location by the fjord gives a very fresh outdoor climate, from the smell of sea and the windy weather. Later we experienced that it is always windy, and it can be freezing in the winter. Those who had outdoor work seldom wanted to move inside again. It had something to do with the roughness and the freedom of the work, and the feeling that this was where the important things really happened.

The offshore yard specializes in steel constructions for offshore installations for the oil and gas industry in the North Sea, such as *jackets* and *production modules. Jackets* look like giant stools. 80–90 meters tall, they are put on the seabed and serve as a foundation for offshore oil and gas rigs. *Modules* make up the central structures above sea surface of rigs and other installations (production units, etc.). Pipes (for oil, gas, water, and air) are produced both as sub-parts for jackets and modules, and as separate products for other customers in the offshore market. *Spools* are particularly important parts in any offshore pipe system: Elements with elbows, fittings, branching and joints.

The company had a long and rather incoherent history of company development activities. The majority of the initiatives came from the owners or the corporate level. In 1996, the local management decided to devote financial resources and intellectual energy to redesign the company in line with the concepts of Business Process Reengineering (BPR). A process orientation of the workflow was seen as the key to achieve increased efficiency and productivity. A fundamental must for AMV was enhancing the position on future markets. In the summer of 1996, an internal project named "Offshore yard towards the year 2000" (O2000) was launched. The local unions were informed about the project, but not involved in the strategic and planning decisions. This turned out to be an important factor for why the O2000 emerged purely as the managements' project.

Our entrance ticket was a linkage through the two engineers in the research team. They made their first contact with the yard through a research project on enterprise modeling. Both of them had a former relation to the company as employees, one as a plumber, and the other on contract as an engineer. They entered familiar ground and could therefore provide the social scientists with a lot of information on company history and company actors. The social scientists were in a way forced upon the engineers. Their modeling project had been granted money on the prerequisite that social science was included in the project. This opened the way for ED2000, and in 1997, organization development was established as a separate sub-project in the company's development project. The social researchers knew the company almost solely from the newspapers. The research 'contract' with the central company actors was unclear, and the company actors as well as the engineers had little experience with social scientists doing work research.

In the early phases, the engagement had a clear technical focus. As mentioned above, the research team at AMV consisted of two (sometimes three) social scientists and two engineers. Initially, it was the two engineers who had a project with AMV, with a technical agenda. In the development activities at the yard, the most appreciated kind of know-how was technical. Technological and management knowledge and competence was the basis for most of the communication. All central actors had some sort of technical background; the CEO had his education from the Master Programme in Engineering at NTNU, and almost all members of the development groups were either skilled operators or engineers. The accepted language was accordingly technical jargon. As the social researchers moved in, they found it difficult to introduce themselves and their perspectives on the agenda. Non-technical issues, or non-technical perspectives on technical issues, were simply not seen or acknowledged.

Another difficulty was created by the big differences in expectations about the role of social research in the project. The social researchers' agenda was to improve the development group's ability to analyze, reflect on and learn from both company everyday life and the development activities. For the engineering researchers and the company actors, the role of the social researchers was a *therapeutic* one. Once they had analyzed a problem and figured out how it should be solved, they wanted 'the softies' to move in and talk to the people who would be affected, pat their backs and listen to their complaints, in order to increase the likelihood of getting the engineers' solution accepted and implemented. The social researchers gradually grew impatient, and eventually they succeeded in creating space for their perspectives in the project.

The engineers were not very impressed with the social researchers. Although social scientists repeatedly were asked, they were reluctant to come up with clear prescriptions or recipes for 'good management' or 'good work descriptions' for the foremen.

The organizational challenge eventually was to develop an internal and external organization so that all work processes could be done with a minimum of grievances. There was a need for more flexibility in the organization of work and the production system. The level of uncertainty (production, human resources) had to be reduced. There was a need for implementing standards, especially in engineering and construction. In general, the aim was to arrive at a better workflow. Enterprise-modeling and organization development were the tools necessary to achieve the company's goals. This gave us admission to the internal change processes, and the ways the different company teams handled them.

The integration of the efforts and research agendas of the engineers and social scientists had a slow and difficult birth. The members understood what they individually were struggling to achieve, but few bridges were built directly linked to the project activity. Also, there was a certain strain between the action oriented, quick result approaches of the engineers, and the more reflective and long-term approaches of the social scientists. A main challenge in this picture was to increase communication and co-operation across the divides between the actors.

The project at the yard has contained many elements. We have conducted field observations and interviewing. We have conducted technical analyses of production efficiencies and assessed throughput times. We have arranged for bringing in experiences from other companies and their ways of handling parallel challenges. Based on data gathered and analyses carried out, we have arranged many meetings across organizational divides, and conducted seminars and search conferences with a broad participation, reflecting on local challenges and contemporary practices. We have proposed alternative models of dealing with troublesome tasks.

In the end we worked closely with shop stewards, production engineers, management and the people at the human resources division. This process had an interesting development. In the offset, the cooperation within the research team was fairly difficult. It took a long time before the initial suspicion and lack of real communication was worked through. Gradually mutually respect emerged, and at the end of the three-year co-operation, the research team approached something that could be identified as mutual and fruitful co-operation. Maybe the breakthrough came when team members realized that they needed the skills and knowledge from other professions in order to be able to be smart actors in working with enterprise development.

At the closing of the project in March 2000, the whole project group met to summarize the learning from the three years of project co-operation. They regretted that the project had not taken better care of human resources and organizational issues. This was said both as an appreciation and as a critique of the role the social researchers had been playing. It was an appreciation in the sense that the project would have been a better one if the project group had put the social researchers' perspectives more in focus. It was a critique in the sense that the social researchers could have played a more pro-active role instead of acting as reflective analysts, sitting in the back seat.

HÅG — The office chair Producer

The chair-producer's trademark is excellence in design and fast delivery. The whole production facility is imprinted with unusual design effects, bright colors and nice furniture. The chair producer's vision statement "different and better" underscores this point. Their production system is geared to be able to deliver a chair anywhere in Northern Europe within five days from when the order is placed. The company is highly successful in its market niche, and is currently bringing a new generation of chairs to the market. The company was recruited on the basis of a former relationship with the engineering researchers. That research team had over some years restructured the production system from a conventional batch production system to a Kanban and Just-in-Time based system. This transition turned out to be very successful. The throughput increased and the delivery time was reduced, but there were still some technological problems to be solved related to integrating the information technology with the JIT production control system. A specific problem was caused by daily fluctuation in orders, as the company was not keeping an order reserve. The whole idea was to expedite an order immediately.

The transformation to the new production system was done without paying any particular attention to potential changes in the organization. The "old" organization was not particularly well adapted to the new production system. It was fairly evident that there was no unified design of technology and organization. However, the new production system led to improved competitiveness both in domestic and international markets.

The R&D challenges at HAG were to improve the production planning system, the information technology system and the organization of the company in an integrated perspective. Our working relationship with the company started in the early 1990s, just after the implementation of the new production system. Our legitimacy was based on the production engineers' work. In the first meeting with the company it became clear that the technological solution functioned quite satisfactory, but they could see some signs of a miss-match between technology and organization. In addition, problems were created due to variability in daily production. This initial discussion created a shared understanding between company people and researchers to question the inflexibility emerging in the production system.

We started our engagement in the company by running a conventional assessment of the enterprise. The social scientists played a dominant role in this work and the engineers functioned as key informants and discussion partners. This "sounding-board" co-operation worked well, both as a corrective to the process of making sense of the company and as a ground for mutual learning.

After this initial assessment we continued discussions on how to proceed. It was quite difficult to find a point of entry that immediately resonated both for the local company and for the research team. After a fairly lengthy discussion, the next step became a survey based Quality of Work Life assessment. The questionnaire was developed, and at this time the engineers in the group actively participated in the work. Due to strong support from the trade union and the management, 99.5 percent of the employees returned the questionnaire. The major results of the climate survey were an identification of a lack of visible leadership. Top managers, middle managers and foremen were criticized for their non-presence in day-to-day manufacturing. Another key result was workers' lack of respect for superiors. Both findings could partially be explained by the very high growth-rate of employees over the last years.

The structuring of the feedback turned out to be of major importance. This process was organized as a four-stage process. First, an in-depth presentation with the local project team, then general feedback sessions for all employees, followed by the researchers walking and talking with interested workers on the shop floor. The fourth stage was a presentation at departmental level where both management and workers were present. These interpretations and deliberations on the findings were not only important for the research team, but hopefully also for the company. This process created a voice for bringing forward how the employees judged their Quality of Work Life. The current focus for the work is now on leadership development and reorganization of the production system. We have now been asked to prepare a comparable survey for the entire national and international organization. Based on the survey findings and the initial assessment, we were embarking on concrete developmental activity.

Just as was the case at the yard, the research team at HAG has varied over time, and also, the project co-operation between company and researchers started out with a fairly technical focus. But then the ED2000 was introduced as a separate project from the ongoing project on implementing a new production system. The research team of ED2000 at HAG first consisted of a social scientist and an engineer working on production planning and control. From the very outset, they really wanted to co-operate, but they found it quite demanding. They discovered the great disparity between engineers' and social scientists' ways of interpreting. They hardly found that their views overlapped. As they reported, they did not necessarily disagree, but they were not seeing the same things. They also differed on to what degree they wanted to be directive. As the researchers themselves put it:

"While the engineering side immediately jumps to a solution, the social scientist uses most of the time trying to interpret the situation in different ways, bringing in new information, asking about reactions from the person who received all the cards, asking what kind of work situation they both have, whether they have any kind of responsibility in their job and what the degree of variation in his work situation is. But we had to ask the social scientists several times before anyone suggested any solutions."

Their ability to co-operate across disciplinary boundaries was the first proof of the assumption about multi-disciplinary research strongly held in the Trondheim module. They were able to combine their analytical perspectives with being deeply embedded in the company's practice. One of them stood in the production line for two weeks, the other for a total of five weeks, all for the purpose of embedding their analytical and problem solving skills in the practice where it was to be applied.

A crisis was about to occur when both had to leave the project at the same time. Two other researchers in the module were to take over the tasks and responsibilities of the first two. Quite understandingly, this change of personnel was not very popular at HAG in the beginning. But gradually the two new researchers, who both were social researchers, were able to create a role for themselves that the company could acknowledge. In this phase of the project they were working on issues related to Quality of Work Life. In the third period, one researcher was running a training program for middle management.

Over the whole period of ED2000's engagement at HAG, the company has had engineering researchers in a separate project, aiming at developing next generation office chairs. The co-ordination has not been overwhelmingly strong between ED2000 and this project. This applies both for the researcher side as well as the company side. This shows how hard it is to maintain trust, co-operation and co-generative learning across functional divides or disciplinary borders.

Norsk Hydro Sunndal Aluminum

Norsk Hydro Sunndal (HAS) was well known to the research team. The module leader had a project with the local union back in the early 1980s. Later Norsk Hydro Sunndal was approached to host first year engineering students in their effort to understand issues of organization and leadership. Later the smelter was enrolled in a Ph.D.-program focusing on the operation of chemical production plants. One of the Ph.D. candidates was linked to HAS, and used the data from that engagement as the basis for her thesis. She wrote her dissertation on continual learning processes, and we were frequently called in to work on issues of enterprise development. Gradually the company became interested to join in for the ED2000 program. The core area of attention for our contact persons was the creation of a leadership development program. They had run the first cohort based on utilizing their own resources, and were now embarking on the second program. The first development program was organized as a corporate activity, but now it had changed to a local responsibility. We were enrolled as partners in that process, and we worked closely with local actors in the company, both in planning the program, and in running sections of the leadership development activity.

A cornerstone in the program was that leadership development had to be connected to the local situation, and that development of leaders must involve development of local organization. In the planning of the program, each participant was given the task of running local developmental activities. That activity functioned as a ground for exercising new models of leadership, but also to take leverage for leadership development as organization development. Through active involvement with their own subordinates and colleagues, the idea was that the OD activity hopefully would result in good quality leadership and fragments of a new organization. As part of this leadership program, the participants were invited to present their work in a guest lecture in an OD class at NTNU in Trondheim. The group took on this task as a collective responsibility, and made a good presentation in Trondheim. This created an interesting new link between a university system and local company activity.

A team of social scientists conducted the activity at HAS. It originated as a prolonged activity with a focus on leadership and organizational issues. During our engagement, we made two attempts to introduce engineering researchers at the site. Our intention was to convince local actors that engineering skills could contribute to the local projects. In both instances we negotiated the organization of meetings where different issues were to be discussed. One such issue was to introduce risk analysis as a planning tool, and the other issue was health and safety in designing production systems. Both meetings went well, and everyone was satisfied, but nothing more happened. We never managed to create a research perspective that included both engineers and social scientists. We probably never managed to enter a project of core value to the organization, or it perhaps was simply that our engineering perspectives was neither inspiring nor considered to create energy for inclusion. A third factor might be that HAS had different channels and different institutions that were used to engage engineers.

Gradually the activity shifted towards engagement in corporate activity related to leadership and organizational development, both within the aluminum division and corporate headquarters. This activity is still running, and plans are made for a future extension to involve design of green-field sites and top leadership development. This development emerged by itself as a consequence of the long-term engagement within the corporate structure of Norsk Hydro. The activity has not been a mainstream and traditional development activity in the perspective that ED2000 has envisaged. There was no up-front agreement between the local trade union and management related to our engagement. The engagement evolved by its own dynamic, and was based on this long-term co-operation and contact. Only in the later phases of the project were the local union representatives enrolled. That followed naturally from the company's involvement in the Trondheim network. From then on, the local trade union became visible, and hopefully got an understanding of, and an involvement in, the developmental activities related to the leadership development program.

The emerging transdisciplinary work

The initial goals for the module were fairly conventional as they stressed issues of co-operative trade unions and management efforts to enhance company development in a multi-professional setting. We had some ideas in the offing, but nurtured by the communication process with participating companies and within the research team, a new research direction gradually emerged. The final conceptualization of our research platform resulted from the work of the Aker Verdal research team. The rationale is that there are parallel structures at company level (production engineers and management) and within the research team (engineers and social scientists). The conventional communication pattern has been between production engineers and research engineers, and between management and social scientists. What is conceptualized is a much more complex situation, where communication channels are opened in four directions. This creates a situation where dialogues between different professions are paralleled by communication between the same professions, but across institutional boundaries. All together, this created the basic structure of a transdisciplinary mode of knowledge production.[2]

As the work in the module got off the ground, the goals moved toward a focus on integrated enterprise development. The concept of integrated enterprise development was identified along two variables. The first is already mentioned, namely working on issues that were important for the enterprise's business activity. The second was to take on a holistic approach. In the Trondheim module, this came to mean a joint engineering-social science approach to company development. The core idea was transdisciplinary research based on working jointly on the same issues. We had a very clear understanding that transdisciplinary research could not take place unless the researchers shared the same *praxis*. This meant that

2. See Gibbons et al., 1994.

engineers and social scientists jointly approached the actual problem to negotiate a way to deal with the "problem", as they gradually got an insight of how the different professions were thinking and working.

Our aim was to create new transdisciplinary knowledge based on the collective learning of a multi-professional researcher team. We wanted to create a common learning arena through engaging in core change processes to create useful results for the company. But the major knowledge production that took place in the module reside still at company level, contextualised and hopefully relevant for practical problem solving.

The unexpectedness of networking

In initiating the work in the module, we had no focus on networking among our participating companies. The politics of ED2000 forced us to engage in constructing a network among the participating companies. More or less reluctantly, we started preparing for the first network meeting. It was held in Trondheim, and representatives from the initial five companies participated. The meeting was scheduled to last for a full day, and was constructed around presentations of research and company developmental perspectives. One of the issues was to create dialogues both between researchers and company representatives, and between participating companies. Obviously, the latter were more successful than the company-researcher engagement. The gut feeling in the research team was that this meeting was a fiasco. We neither managed to create energy among participants, nor a burning engagement from ourselves for networking.

We licked our wounds for some months, trying to carve out a stance towards networking. The attempt could remain a failure, and we would continue with a focus on company issues. The board of E2000 would probably dislike this solution, but our judgment was that we could get along with it. Maybe the reason for making another effort was the pain of having created a fiasco. By the end of the day we were engaged in redesigning the whole concept. First of all, we saw that networking demanded careful planning. Second, we relocated the meetings to the company sites, and we included both professional issues related to business development, and a cultural program, added to the value of participants being able to visit each other premises. This was a recipe that turned out to be quite successful.

The planning of network meetings gradually became a joint company and researcher task. The network attracted new participants, basically enrolling companies that we had some kind of former relationship with. From a starting point of bringing together some 15 company people, we had at the end of the ED2000 period almost 50 participants from the company side. We have experienced that the network has powerful learning possibilities across companies. In addition we have created a ground for learning between a specific company and the researcher group, and between the network of companies and the researcher group.

Teaching as an integrated activity

A key goal was the integration of university staff with SINTEF researchers in enterprise development. We added a dimension to this, as we wanted to integrate the education of students in the module's enterprise development activity. We had for some years been running a program for engineering students in technology management. This program was now expanded to enroll students from social sciences as well as more traditional production engineering. The program has been running since the early 1990s, and is now more popular then ever. The DEMON (Democratic Learning in Network) is intended for students in the final years of their study program. For engineering students, participation in the program includes a large project in the fourth year and doing the thesis work for their master degree in the fifth year. For students in social sciences, DEMON is the vehicle to the master degree. The students have their work closely linked to company activities.

A dominant feature of the program is the ability to link academic work with practical development work at company level. A core value is to link practice with theoretical reflection, thus enabling the students to become well read practitioners who can combine theory and practice in their future jobs. The ideal is to have the students work closely with the ongoing, company-based OD activity. Some times we succeed in this, but in other situations the students are more rudimentary, coupled to the ongoing activity. Students are divided in groups, and each group is assigned to one specific company. In parallel to the field activity, the students meet with the module staff once every month. These seminars last for half a day integrating theoretical reflections with the students' experiences from companies. We consider it to be a major challenge to train new generations of engineers in the "Scandinavian" way of working with enterprise development. This is potentially the most promising strategy to create a platform for participative developmental strategies in work life.

The ED2000 Board

The relationship with the program board was certainly not always easy. We have already discussed in detail how complex the initiation phase was. Members of the research team in Trondheim experienced this as frustrating and unnecessary. Later the relationship to the board and program secretariat changed in a positive direction. In the end, the administrative relations were pragmatic, functional and supportive.

An issue that the board has not handled very well is the distinction between influencing the research activity in the module, and the participant modules' expectations of being in self-control. This issue is particularly important and critical in a program that is founded in an ideology involving participative company development. Strong impact from the board in the beginning of the program period could be legitimized, but when the overruling modes of the board continued towards the end of the program period, a fundamental problem of legitimacy emerged. We experienced that in the process of applying for grants for the final year. Without any explanations, the board structured the modules' internal activities by imposing their view on how resources should be used locally in a reduced budget. In a program on participative enterprise development this is not a very sensible activity.

One excellent feature of the ED2000 program was its length. It gave us an opportunity to work with a long-term (four-five years) focus. Especially in the contract researchers' situation, these five years have secured a sustained work over the whole period.

Reflecting on reflections

Our learning has basically been on three levels. A core theme in the module work was on multi- and transdisciplinary work, on network creation, and on integrating the teaching of undergraduate and graduate students in enterprise development.

Multi- and transdisciplinary knowledge

A central objective in the Trondheim module was to create options for multi-disciplinary research that eventually could lead to transdisciplinary knowledge creation. Our achievements are only the start of the journey towards trans-disciplinary knowledge. This has been a much more challenging effort than we anticipated in the initial phase. We underestimated the time that was necessary to create the premises for multi-disciplinary cooperation. Professional knowledge involves strong social constructions that are very persistent, and any crossing of borders between pockets of professional knowledge are suspicious, to put it mildly.

Our first experience was negligence and lack of respect. Engineers ran their game, while social scientists too easy became spectators on the sideline. Bridging the gap between different professional positions demands time and persistence. It takes a long time to be able to create a common ground, and to utilize this to generate new insights across conventional knowledge boundaries. We spent much energy in reaching a position where we could generate knowledge across professions. Actually, it was only at the end of the program that trust and mutual understanding shaped the background for co-generation of knowledge.

One of our major findings was that professions also ruled in the companies. In retrospect, this seems to be a self-evident position, but this was not explained anywhere in the literature on enterprise development. As the research group was multi-professional, so were also the company actors. Engineers, HR people and economists all had their own models. We can identify four layers of co-operation. First, it is the multi-professional work, both at company level and within the research team. Second, co-operation within professions, but across company and research institutions. Third, the potential mutual learning between company engineers and outside social scientists, and between local enterprise management and research engineers. The fourth level indicates the co-operation with all four stakeholders in the same process. Our learning has primarily been related to co-operation inside the research groups.

Multi-professional co-operation was at the outset expected to depend on concrete problem-oriented work. We have learned that the process of co-operation took a long time, and this was partly due to not working on the same concrete problems. Our experience was that the co-operation potential improved very much when we started working together on the same concrete issues, and that gradually became the situation we moved towards.

Networking

There was no intention at the outset to really engage in networking activity. We dragged ourselves to initiate networking activity. After the first failure, we decided to engage more seriously in the effort. As time went, it clearly became a successful activity. The number of enterprises attending increased throughout the period. How can we explain this development?

Many factors can account for the result. We clearly met a need for communication and learning between the participating companies. The companies that later joined in sought an arena for information exchange and learning that probably was motivated by their struggle to develop their own organization. Clear indications show that companies had a lively exchange, where experiences and ideas were traded. When the contact first was established, then it was easy for the participants to directly contact other companies when the need was felt. A second factor that could account for the success was the composed agenda, both sharing enterprise experiences and having professional researcher input. This created a situation where the audience both could learn from practice and be able to dig into research-based knowing. A third factor was participation as a way to keep in touch with future development in the area of enterprise development. Through the activity in the network, it is possible to participate in future research and developmental work in enterprise development.

Teaching

A formulated goal for the module's work was to integrate teaching in our research and developmental work. The argument was the importance of training future professionals in participative developmental work. We linked the students primarily to existing projects at company level. We mainly had positive experiences from running the DEMON program. Students are given great responsibility when they are invited to take part in ongoing developmental work. It seems most likely that this pedagogical approach has been quite successful. When we link students to ongoing developmental activity, we create a wonderful pedagogical situation linking theory and practical problem solving.

Finally, it is amazing by the end of this project to have a strong personal experience of how teaching, research and practical problem solving created a continuous learning spiral, where each of the activities supported and enriched the others. It made teaching richer and more grounded, it supported research because you had to teach students who were not familiar with the field, and the common ground was a shared practical problem situation.

Part II

Insights

Researchers' collaborative reflections on ED2000

Morten Levin

In this second section of the book, the intention is to present the insights that were gained through this five years' program. The major idea behind this book is to have the participating researchers collectively develop the broad line of new knowledge that emerged through this action research. The authors worked together over a period of two years to reflect on and investigate ED 2000. The basis was a shared understanding of how research developed in the individual modules. These descriptions created the backdrop for a critical assessment of the benefits and downsides of action research on enterprise development which ultimately led to the insights that focused the attention on the issues presented in the following chapters.

In Chapter 10 the focus is on how ED2000 emerged as a program with seven different modules, where each module story had its specific ingredient. In this chapter we reflect on how the board gradually developed a program through different management strategies. Chapter 11 has a focus on how the modules struggled to create a research practice that is aligned with the expectations and the context of ED2000. The twelfth chapter investigates the creation of regional developmental coalitions, where the purpose was to shape a research activity that could enhance regional economic development. One of the major objectives in ED 2000 was to improve the innovation capability of the participating companies. This issue is addressed in Chapter 13, while Chapter 14 is devoted to a discussion of the potential contradiction or alignment between democracy and enterprise development. Finally, Chapter 15 pulls all the threads together, aiming at creating advice for future action research on enterprise development.

Chapter 10

The changing program

Controversies and cooperation

Morten Levin and Jarle Løvland

Introduction

ED2000 was an atypical program in the Research Council of Norway. It was created outside the research council, and was integrated in the Council's portfolio as a complete package. It also presupposed co-operation between the industrial and energy research division and the division for social science research. The third important element of the program was the board's ambition to impact the direction and methodological basis of the research that it funded. According to conventional practice, research proposals are judged for quality and relevance before any money is granted. Then the engagement from the Research Council usually was limited to following up on compliance with plans and the actual spending of money. The ED2000 board had ambitions to impact the program though involving themselves in the design of research in each module, and in continually monitoring program development. A special focus was on the relationship to participating companies, both related to management and to the local trade union. This ambition was remarkable in a program where a core value was participative approaches to enterprise development, as the commitment to participation would certainly be challenged by the board's aim to impact the development of the program.

In the first phase of the project, the board engaged in discussions with each module in order to shape their individual research focus. This was at times confrontational, with hard discussions, where it was obvious that the board of ED2000 knew where the power (and money) was. In addition, the program board and secretariat was committed to a much more extensive follow up than was accepted according to standard procedures in the research council. Members of the governing body visited, throughout the research period, both the research groups and participating companies. Based on this monitoring activity they developed an understanding of the program's strength and weaknesses through their own investigations. There are probably few other programs within the Norwegian research system that have been monitored like ED2000.

This is the story that will be communicated in this chapter, and those experiences constitute the basis for reflection on the organization and leadership of research programs.

The creation of the ED2000 program

The ED2000 was initiated through co-operation between key researchers at the Work Research Institute in Oslo, the Federation of Employers and the Federation og Trade Unions. The Work Research Institute had worked with action research in industrial settings for years, and ED2000 was launched as a new major initiative to revitalize systematic change efforts in Norwegian work life. The program had strong supporters from the Norwegian Federation of Employers and the Norwegian Federation of Trade Unions. Without their engagement, support and lobbying activity, ED2000 would never have got off the ground. This group formed the core issues of the program, and subsequently the program was presented to the Research Council of Norway, more or less as a complete package. In the science foundation, it was introduced as co-operation between the division for "Culture and Society" and the division for "Industry and Energy". The idea was to integrate social science, applied engineering and economic research in one program with the specific goal of researching enterprise development. The methodological approach was expected to have a heavy leaning toward action research. In the original invitation to potential research institutions, only four of the present seven modules were invited. These four research institutions were the ones with former experience in action research in work life.

The core goal of ED2000 was "*to develop knowledge about strategies, methods, work structures and infrastructure to initiate and support the necessary development processes enabling Norwegian enterprises to achieve a leading edge position in international competition*". The program was intended to support the following activities:

- new development organizations in the participating enterprises
- new inter-organizational structures
- concepts, evaluation frameworks and international forms of co-operation facilitating a better comparison of results regarding the international and Norwegian development front in enterprise development
- examples of further development of the Norwegian co-operation model, encapsulating new development directions in thinking connected to productivity development, giving Norwegian enterprises competitive advantages through developing advanced strategies of marketing, product development and production

– business ideas within areas such as work environment development, participation and motivation, capable of transformation by means of enterprise and network development

In the following table a summary of the operational characteristics of the program is presented.

This table identifies the different stages of the program development, and the different phases in operating ED2000. The program had a long story prior to 1994, where ideas and plans had been developed over a long period. Central in this work was Professor Bjørn Gustavsen and the social partners in the labor market. When they had developed the framework for the ED2000 program, it was handed over to the Research Council of Norway. It was not only in its creation that ED2000 differed from most research programs, but it was also managed and led in a fairly unconventional manner.

The creation of research modules

The program was intended both to integrate already existing action oriented work research groups, and to include regional institutions in order to create a broader national basis for this type of research. Four institutions were mentioned in the tender, all of whom had been engaged in work life research. The Work Research Institute in Oslo and the Norwegian University of Science and Technology (NTNU) and the affiliated research organization (SINTEF) in Trondheim carried the tradition of Norwegian action research in industrial settings, while the Norwegian School of Economics and Business administrations (NHH) in Bergen and the Norwegian Business School in Oslo had been engaged in conventional research on work life and business development. The Business School in Oslo never submitted an application to the program.

Rogaland Research was the first module to be given a grant from ED2000. They had combined an application to ED2000 with a proposal to the Work Research Fund of the Confederation of Employers. The perspective on network development and the implementation of international management concepts in the Norwegian industry (Total Quality Management) attracted the board of ED2000, and the Rogaland module received the biggest grant of all participating modules. None of the other modules were granted funding until after an extensive process of negotiation. The NHH application was seen as being quite close to the application from the Institute of Applied Social Science (Fafo). The board initiated a merger between these two modules, aiming at shaping a unified approach to research and development activities. The modules responded by creating one joint application that integrated both original research perspectives. Their research focus came to be on union and management co-operation in large multinational companies. The

Table 10.1 Program chronologies

Period	Program phase	Focal areas and activities
Up until 1994	– *Program conception and initiation* – WRI, Confederation of Employers and Federation of Trade Unions negotiates ideas for a new program Plan introduced to the Research Council of Norway	Creating the main ideas and concepts of the ED2000 program Mobilizing external partners and involve some relevant research institutions.
1994–1996	– *Module development and partnership building and negotiations* – invitation to initial research institutions – regional modules – Industry network activities Negotiations and target outcomes	Initial invitation to key research institutions early 1994, regional module initiatives and negotiations on research and industry focus, module building
1995–1997	– *Module process activities — part one* – Enterprise development support Networking activities/local relation building	Developing industry network and interchange between research groups, enterprises, and networks,
1996–1998	– *Mid-term evaluation* – Design and implementation Outcomes and perceptions	Quantitative and standardized evaluation based interventions from board and secretariat Change in evaluation focus
1998–2000	– *Adjusted module activities — part two* – Enterprise development support Network building Inter-module learning	Changes in modular activities, formation of research cooperation and learning between modules
1999–2001	– *Finalizing activities — continued activity* – Research focus – Strengthened inter-modular learning – International benchmarking Process and further development	Centrally and module supported activities to further development of enterprise development knowledge building and cooperation, evaluation and international relation building

Trondheim module had to struggle for a long time to get their proposal funded. In the first round, the feedback was that it was too conventional, in the second attempt that it had a fairly uninteresting perspective. The third and accepted perspective was on integrated enterprise development combining engineering and social science knowledge in the same process. The Tromsø module had no former experience in work research. The research group in Tromsø had formerly worked on projects in the fish processing industry related to its process of TQM implementation. With strong support from the fishing industry, the local research institution and the University of Tromsø the application was accepted relatively early. The Fafo and Northwest-Forum (Fafo/NVF) module was atypical. The learning network was up and running on the Western coast of Norway, but the affiliated research institution was located in Oslo. This relationship had existed for a long time, but the board of ED2000 wanted to link the NVF activity more closely to an educational institution. After long and complex negotiations the result was a Fafo/NVF module, but with a group of researchers from different institutions closely affiliated with the program. The WRI in Oslo was heavily engaged in the making of ED2000. Many of the models and structures in the program can clearly be traced back to years of work at WRI. However, the application from WRI did not receive an immediate positive response from the board, and the WRI researchers had to fight for a long time to get funded. Finally, the Agder module was the last group to enter the program. Their entrance was based on an intense round of lobbying. Local industry, the Agder College, politicians and the social partners all put their pressure behind the creating of a module in Southern Norway. One year after the others, the Agder module succeeded and entered the program.

The governing body — The board and the secretariat

The program established a very untypical governance structure. One should bear in mind that this program was created with strong support from the social partners in work life. Both the Trade Unions Council and the National Confederation of Employers were heavily involved in creating the program, and when the program was up and running they also financed a proportion of the program. In addition, these two organizations represented the "recipients" of the research activity, namely Norwegian business life, and they already had a joint committee responsible for business development activity. The social partners played a dual role, as they were both funders and formal representatives of the management and unions that would benefit from the program.

The board was elected according to standard Research Council procedures, and hence it was composed both of industry people and researchers not actively involved in this particular program. An industrialist with an expressed interest in research headed the board. The social partners on the labour market were represented, basically with the same actors that were involved in creating the program. In addition two professors and one work life researcher from abroad made up the board. The board created a secretariat that took on the responsibility for the daily operation of the program. This secretariat consisted of representatives of employers and unions in addition to the program director in the Research Council.

The secretariat had operating responsibility for running the program, while the board took on formal responsibility both to decide on grants and to monitor the activity in the program. Given this construction, it was obvious that the secretariat had quite a substantial influence, not only over the daily operation but also on more fundamental policy and management issues. The secretariat turned out to express and exercise professional opinions and practice in work research, and they were obviously a key factor in the program's learning system. They communicated directly with the research groups on issues related to participating companies, and to positions and views expressed in the board. They played an important role in the communication process between board and modules, as it enabled an increased understanding in modules of how the board was thinking and acting. This was certainly important for creating synergy between the board and modules, but also between the modules. The secretariat for its part gave the board feedback on the attitudes, arguments and positions held in the modules. That also had the potential of giving the board an understanding of what the active researchers were thinking, and how they operated. Throughout the whole period, the secretariat kept good contact with the participating companies. These visits were important for monitoring the daily operation of the program, feeding back information both to modules and board.

Daily operation of ED2000

The program ended up funding seven modules. Each research group had negotiated its own agenda with the board, and was deeply engaged in local work. From this perspective the program operated in a very conventional manner. This was at least the situation in the initial phases of the project. The researchers had heard something about an annual program conference, and about the intention to arrange regular meetings between module leaders. In the first two years of operation, these meetings were quite unexciting. In addition, the annual program conference was organized in a fairly conventional manner. The conference was a one-day event, and had a number of speeches, followed by a discussion that was expected to include both practitioners and professionals. The conferences attracted mainly researchers and officers of national institutions relevant for work life. Participants from the industry never dominated the crowd. In the first phase of the program, the module leader meetings were also close to being boring. Module leaders met, discussed an agenda set by representatives of the secretariat and traveled back home. As information exchange it worked reasonably well, but as a forum for mutual learning it was pretty close to a waste of time.

A breakthrough in the program came in its second year of operation. A module leader meeting was held in Stavanger. The major issue on the agendas was a mid-term evaluation. All module leaders were upset. It was considered to be commissioned too early, the design was mainly for external political purposes, and the suggested data was considered not very relevant for the actual research. However, the conflict with the board and secretariat was productive, and this was probably the single most important meeting of the program. The confrontation resulted in a better understanding of the political strategies the board held, it was the first stage in the process of shaping a community of module leaders. In fact, the module leaders "co-opted" the mid term evaluation, making it a fairly uncontroversial issue. The meeting ended with a joint dinner, eating "lutefish", a traditional Norwegian Christmas course. From then on, the "lutefish dinner" became a core cultural element of the program.

This event marked a change in the program. For the first time, a sort of collective learning environment emerged. The modules became aware of each other, and the initial, fierce competition weakened. In other words, this was a phase where co-operation and mutual learning slowly could be developed. An important barrier was passed when all involved researchers were invited to a joint meeting. The meeting addressed key administrative and research issues and there was ample time for discussion and networking among the participants. All participants expressed their satisfaction with this meeting, and they looked forward to having further contact with colleagues. The program only held one more meeting between the participating researchers. That meeting was not as successful as the previous meeting, as it was focused on research publications from the project and did not address operational research questions to the same extent. In addition, it lasted only for a day, and gave few options for networking among researchers.

The module leader meeting rolled along, and was with one exception very constructive. In the third year of operation, the secretariat wanted to initiate publication activity. The module leaders were presented with a fixed structure for a book where specific chapters were assigned to each module. This was certainly not a smart move, and it violated the participative touch that had emerged within the program. The conflict was settled without lasting consequences. The result was of course that new issues were added to the publication plans.

The management of research

Management of research has traditionally tended to be viewed as a pure administrative task. The funding body develop strategic initiatives, which later result in programs with specific perspectives and goals. The essential function of research councils has often been viewed as one of creating strategic programs, and then to make sure that the best applications are funded. Once a research group has passed the test of getting access to research money, management activities from the council stress the follow up of initial plans, monitoring that the spending of money is according to rules and regulations, and that the program delivers what is promised. This is a very bureaucratic and fairly static way of administering the use of research funds. The governing body of ED2000 took a more dynamic and active management approach. They clearly wanted to exercise leadership, as their ambitions extended being passive recipients of applications. They wanted to impact the actual design of the research in the modules, and they had ambitions about involving specific institutions in the research program. This was certainly not the standard operating procedure in the Research Council of Norway. To use an established distinction in the literature on leadership (Northouse 1997, Levin et al. 1994), the governing bodies of ED2000 took on *leadership* instead of *management.* A quote from Northouse can illustrate the difference between leadership and management (Northouse, 1997, p. 8):

> "The major activities of management get played out differently than activities of leadership. In planning and budgeting, the emphasis of management is on establishing detailed agendas, setting timetables from several months to a few years and allocating the necessary resources to meet organizational objectives. *In contrast to this, the emphasis of leadership is on direction setting, clarifying the big picture, building a vision that is often long term, and setting strategy to create needed organizational changes.*" (Italic by the authors)

Our intention here is not to present a thorough discussion of the very diverse and scattered literature on management and leadership. Major lines of this literature are structured in, for example, the books by Andersen (1995) and Northouse (1997). These modes of structuring different strands of thinking in leadership and management are in themselves interesting, but for the purpose of the discussion in this chapter, the distinction between leadership and management would be sufficient for understanding key issues at stake in leading a research program.

The exercise of leadership in a research program forces one question to the surface. What kind of organization is a research program? In many ways it is easier to identify what it is not. It is probably not public administration, it is certainly not an industrial organization, and it does not look like an institution of higher education. In spite of these difficulties, we cannot avoid wrestling with how to characterize a research program. First, it is evident that it is a form of work organization, as it produces research, publications, and Ph.D. graduates. Second, the structure of a research program is certainly a loose coupling of actors. The weakest tie was obviously between different research modules, while there was a strong tie between the governing body and the modules and of course between researchers within the modules. The strength and power is predominantly embedded in financial relations. The board has de facto total control over the funding, but that does not necessarily grant the ability to directly steer the research activities.

Research depends on creative and intellectual processes in a given organizational environment. It is possible to control the research context, but creativity in research is primarily under total control of the individual. Third, social processes impact the values and belief in the community of practitioners, which again impacts the individual researchers. Such processes cannot be directly controlled or influenced by the board of the program. In reality, the board of a research program face a situation where their basic power is to include or exclude a research group, but if they intend to influence the operational research processes they must exercise a more elaborate management.

Leadership in this loosely coupled and hierarchical power structure is fairly complex. Many of the modern ideas of leadership are expressed as mentoring, teaching, empowering, etc. Important in all these approaches is that leadership is relational, as it depends on mutual understanding and accept. A statement from a leader in a particular direction has no effect unless it is understood, accepted and acted upon by the subordinate. When an idea is "built" into the head of the subordinate, it creates a direction that fundamentally directs the individuals' actions. On the other hand, interpreting leadership as a relational process implies that the exchange also impacts on the leader. The whole leadership process takes on a form of mutual learning. It is hard to see that the process of relational leadership can function unless leader and subordinates join in the same learning process.

Given this general picture of the kind of an organization that a program can be interpreted to be, and what can be argued to be the core leadership in such programs, we can identify at least three different modes of leadership. All have their characteristics, problems, possibilities and pitfalls. The basic argument for this taxonomy is that it invokes three different types of activity on the part of the governing body. As a consequence of this, it will also create different responses and activities in the modules. These three forms for impacting local research groups are generated by differences in the application of power, of communication strategy and of co-operation.

Leadership 1: Pressure

The governing body uses its power position to force the research modules to align their activity in a preferred direction. The big "carrot" in such a process is of course access to research grants. The governing body controls the use of this genuine power position that enable them to shape the overall direction of the program. Writing, rewriting and negotiating proposals might be major factors in this process. This is obviously something that has an impact, because the underlying power position is evident for all participants.

Strategy 2: Monitoring
When a program is up and running, the board can decide to be very active in the follow-up of the module activity. This activity will not be limited to the formalized monitoring system of the Research Council, but can involve frequent contacts and discussions, not only with researchers, but also with management and union representatives of the participating companies.

Strategy 3: Developing
A third leadership opportunity is to enhance the professional development and to co-ordinate ongoing research activities. The core idea is to mentor, support and train researchers in order to make them capable of meeting the demands forwarded by the program. This is leadership through training, learning and mentoring. Power is not a dominant factor in this type of leadership, as various intrinsic factors are what are the key factors. Leadership is not there to direct, but to enhance the researchers' ability to reach desired goals. This type of leadership has a focus on developing researchers to make them capable of reaching desired goals.

Pressure

The initial phase of the E2000 project was unconventional. A number of selected research institutes were encouraged to submit proposals. At the outset, the initiation was quite an open invitation. Participatory approaches to enterprise development was to be understood as mandatory, as it was expected that the modules also should support the construction of learning networks, linking both companies and researchers in the developmental process. Some of the modules were given a hint that a regional dimension would be important, while others received less specific directives.

The aspiring modules wrote their applications, and the negotiating process started. Depending on who had written the application, the pressure took on different forms. The two first applications written from the Trondheim research group were not received particularly well. The first one was based on industrial networks in the southern part of Norway. The regional research institution had also submitted a proposal, and the board wanted to create co-operation between these two institutions. They called for a meeting, but the research groups did not manage to develop a strategy for co-operation. The result was that both institutions were sent back to the drawing table in order to create a partnership. This co-operative effort, which probably is the most difficult of all construction processes in research, did not work out. Actually, the pressure did not work out at all.

A second attempt to force co-operation upon researchers was related to a research engagement in Norwegian multinationals (Corporations or Norwegian branches owned by international corporations). Based on an application written at the Norwegian School of Economics and Management, and one written by Institute of Applied Social Science, a co-operative effort emerged. Pressure from the governing body forced this co-operation upon the researchers, and it lasted until the field vanished when the company broke the research contract.

The conclusions of the mid-term evaluation by the program secretariat and board, was also the direct reason why the co-operating research group in Bodø, which was formerly instructed to co-operate with the Tromsø module, left the program at the end of 1997. Other modules engaged in similar considerationsl. However, some points and conclusions from the secretariat evaluation were followed up and implemented by the modules during the last stage of ED2000, although they strongly disagreed on the methodology and use of the evaluation.

The "pressure" strategy was an interesting phenomenon in a program aiming at participative approaches to enterprise development. The whip was clearly present in both situations, and a first superficial analysis would end up with the potential conclusion that there was a clear contradiction between the stated values of the program and its operational modus. What the governing body instituted as a practice in this first phase was clearly not participative, and it would result in a total crisis if this mode of acting had continued throughout the whole program period. When the Agder module and the Trondheim module never came to terms, neither of them were granted any funding. Later, both of the modules re-entered the program, but then with a different agenda. For the Agder module this was not a very different agenda, but they succeeded through lobby activities by mobilizing many different interest groups in the region. The Trondheim module came back with a quite different proposal, shifting the focus from regional networks to multidisciplinary development.

Monitoring

The governing body of ED2000 included both a board and a secretariat. The two groups obviously had a division of labour between them. The board had the formal responsibility of monitoring the total program activity, including making decisions on grants and being responsible for the total operation. In this role, the board had a fair distance to the operational activity in the program. Members of the secretariat participated quite frequently in the more external oriented activities of ED2000. It was more the rule that the secretariat visited local modules when seminars and conferences were organized. These visits were well received, and played the important role of both creating legitimacy for local activity, giving national support to local work and last but not least they were a sign of genuine interest in local activity. Undoubtedly, all this was basically considered as a very supportive activity in the program, and it was generally very much appreciated by the researchers in the modules. This activity was more extensive than what was common in programs run by the Research Council of Norway.

A second form of conventional monitoring was to run surveys. An almost catastrophic attempt was made in the second year of the program's operational period. The governing body had at that time figured out that they needed some sort of hard evidence of the ongoing achievements of the program. In order to meet what the governing body experienced as heavy external pressure, they mandated a survey. The idea was to collect data both from the activities in the modules and from the participating companies. Questionnaires were created and presented to the module leaders at a meeting in Stavanger in the early fall of 1998. At that point, the program was on the brink of breaking apart. The whole idea of collecting data based on questionnaires to gather information on highly complex social change processes, was regarded as a contradiction in terms by all of the module leaders. Most of the activities were in a fairly early stage, some of the modules had hardly begun their work, and the participating companies were asked to spend time and energy on issues certainly disconnected from their own development activity.

The arguments were plentiful, and the social temperature at the gathering was quite high. The real question for the module leaders, even though not really discussed openly, was whether it was worth while continuing working on the program. This conflict was constructive in the sense of naming some of the tensions between the governing body and the researchers. The results were quite productive but not through taking this survey seriously. An elegant move by a couple of the module leaders who volunteered to improve the survey, turned out to be perfect sabotage. The whole issue of a midway evaluation based on survey research fell more or less dead to the ground. However, the important effect of this meeting was the acknowledgement that external pressures and needs of the ED2000 created a collective and supportive attitude by the module leaders. This was probably the single most important meeting in the whole program, even though the formal outcome was a disaster.

The third and probably most innovative part of the monitoring structure of the program was shaped by the secretariat. A two-person group, one from the Confederation of Employers and the other from Federation of Trade Unions started frequent visits to companies and modules. This turned out to be a smart decision. Through visiting companies and modules, they were able to gather important and complex data necessary to make sense of the progression in the program, through taking on this third party role. They could create a self-reliant understanding of the program achievements. This activity was certainly well received by the modules and probably also by the companies. The most important effect was not the "evaluation" aspect of their visits, but the discussions between the governing body and the local modules that accompanied all these visits.

This was not a one-way communication. As the governing body learned about the development of the program, the researchers learned about the governing body. An insight in discussions and debates related to the program was an important part of total program alignment. These communications did not deal with formal debates in the board meetings, but related to communication in and around central program activity. Local modules had an opportunity to get a better understanding of the political and substantive issues of the program, and the researchers had an opportunity to convey their views. This monitoring "on the road" was really a key factor in gradually shaping a unified program. In terms of dynamically leading a program, this activity was obviously aligned to the core value of participative change processes. Module leader meetings gradually came to work in the same direction, but the discussions were often too evasive. The positive effect of the Stavanger meeting was the creation of a social space that was that was open and safe enough to allow contradictory positions to be played out. Instead of considering conflicts as disruptive, they became productive, even though they were always risky.

Perhaps the most important outcome of the mid term evaluation, was the role it acquired as the common enemy to all the modules. The module leaders neither accepted the evaluation format with strong focus on hard facts rather than processes, nor the missing considerations of local module preconditions and demands affecting both the short-term orientation, and the achievements both in terms of published research and action outcomes. This evaluation also changed the module leader meetings. In the initial stages of the program, the function of the module leader meeting was mainly an efficient way for the secretariat to co-ordinate the program development. Due to competition between modules in the early stages of the program, it was only after the Stavanger meeting that self-governance through mutual and collective efforts found its place within ED2000. This came about as a consequence of the monitoring function of the program. Furthermore, it is important to acknowledge the positive impact of leadership through monitoring.

Developing

In the construction of the program, some emphasis was put on creating learning opportunities for the researchers. Efforts were made to have the researchers meet and potentially learn together. In the first two years, this activity was fragmentary in terms of making it possible for researchers to meet and discuss professional issues. The only arena for communication and learning was the annual ED2000 conference. Many of the researchers met at those conferences, and discussions were abundant over lunch and between presentations. This was in itself a nice opportunity to exchange experiences, but it did not give room for in-depth, mutual learning. In addition, the presentations where individual research groups communicated examples or cases from their own work of course gave a very traditional opportunity to learn from others' work. One should not underestimate the effect of these presentations and communications, but time could probably have been used better.

A much stronger initiative was launched at the end of the fourth year of operation. All researchers were invited to a workshop with a special focus on mutual learning in the community of participating researchers. The program was constructed to achieve this: the chairman of the board gave a presentation of core issues and opened up a dialogue. This meeting, which lasted for one and a half days, gave ample room for communication across modules and professions. Together with the staged discussions in plenary and group settings, most of the researchers found themselves deeply engaged in intellectual exchanges with colleagues. In addition, the chairman of the board invited the research group to actively discuss his major strategic challenge. The company he was president of had just acquired another industrial group, and his major concern was how he could create a strong new company. This created a lively discussion among the participants dealing both with practical challenges and theoretical issues.

This was a very successful meeting. The overwhelming majority of the participants found this a fruitful and worthwhile workshop. Arenas like this workshop created the necessary backdrop for the type of intellectual exchange that has the potential to link different program activities. The command-model inherent in the application of pressure might easily direct the extrovert activity in a desired direction, but a real and lasting change of direction can only emerge from communication processes which involve real intellectual exchange.

A second researcher workshop was organized a year after this first one. The theme was the development of the joint publications from the ED2000. This workshop had a much narrower focus on writing up the research. As a practical instrument it worked well, and it also gave room for mutual discussion and design of the publications and books that eventually would come out of this program. On the other hand, it had much less impact as an arena that could set the intellectual agenda for the program. It was simply too late for that.

Conclusion — Organization and leadership of research

ED2000 was a program on participatory change processes in Norwegian industry. The founding idea was that labor and management should co-operate in enterprise development work. This should therefore be a legitimate standard of reference when reviewing the organization and the leadership of this program. It is difficult to accept that a program on participative change should hold one standard for the activity related to activity at company level, and a different standard for the operation of the research organization. Obviously, the reflections on the developmental process of ED2000 must take place in the perspective of participative changes.

There is not much work on evaluation of programs that focus on organizational and leadership processes In the literature. Evaluations have traditionally focused on the management of programs, but few if any have taken on the perspective of viewing programs as organizational bodies. It is for example quite interesting that when Nashold et al. (1993) evaluated the Swedish LOM program, the internal program developmental issues were not dealt with at all. In fact, there is not enough published on this topic to make good comparisons. This in itself is an interesting fact.

The history that is presented of ED2000 in this chapter focuses on three different strategies used in the leadership of this program. Direct pressure was used in order to create a local research agenda that would be in line with the perspective that the governing body really wanted. For the modules exposed to this strategy, it was experienced as provocative and as a power play. It was too obvious that if the modules really wanted to get funded, they had to follow the intentions of the board. This was of course not unfair. The ED2000 was a program with a specific aim, and it was the responsibility of the governing body to make sure that this aim would be reached. The problematic side of this strong intervention aimed at impacting the local agenda setting was that it hardly could be identified as a participative dialogue. In a participative change process it is of course not illegitimate to use power, but it must be based on a dialogical relationship between the actors. Power relations are present in any organization, but in participative change processes, the power has to be visible and explicated in a communication process between the parties. Dialogues are necessary for creating a mutual understanding between power holders and subordinates. In the early phases of ED2000, these communication processes did not take place. With a little exaggeration one could state that the chain of command was activated, and the modules had to obey. The initial and controversial stages of the program could have benefited much from spending more time on dialogues creating a mutual learning situation. The board would probably have benefited more from a well founded understanding of the local research context, while the prospective modules would equally have benefited from having an in depth understanding of the perspectives held by the governing body.

The monitoring process of the program was much more successful. It is unclear how meticulously this was planned. In any respect, it was really an interesting and important innovation on part of the secretariat to visit companies and modules.

This created a very fruitful dialogue that shaped the ground for mutual learning. Through this activity the modules felt that they had a voice in the program, and also that they could learn how the governing body was thinking. This monitoring could have taken on the form of strict management control, but through the "modus operandi" chosen by the secretariat it created fruitful feedback for local research. We do not know how this monitoring affected the participating companies, but we have good reason to believe that the process was equally important for them. The local partners had an opportunity to review project activity independent of researchers' presence and this shaped an arena that is important in this kind of action research. The midterm evaluation was a total fiasco in terms of impacting the performance of the program. On the other hand, it created, albeit not intentionally the breakthrough moment in the program. Through resolving the deep conflict this evaluation produced, a new and collective spirit was born. This conflict was probably the most important single event in the whole program.

The second half of the program had a different participative profile. The leadership of the program was at this stage geared towards communicative processes. We have already discussed the monitoring activity. What turned out to be key factor in the "developing" modus was more successful meetings between governing bodies and participating researchers. One important outcome of this activity was increased learning between participating researchers and the governing body of ED2000. The other equally important outcome was the ability to create a network among the researchers. Creating an opportunity to meet paved the way for a collective understanding of working in the same program and to discover similarities and differences, all of which created a potentially rich learning environment. It was a common attitude of these moments of mutual learning, that they were important and that the participating researchers wanted more. These processes were also vital if the ambition was to create a momentum for collaboration between researchers interested in action based research on enterprise development.

Has ED2000 been a research program that held the standards it is reasonable to demand from a participative standpoint? This question has a two-fold answer. In the first phase, the exercise of power from the governing board made participative aspects fairly invisible. The communication process was moderate, and demarcation line between power holders and subordinates was too strong. However, we do not say that power is either illegitimate or should not be used. The whole point is to integrate power in communication processes. The second phase of the project, where monitoring and developing became a more profound characteristic of the program, shaped a fruitful ground for participation. The ED2000 turned into a research program that scored high in terms of participation.

Chapter 11

Creating new research practices

Lene Foss, Henrik Kvadsheim and Johan E. Ravn

Introduction

In order to enhance and disseminate its agenda on a national level, the ED2000 program wanted to establish regional research teams, or modules as they were termed. Researchers from local research institutions formed a team focusing on enterprise development, attracting local enterprises and conducting action research. This chapter deals with how a new research practice was established and sustained. In the relatively small research institutes in Norway, this practice implied recruiting researchers across institutional or departmental borders and having them to work together for a five-year period. This meant that the modules needed to involve researchers from a variety of academic disciplines, like sociology, political science, organization theory and management research. The involvement of researchers from diverse backgrounds generated new experiences for most of the participating modules. The researchers both had to keep up legitimacy in the research community as well as prove practical relevance for the participating companies.

Action research is a research strategy by which knowledge generation is embedded in practical problem solving. It covers a broad set of tasks to deal with, from field intervention to analysis and theory building. To handle this, some modules tried to develop division of labor within the researcher teams, whereas others tried not to. In both cases, the modules had to handle heterogeneity, understood as differences among the members of the research modules and their stakeholders. The modules also had to face the legitimacy issue regarding research communities. The researchers had to answer questions about scientific rigor from their peers in the various academic camps. Action researchers have always been exposed to this issue, but most of the researchers of the ED2000 modules were new to action research, and therefore new to this challenge.

The modules differed in how they composed their research teams, and how they related to their enterprises and external stakeholders in the ED2000 project.

For most of the modules, ED2000 was their first move in establishing research projects to address development needs of local enterprises. Research based on multidisciplinary teams was also an unfamiliar practice. ED 2000 asked for a hitherto unknown level of heterogeneity in the researcher groups. Heterogeneity has both positive and negative elements. On the one hand, it creates opportunities for new ways of intervention, reflection and learning, and therefore it can catalyze work life innovations. On the other hand, heterogeneous research processes risk becoming laden with confusion, misunderstandings, conflicts and fragmentation, just as unable to handle practical problem solving as to produce new knowledge. In order to gain legitimacy among the enterprises and in academia by producing sound research results, the challenge for the heterogeneous research teams was to handle research and practical relevance.

The above focus leads us to ask the following questions in order to signify how collaboration in a module research practice was shaped:

- How did the heterogeneous research teams legitimate their approaches vis-à-vis the research environment and companies? How did their heterogeneity affect the modules' projects? Did it result in creativity and new ways of thinking and acting? Did it reform prevailing models of action research? In short: Did the module design enable us to move beyond the research paradigms of the different disciplines?
- What do the experiences with regional module design tell us about how heterogeneous research teams should organize themselves in order to meet both the requirements of practical problem solving and theory building? Does this regionalization make sense?

These questions will be addressed by reflecting on the experiences of three differently composed modules: Tromsø, Trondheim and Rogaland Research (RR). These modules were chosen because their very difference is likely to illustrate the complexity of heterogeneity and legitimacy in various ways.

The Tromsø module was a multidisciplinary composition. It was an attempt at a new research practice, since most of its members had a strong disciplinary identification. What they had in common was a focus on one particular trade: the fishery industry of Northern Norway. The researchers had few prior experiences of working together in the field. The module's work took shape as a close encounter between academia and small to medium sized enterprises. This kind of meeting between research and practice was a new experience for both sides.

The Trondheim module was also multidisciplinary, composed of social scientists and engineers. The social scientists came from a department where action research had been an established work tradition. The engineers of the group were used to being involved with problem solving in companies, but they had no action research experience. What was new to both social scientists and engineers was to co-operate on work in company settings and in research. This type of co-operation turned out to be a new experience also for the companies, and learning in trans-disciplinary settings became a key focus.

The RR module was composed of social scientists and consultants. Just like in the Trondheim module, co-operation across professional or disciplinary divides was a key challenge. In addition, a central problem for the RR module was handling several types of obligations and interests within the program's local stakeholders. It became important how to run this heterogeneous group through the establishment of 'multi-level' arenas for reflection and negotiation. A key challenge for all modules was to define roles and a division of labor within the researcher teams, in order to run processes of development work hand in hand with conducting solid trustworthy research.

Challenges of multidisciplinary module construction

Heterogeneity is important in order to understand the organization of the modules in ED2000. We use it here to denote the variety of academic disciplines involved, the differences in the construction of the research teams, and the differences across research teams, as well as to highlight various reflection-action opposites. We propose that the concept of heterogeneity has both a quantitative and a qualitative aspect. With quantitative heterogeneity we refer to multiplicity, for instance by having a whole set of voices included in a dialogue on change. An example would be an arena on which social researchers meet. Despite their differences, they do have some common traits and interests. Qualitative heterogeneity, on the other hand, shows more *diversity*: The voices included are not necessarily very numerous, but they are deeply and thoroughly different from one another. An example would be an encounter between a desktop social researcher and the manager of a small family-owned business in a rural area. Their work lives are worlds apart.

Heterogeneity has a double mission in an action oriented research project. Some degree of heterogeneity can secure a broader analytical approach to enterprise development. It can further be of practical value for the firm, as researchers from different disciplines may look differently at the variety of factors that are salient for enterprise development. Heterogeneity can also allow researchers different roles in a team, i.e., some can work with communication processes, some can work with work place redesign, some can look into the organization structure. Too much heterogeneity, however, can be a disadvantage when a team needs to make an impact. It can have a negative effect on the ability to stand together and form consensus. The greater disciplinary difference between scholars, the more difficult this becomes. At least since Thomas Kuhn (1962), it has been referred to as the so-called *incommensurability* between various epistemological stands. All understanding is theory based, and there is no "objective" point from where various epistemological positions can be compared (Kuhn, op. cit). Through a different line of arguments, Habermas arrives at a parallel position: it is impossible to separate the process of knowledge generation from our human interests. Thus, all knowledge is essentially value based (Habermas 1972). Given a qualitative heterogeneity; we cannot expect team members to share all values. This is in short the predicament heterogeneous research groups face. There are two ways out of this difficulty: One is to continue along mono-disciplinary paths, making sure that the various stands do not conflict too much. Another strategy would be to find a way to handle heterogeneity. Flood and Romm (1996) argue that the incommensurability created by heterogeneity does not need to be solved or dissolved, but it must be managed or handled. Heterogeneity is surely a double-edged sword. On the one hand, it is a state that enables creativity, variety and innovation. On the other hand, heterogeneous research teams risk becoming paralyzed due to an incommensurability that renders any joint action impossible.

Habermas' (1972) claim about knowledge as essentially value based also raises the issue of *legitimacy* for us. Legitimacy is a legal-moral concept, and has to do with both lawfulness and rightfulness. An institution or action is legitimate if it is judged (by those who subject to it) as just, and in accordance with common ideas of morality. The concept of legitimacy is commonly linked to the concept of authority. Authority is seen as a legitimate exercise of power (Weber 1990).[1] We find Parsons' concept of functional authority useful, i.e. that a person/group has legitimacy in terms of his/its expertise, knowledge and competence. This concept of legitimacy is relevant to the understanding of construction and development of the modules in this chapter. Based on their expertise and knowledge, the modules created a research profile that the enterprises acknowledged. There is often scepticism in the field with regard to research, the assumption held being that academics are unable to come up with something that is of immediate use for local problems in the field. The researchers' competence will be put to the test; the enterprises need to know "what's in it for us?" Further, the work of the modules needed legitimacy in relation to the general research environment. Research requires that researchers legitimize their work vis-à-vis their academic colleagues, both at a national and international level. Academics handle this by keeping up with the standards of scientific research, and by publishing their results for other

1. Weber (1990) distinguished between three types of legitimacy: (1) Traditional authority, (2) Charismatic authority and (3) Legal-rational authority. Parsons in the introduction in (Weber, 1964, pp. 60–61) invented a fourth type — functional authority — which we find is the most relevant for the issue at hand here.

academics within the research paradigm they want to belong to. In creating legitimacy in a regional context, the modules therefore had to fight both the professions and the dominating research paradigm.

It is a challenge to produce something practical, and in addition to meet the academic requirements. The challenge in constructing and developing modules is therefore about how to gain legitimacy in two spheres — the academic and the practical. Because of the close interaction between theoretical perspectives of research and the concrete challenges of practice, any action research project will be a heterogeneous process. For the same reason, issues of legitimacy will surface as a challenge the people in the project. The aim of action research is to bridge the gap between "field" and academia, by producing new knowledge that solves practical problems, as well as contributing to the goals of social science (Elden and Chisholm 1993; Greenwood & Levin, 1998, Rapoport 1970). Most action researchers would also hold democratic inclusion to be an important goal, alongside with problem solving, problem learning and the quality of the social research (Greenwood and Levin 1998). This implies that action research needs to legitimize itself, both in the academic and the "practical" world. To legitimize action research as "research" has been action researchers' difficulty, as their work never has been fully accepted by the camp of traditional social scientists.[2] A key challenge for ED2000 was therefore to overcome this criticism, and the multi-disciplinary design of the research groups made it harder than ever to do so — towards traditional social science camps.

At the same time, the more orthodox disciplines also face a legitimating crisis[3] these days — at least we can observe that normal science more often than before is challenged. Critical views on traditional mono-disciplinary research have developed in the research camp, also outside of action research strongholds. It has been argued that academia's traditional ways of understanding knowledge production does not account for it all anymore. On an epistemological level, for instance Luhmann has argued that the late modern society has differentiated itself into subsystems that do not share a common logic or paradigm (Luhmann 1989). Different disciplines or professions have differentiated themselves away from one another, and their internal knowledge bases are marked by opaqueness when seen from the outside. The question of what kind of discourse that is to take place across disciplines or professions cannot be solved easily, since no knowledge or epistemology is overarching the separate sub-systems. In a world where economy and politics seem to be more and more integrated on a global level, and where people more and more experience how various phenomena are interlinked, traditional mono-

2. For a discussion of this based on Norwegian action research, see (Bødtker Sørensen 1992) and (Pålshaugen 1992). For an international debate, see (Whyte 1991) or (Greenwood and Levin 1998)

3. See (Habermas 1973)

disciplinary approaches simply cannot deliver the answers. The question of how to handle this is discussed by Gibbons et al. (Gibbons 1994). They argue for what they call "the new production of knowledge", a mode of knowledge production that relies on a "transdisciplinary knowledge paradigm." Gibbons et al. define transdisciplinary knowledge as "Knowledge which emerges from a particular *context of application* with its own distinct theoretical structures, research methods and modes of practice but which may not be locatable on the prevailing disciplininary map" (Gibbons 1994: 168). Knowledge production of this kind is by necessity situated in processes of practical problem solving. It involves a multiplicity of disciplines or professions, mutually interpenetrating one another's research questions, preferred practices, methods and even epistemologies. With this approach, Gibbons et al. address the old clash of interests (antagonism) between practical relevance and scientific rigor by proposing a kind of bridge that involves a new mode for producing science (rigor) in a transdisciplinary manner, embedded in practical situations of problem solving (relevance). In such an approach, disciplinary heterogeneity is no hindrance to rigor, quite the contrary, it is what can give research its legitimacy.

Even though disciplinary heterogeneity is desirable, it does not make it simple to deal with. The most promising way of doing so seems to be along the mode 2 knowledge production proposed by Gibbons et al. (Gibbons 1994): transdisciplinary knowledge production embedded in practical situations of problem solving. In the research projects of the modules discussed here, we can observe attempts at creating such transdisciplinary spaces or arenas: knowledge production embedded in processes of transdisciplinary problem solving. It can also be argued that the work of the modules have tried to move beyond this, because of attempts to bring not just researchers, but also the organization members (the task owners) into the knowledge generation process. Such a design faces heterogeneity not just through letting diverse research disciplines confront one another, but also through bringing in interests and knowledge systems of the task owners.

Prior experiences with action research and teamwork in the modules

A new research practice never starts from scratch. By the very nature of research, researchers bring with them prior education and experience into a new research setting. As stated in the history of the Tromsø module, researchers in the team were very heterogeneous with regard to academic background. This heterogeneity was partly due to the fact that the module in the first couple of years was clearly divided into a productivity and benchmarking group working from an economist's point of view, and a group oriented towards sociotechnical theory, institutional theory and network theory. The heterogeneity was strongest in the projects' 2–3 first years, and it was difficult because there were few persons available for building legitimacy in the enterprises. Over the years, after some turnover in the research team, and after working collectively in the field together, and through that learning from one another, the disciplinary distance became less prominent. However, a dividing line between benchmarking researchers and those researching on intraorganizational issues always persisted. On interorganizational issues, there was more overlap between researchers from different disciplines.

The Trondheim module recruited its members from four different departments of the Norwegian University of Science and Technology (NTNU) and SINTEF, a non-profit research organization closely linked to NTNU. Those four departments represented a fairly wide range of competencies, spanning from industrial and production engineering, via health, safety, organization and leadership, to general sociology and political science. In the Trondheim group, several of the researchers were familiar with action research. In this view, the work of ED2000 should have its roots in what can be called the "Scandinavian Model".[4] However, the module tried to develop this tradition further in an attempt of having engineers' support in maintaining the dual perspective: not just social perspectives on technology, but also technical or engineering perspectives on the work system. The engineers' prior mode of work was focused on an expertise model. The assumption was that the role of the researchers was to analyze the company, and based on this to develop a company redesign and carry it out. In the individual projects, these two interests were to meet, and not without conflicts.

The initial main challenge in the RR module was to handle different research-practices in their module, expressed by the diversity and clash of interests between social science researchers and 'business consultant' researchers. Those were organized into separate departments at RR, with different attitudes and understandings of the right way to conduct business-related action research. A continuous discussion between the RR-researchers participating in the module-work dealt with matters of how the researchers should intervene and influence the development processes in the participating enterprises, which were initiated as a central part of their module work. The consultants preferred a research practice which mainly focused on business-techniques and expert advise to the companies. This practice would lead to close relations, characterized by usefulness and confidence between the researchers and the enterprises, and thereby building legitimacy

4. The main elements in this model are as follows: (1) institutionalised cooperation between employers and trade unions (and the state); (2) sociotechnical thinking: the interrelationship between technology and work organization shapes the working conditions (Trist and Bamforth 1951; Trist 1981) (3) an effective work organization is based on a good sociotechnical fit, and it is developed through a participative change process involving all relevant parties in the organisation.

among the participating enterprises. The social science researchers highlighted the problems of combining "the advising role" with critical research. For them, "the advising role" in the enterprises would make them committed and responsible for the development in these enterprises, and thereby make it difficult to evaluate the actual outcomes and thus legitimize their research for the academic community.

The Tromsø module was perhaps the one where the researchers had least intervention experience, but where all could gather under social science banners, a module marked by quantitative heterogeneity at the outset. In both the Trondheim and RR modules, a clear-cut division in two main camps could be observed, across which few core epistemological assumptions were shared. A more deep-seated or qualitative heterogeneity marked these research groups.

The construction of the research modules

To design a research module involves both developing an internal structure as well as taking the external constituencies into consideration. Its internal structure involves research themes, different types of researchers, and a special type of "vocabulary" in its interaction with the enterprises. External constituencies represent resources that an organization is dependent on (Pfeffer and Salancik 1978). For a research module, these are access to local business networks, branch organizations and work life organizations. Internal as well external elements are therefore crucial in constructing a regional research module.

Internal elements

The Tromsø module consisted of social scientists, i.e. there was no qualitative heterogeneity in terms of professions (consultants and engineers versus researchers). The construction of the module was built around the brave attempt by the social scientists' to familiarize themselves with the problems of the industry by "going native". On the industry side they were more used to working with private consultants than academics. As for the researchers involved they were not used to working as a team. In addition, the module recruited graduate students for doing fieldwork in the companies. Internal cliques emerged within the module, In one way this was effective as it focused on the firms needs on special issues (i.e. intraorganizational issues) and thereby allowed for building competence on related ED topics. Because of the initial strong emphasis on productivity enhancement, these cliques also were inefficient in the sense that it created too much heterogeneity within the module. Consequently, the Tromsø module did not function as one team. Coupled with a high turnover in the module, it took years before the module gained a solid internal structure. The construction phase was the module's darkest chapter.

The Trondheim group's research projects were designed as task force dyads: A team of researchers was engaged in each of the companies. In most cases, this team was heterogeneous, composed of engineers and social researchers. At the company side, there was a corresponding team of insiders. The project teams were thus made up of people belonging in different worlds. If we take a look at the objectives of the research projects we can observe a similar diversity. On a general level, both parties address the organization and the production system, but in different ways. The vocabulary of social scientists focused on topics such as innovation, job content, participation, and leadership. The general objective as conceived by the social researchers was to establish and enhance processes of learning for company actors (managers, shop stewards, human resource managers and production managers) and researchers (engineers and social researchers) allowing new knowledge to develop on the interdisciplinary learning arena. This knowledge is based on and embedded in the work of each of the task forces who are cooperating on development efforts in each of the participating companies. For the engineers, the understanding was more focused on problem solving and expert advice than on facilitating reflection and learning. Engineers are traditionally concerned with issues such as productivity, benchmarking, production control systems, IT systems, or quality control systems. In the individual projects, these two interests met with the companies' various interests. Concrete research objectives were focused on areas such as management training, developing new production layouts, new forms of work organization, upgrading the operators' skills and jobs and work climate studies.

The RR module also designed heterogeneous research groups made up of social scientists and consultants. These groups were supposed to participate as facilitators for the development processes in each participating enterprise. The group's main contribution at the network-level was arranging and participating in network meetings, partly as lecturers, partly as discussion partners, and partly as participant observers. They also had to operate as process facilitators and advisors for each participating company. For the consultants in the research group, it was important to follow up the development process in the enterprises by visiting them regularly, listening to their needs and advising them how to run the internal development processes. For the social scientists, it was more important to behave as neutral observers, discussing with the process responsible people in the enterprises, but not committing themselves to the enterprises' developmental processes. Instead they argued that the research focus should be on different structural conditions and actors who continuously supported or counteracted the development processes. In this way they also ended up with emphasizing and reflecting upon the RR-consultants as well as their own role in the development processes.

The construction phase of the modules involved recruiting researchers who not only had to serve the various ED needs of enterprises collectively, but who also had to function as a coordinated team. Within a broad-scoped action oriented research program, this was a cumbersome process for several of us.

External constituencies

In action research, the knowledge of the research scientists and actors in the field is seen as having equal status (Pålshaugen 1992) and complementary to each other (Elden and Levin 1991; Foss and Moldenæs 2000). Since the ED program is based on an action research oriented approach, the external constituencies or stakeholders become important in legitimizing of research. The dependency of a highly collaborative process between researchers and the members of the study (Greenwood, Whyte, and Harkavy 1993) implies that access to enterprises and the trust needed from outside stakeholders is significant.

The Tromsø module gained legitimacy in the fish processing industry, partly because those relations were already established with the Norwegian Institute of Fisheries and Aquaculture (NIFA) and the Norwegian College of Fishery Science (NFH). To concentrate on one industry was efficient in order to get access to enterprises. The module got assistance from branch organizations connected to this industry, the Fish Producers Association (FPA). The focus on one industry was also efficient with respect to establishing the research team. Most of the researchers recruited into the team had experience from fisheries — and aquaculture. Because the research team was very heterogeneous, the focus on one industry made the task somewhat easier. With respect to legitimacy, the focus on fish processing enterprises in the northern region, made it easier to identify and "recruit" firms, and to let the "word of mouth" strategy work for the team. The Tromsø module was less successful in engaging the regional work life organizations like the Confederation of Employers and the trade union. The lack of connection to these organizations was unfortunate, as the industry is known for its limited collaboration with the unions. A connection to these regional organizations could have helped promoting the enterprise development projects as joint responsibility between "managers" and "workers" in the enterprises. With regard to networks, there was no established, formal network of fish processing firms available for the module. However, as one of the firms was situated in a community with a long history of collaboration, the team was able to follow up firms working together in a more informal network. As other firms in this town were recruited to a project close to ED2000, the module ended up with firms situated in only two areas, making it possible to follow the ED processes with reference to issues and events taking place in those two local communities.

In the case portfolio of the Trondheim module, there were significant differences between the companies. They differed in industry, markets, products, technology, size, structures and cultures. The recruitment of the companies took many forms. Recruiting companies was also a process of getting to know each other within the research teams of the module. Most of the companies signed up because either the engineers or the social researchers had a former relationship with them. Prior relationships also framed the expectations of the research agenda. In companies recruited by the engineers, the initial expectation would be an involvement with a technological development project. In companies recruited by social scientists, they would hold expectations about organization redesign, workplace development or analyses of leadership performance. We made it a prerequisite that both management and the local trade union representatives should agree upon the project and take part in the work in all the projects. The module ended up working with five companies: an offshore construction yard, a chair producer, an aluminum smelter, a subcontractor in the gas turbine industry and a sausage factory. Without having worked together for very long, we quit the co-operation with the gas turbine subcontractor. After about a year and a half, the work in the sausage factory came to a halt as well. At the same time new companies were recruited to the network.

RR didn't face the same challenges with regard to the recruitment of enterprises. Close connections to enterprises in the region had since the establishment of the RR institutes in the 1970s been an important precondition for the initialization of research activities in RR. Conducting project work for private enterprises was the core activity for The Department of Business Development in RR. Even before the initialization of the ED2000 module, the RR consultants had established collaborative relationships with three different enterprise networks. Nevertheless, conducting project work in private enterprises was not enough to fulfill the requirements of the ED2000 program. The module also had to include social science researchers to include scientific based question and perspectives together with the aims of the business development consultants. Together they managed to construct a module larger than any of the other ED2000 modules; including three enterprise networks involving different industries, several funding agencies, stakeholders and target groups. This also resulted in more external obligations and varying expectations compared to a module with fewer and less diverse external constituencies. A main challenge for RR was therefore how to cope with all the different stakeholders and target groups related to the module, and to create legitimacy for all of them.

The construction phase was for several modules a difficult puzzle because their internal heterogeneity had to match the needs of their external stakeholders. The construction phase involved collaboration with external constituencies, such as companies, networks, industries and work organizations. Without ties to such important sectors, enterprise development projects may be difficult to pursue because they need to earn legitimacy also outside the individual enterprises. The fit between the modules internal structure and the needs of their constituencies was hard to construct in advance, and had to be played out in relation to enterprises, organizations and networks. Flexibility then became a key issue. This certainly came along as the modules grew and developed over time.

Development and consolidation of the research modules

For Tromsø as a newcomer in action research, it was important to develop a profile that both developed legitimacy among the companies as well as in academia. This duality needed balance between fieldwork and reflection through writing texts for the academic community. The module needed relatively long time in the field before they were able to communicate their experiences and findings to an academic audience. The researchers' time and resources were in the first three years allocated to close collaboration with the enterprises, in order to learn action research and to train students.[5] In general, senior level researchers published most of the modules' academic work. Junior researchers were introduced to publishing as co-authors, implying that most of the published work from the Tromsø module in fact is collective work.

One challenge related to publishing was that the fieldwork did not always allow enough time for observation and interviewing, which often was needed to be able to fully describe and analyze ED processes. The fish processing firms have turbulent day-to-day operation, and the researchers were not always able to collect the necessary information on their visits to the firms. Also, the geographical distance between research and enterprise was a hindrance for the team, as the module could not afford to have the research team staying in the field for long periods of time.

The module emphasized taking the enterprises' own formulated problems as a point of departure for the research. Legitimacy was therefore mainly built up in those firms where the research team was successful, in creating a dialogue and a common understanding of the ED. Since the industry was very unfamiliar with the approach, legitimacy was particularly sensitive to the communication between researchers and enterprises. One part of the problem was to be able to "speak the same language". Another problem was to agree on research questions that the firms needed to have solved, which also fitted into the module's analytical scheme. A third problem was to be able to follow up ED processes over time. Most of the enterprises experienced turbulent episodes like high turnovers, sudden sick leaves, restructuring processes etc. These episodes resulted in the researchers having to rearrange their focus and resources. As the module lost some enterprises over the years, it ended up with three firms. The firms communicated their satisfaction with

5. Altogether 5 graduate students were trained and wrote their master thesis in social sciences based on fieldwork done in the enterprises.

the enterprise development projects, giving the team a confidence they sorely needed. The three firms' experiences were easily communicated to other firms in the region. In retrospect, this is an example of the advantages of restricting enterprise development projects to one industry in one region. It was effective in creating legitimacy.

A result of the legitimacy earned in the enterprises was a request from enterprises in one specific township to the University in Tromsø to establish an educational program for employees in the fish processing firms and other local business life in the municipality. By the end of the ED2000 period, the township with its 2500 inhabitants, enrolled 30 students to new university courses. Local business leaders saw a need for educating managers and middle managers on organizational development issues.

Initially the Trondheim group did not reflect much on what made the various cases so different from one another. We had no good grasp of the differences of the research teams or how the company actors acted as both our customers and employers. But the conflicts within the research team in one of our cases (the yard) made such reflections necessary, as we needed them to solve internal problems in order to develop our relations with the company actors.[6] We developed a model of the research team with the principal major partners of the research process. We focused on the parallel structures in the company and in the research team. In the company, the principal actor groups were production engineers, HR people, shop stewards and management. In the research team, we had engineers and social scientists. Early in the project, the conventional communication pattern was that the research engineers talked to the production engineers, the social scientists talked to HR people and shop stewards, and the management was to a varying degree involved with both parties. Over time, we saw a more complex pattern of co-operation (and conflict) develop, where cross-disciplinary communication on the researcher side enabled a similar dynamic on the company side and vice versa. Eventually we witnessed cross-disciplinary communication across institutional boundaries. At the chair producer, they requested single subject technical expertise for technical problem solving in the beginning, but that changed. Late in the project, the company experienced a very low productivity in a brand new production line. To analyze the problem, they called for a group of researchers from different disciplines to help them. This call for a heterogeneous research group was a result of the company learning through the project. Initially, they would have wanted to deal with this in a purely technical manner. In some of the other cases, we did not have the same degree of multi-disciplinarity in the research team.

6. For more on this, see (Elvemo and Munkeby, forthcoming)

Neither did we achieve a similar kind of cross-disciplinary communication on the company side. We take this to mean that a heterogeneous or multidisciplinary action research design does not come about by itself. There has to be a certain critical mass present, in the researcher group and/or on the company side, in order to install and sustain it.

Also in the experiences of the Trondheim group, heterogeneity had costs. This was the lack of "a room of one's own" for each of the disciplines or professions involved. The social scientists of the teams observed this on some occasions, and, we suspect, so did the engineers. For sake of communication and consensus, thorough in-depth analysis was lost. For instance, in the case of the offshore construction yard, the social researchers on many occasions left the research group loaded with frustrations, with a sense that "This and that could have been done much better had we dealt with it on our own!" We felt that our analyses and perspectives had to deteriorate to no more than matters of course before the overall group was able to take them up. In spite of this, we still recommend the effort. Within a diverse researcher group, there is not just a difference of opinion due to differences in professional expertise. There is also a multiplicity of ontological outlooks, epistemological assumptions, views on process facilitation and political views (just to name some dimensions on which we differ). Our clients are also made up this way. In the end, the challenges facing an organization are not mono-disciplinary, although we often want to reduce them to such. Heterogeneity of perspectives does not make the group work easier, but it may make the results better.

The RR researchers also had to struggle with conflicts regarding different research practices and requirements for legitimacy through most of their module work. Nevertheless, the important acknowledgement from their story is their emphasis of the composition of the research-teams in the enterprises, which included both consultants and researchers. This composition enabled them to play two roles; an advisor role and a critical researcher role. Continuous opportunities for discussions exemplified by long ferry trips to their participating enterprises, contributed to critical reflections and made it possible to learn from their own practice. The consultants learned about scientific practice, and the social science researchers learned about attaining relationships to enterprises based on usefulness and trust. Presentations, joint seminars and network conferences were frequently arranged and contributed to these reflections. The scepticism among the researchers in the two departments was later replaced by respect for the different roles that researchers and consultants may play in action research. Their lessons highlighted for them the advantage of carrying out action research, not as individuals, but as a divergent team.

The RR story also tells us about internal struggles and conflicts and how to cope with many different obligations and expectations within the same module. The module was partly characterized by internal fragmentation and negotiations between the different research traditions, between actors committed to different enterprise networks, and between different demands from funding agencies and stakeholders (Kvadsheim 2001). Extensive negotiations, lack of common focus and consensus, and the lack of clear module governance may have been the main costs of this heterogeneity.

On the other hand, the RR story is a story of social processes, including the creation of multi-level collaboration arenas at enterprise-, network-, and program level. These arenas created opportunities for reflection-on-action between enterprises, between researchers and enterprises, and between different stakeholders. For the RR-module, the use of action research based methodology represented their common platform for 'naming' (i.e. identifying what has to be dealt with) and 'framing' (setting the problems into a context) issues referring to the different interests, knowledge and epistemology in their module.

The RR story thereby emphasizes the possibilities of handling heterogeneity through the creation of arenas, which should include reflection-on-action activities related to common practice. But their story also emphasizes challenges of heterogeneity related to governing and diversity-management within a multi-composite research program.

To sum up, we can say that the development and consolidation of a module clearly illustrate action research's dilemma between action and reflection. Action research is time consuming, and its aim of contributing to immediate problematic situations in enterprises (Rapoport 1970), leaves research modules many difficult choices. Modules located far from their firms were worse off with regard to allocate lengthy fieldwork in the enterprises. The regional dispersion of the modules resulted in that the researchers were geographically far away from each other, making collective reflection problematic. In retrospect, we see that collaboration between the modules could have been efficient in both understanding and handling ED processes in the firms, and in communicating experiences to the academic sphere. In all three modules, junior faculty were trained in action research methods through their fieldwork. The modules' publishing attempts at the end of the program were significant in also providing academic training.

We have seen that heterogeneity as a design parameter for action research teams can be very productive, but that it has its cost. The Tromsø team showed that a too heterogeneous research team pulled the limit of heterogeneity too far.[7] In a similar vein, it was the larger volume of the RR-module, which made it possible for them play on their heterogeneity as a constructive diversity-strategy for their action research.

7. This shows also that an ED program has clear spatial dimensions, since researchers need to be physically close to the enterprises. This is a point that we will come back to in the end of this chapter.

A legitimate heterogeneity?

The research modules consolidated when they approached closure in 2000. It is therefore relevant to discuss which experiences should be conveyed to future programs.

Moving beyond presently held paradigms

On a pragmatic level, heterogeneity can be productive with regard to developing different views in a group.[8] At the same time, it can be difficult for a very heterogeneous research team to decide on a collective strategy for further research. The size of the team truly matters and research teams should be carefully designed with this in mind. Too much heterogeneity in small research teams can make the focus on ED "mushy". One experience from the Tromsø team was that researchers new to one another sometimes had a hard time in the first "in sale" period in the enterprises, because they could not communicate a consistent message to the enterprises. Too much heterogeneity in a research team can impact the ability to "speak the same language" and to "see the same things" in the field. The experience is that disciplinary training, although giving researchers theoretical and methodological strengths, makes them less likely to give up this framework and be convinced by arguments from a different discipline. Heterogeneity in its most demanding form was clearly a barrier to shared understanding. A minimum level of shared understanding is important in action research: Researchers need to act as a team and not as individuals in competing for the enterprises' attention. To move beyond paradigms requires voices that are quantitatively and qualitatively heterogeneous, which can be a problem small research teams.

Moving beyond paradigms is difficult as long as researchers are mono-disciplinary trained. Research education at the Ph.D level in Norway is still very disciplinary organized. It is difficult to get researchers from different disciplines to move beyond their initial training. One step in this direction is to educate researchers through an action research oriented PhD program, recruiting people with various basic educations. We see this as necessary for being able to move beyond the paradigms that traditional research education creates. The challenge lies in daring to cross disciplinary barriers. Can research teams be successfully designed for heterogeneous projects aimed at problem solving and knowledge construction? This is certainly likely to affect the possibilities for consensus. The greater disciplinary difference between scholars, the more difficult it gets. The most promising way of doing so seems to be transdisciplinary knowledge production embedded in

8. Hannah Arendt (1958) argues that the common best is only possible to identify through a multitude of perspectives.

practical situations of problem solving.

Regionalizing enterprise development

Regionalization of collaboration between business development and research institutions is not unknown in the literature. In a recent contribution, it is argued as follows: "*This lead us to conclude that for maximum efficiency technological innovation, established theoretically and practically, as a socially interactive process, needs to be organized in ways that maximize economic externalities from geographical proximity. This means creating situations where hard (technological) and soft (human) infrastructures and networks enable interaction to take place. Leading, successful examples of this network-based form of nurturing a culture of collective entrepreneurship combine knowledge centers, such as universities, incubators, to nurture small, high-technology, spin-off firms and a collaboratively minded larger firm or firms that will act as the market for new businesses in the difficult start-up and early growth phases of development.*" (Asheim and Cooke 1998: 235).

The question of regionalizing enterprise development deals with both "ideally" constructed research teams and an "ideal" embeddedness to businesses, networks, and trade organizations and local work life parties. As we have seen in this chapter, RR is an example of a regional institution having a good access to a local network and a local industry. The Tromsø module is also an example of the significance of relations to a specific industrial sector and the R&D institutions surrounding the specific sector. Companies in the Trondheim module were basically located in the local region surrounding the city of Trondheim

In order to make the regional aspect more prominent, the program should have a more "local" — and "regional" — coded language in its headings. The question of regionalization of ED is also related to the concept of heterogeneity. Heterogeneity in groups allows for seeing processes and behaviors from different perspectives. A national ED program can be seen as an "institution" covering different industries and research environments. A sound strategy may be to draw on the variety in existing research traditions so that the heterogeneity flourishes among the modules instead of within them. Each research environment and local industry can then pull together and form developing coalitions that are regionally "specialized". Heterogeneity among modules in a national ED program is valuable as it implies building on each research environments' specialties, and on local knowledge for access to enterprises.

Heterogeneity between the modules implies that different teams in different industries downplay the role of internal competition. In the very beginning one could experience that the different modules in ED2000, because they did not know one another, held their "cards tight to their chest". One was afraid that somebody should "steal" concepts and approaches from one another. (If we had known how heterogeneous we actually were, this would probably never have happened!) An implication of this might be that the more regionally based each module is, the more supplementing the research teams can be to one another.

On the other hand, we have experienced that thematic overlap between the modules is very positive because it makes bridging research between the modules possible. In other words, too much heterogeneity can create common ground to meet and learn from one another.

Learning from heterogeneous research

What did we learn about the dynamics of social systems such as work groups and business organizations? What did we learn about participatory research processes? What did we learn about heterogeneity? In our view, all three modules have developed new and innovative ways both field work and for developing knowledge based on this. In this chapter, we have through concepts such as heterogeneity and legitimacy seen how research teams are contextualized in their former research history, their academic ambitions, their disciplinary sense of belonging, and their integration in business life. The research teams struggled throughout the program period. Legitimacy is difficult to obtain, and a new work life project like the ED2000 need legitimacy both in the academic and the practical world. It takes time to earn it. Research modules in a research environment where action research is unknown, like the Tromsø module, have a harder time to get accept for an enterprise development project. With time the research teams learned to live with their heterogeneity as they chose paths to go that gave them an opportunity to enjoy a longitudinal project with long time collaboration with enterprises.

The concept of development coalition (Ennals and Gustavsen 1998a) is linked to the concept of heterogeneity.[9] We would suggest that enterprise development projects should be more heterogeneous when it comes to searching for enterprises. They would not have to compete with one another, but instead be able to learn from one another. This would be in line with the goal of establishing development coalition. As we have shown in this chapter, a diverse research group has both an advantage and disadvantage in action research work. Examples from the modules show that it took a reasonably long time before the research groups functioned as teams. On the other hand, the research groups, due to their broad composition, had the ability to cover several themes the businesses needed. We argue that heterogeneity is a dimension that future modules should consider when constituting

9. A development coalition refers too a cluster of concepts pertaining to the ability of organizations to learn, to innovate, to change (Ennals and Gustavsen 1998a: 15). Inherit in this concept is a network-like function, actors with various resources, shall be linked together and thereby pool its resources together. A central point in a development coalition is "not to become alike but to pool resources, supplement each other, help each other and to provide complementary resources" (Ennals and Gustavsen 1998a: 34).

research teams. Although ED is a multidimensional phenomenon, and different researchers see issues differently, an action based research approach is a teamwork that requires consensus to have an impact. We also advocate future modules to play along with what they see as important sectors embedding the enterprises they collaborate with. If regional modules shall have a mission, they need to play together with institutions that are of importance for the local industry. Without relations to these and an understanding of the essence of development coalitions, ED program can be reduced to internal restructuring without understanding of their exchange relationships with their environment.

ED2000 had an ambitious agenda, both in terms of theory development and practical results. In our experience, to have practical objectives of the problem-solving kind to meet the needs of our clients, was no hindrance to creating research-based knowledge. ED2000 has been about institutionalizing module based action research in conventional research environments, and it has been an attempt of shifting from an individual to a group based action research.

To gain functional authority based on expertise of the research modules, knowledge and competence is based on that the research is situated in an industrial environment. Hence, the enterprises represent a common context judging the research modules' work, without regard to the modules' professional profile. When the diverse disciplines we come from do not offer a shared arena for comparing or judging, the challenges of working in the field force us to establish a shared understanding.

Chapter 12

Networking as an action research practice

Lene Foss, Henrik Kvadsheim and Johan E. Ravn

Introduction

The concept of "network" was central in the ED2000 program. In the initial formulations, a rather broad approach was presented, allowing each module a large scope in conceiving, interpreting, constructing and utilizing networking. A central goal of the program was to link enterprises, in order to strengthen their innovative capacity and business efficiency. The idea was to make enterprises work together in developmental activity, and to create a mutual learning situation.

Implicit in the design of the program was also a network between researchers from the different research modules. A stated goal was to organize research between modules with different research profiles and regional embeddedness, to facilitate mutual learning.

The module stories indicate that the modules struggled in different ways with the concept and aim of networking. The ED2000 program required that every research module should have direct engagement in at least five enterprises, and that these enterprises should co-operate. This challenged the modules in different ways. Would it be possible to establish networks and to arrange collaboration events between the researchers and the networks? Did the network arrangements make it easier or more difficult for the researchers to highlight the research issues from the ED2000 program? And how would this kind of intervention at network level influence the researchers' roles at enterprise level?

In this chapter, the usefulness of networking as an action research practice is discussed based on our experiences in the Tromsø, Trondheim and Rogaland modules. In order to do that, we need an analytical scheme to shed light on our research practice. Three different conceptual positions to facilitate this discussion, an analytic, a prescriptive and a constructivist.

Three approaches to the study of networks

The concept of "network" is multifaceted and multidisciplinary as it is used in anthropology, sociology, organization theory, theories of regional development and marketing. The concept was originally introduced by an anthropologist in the 1950s (Barnes 1954), and has later been developed by sociologists. A classical definition of networks is:

> "...a specific set of linkages among a defined set of persons, with the additional property that the characteristics of these linkages as a whole may be used to interpret the social behavior of the persons involved" (Mitchell 1976, p. 293)

The essence of networks is that the way actors are linked together in a web of connections has impacts on their behavior. According to Powell and Smith-Doerr(1994), there are two approaches to the study of networks. The first one is anchored in sociology and organization theory, and employs networks as an analytical device for illuminating social relations. These relations may be inside an organization, between organizations, or in the environment of organizations. "Network" as an analytical tool is concerned with how structures of relations affect action. One's position in a network both empowers and constrains action. The "who" question concerns which positions in a network structure that has privileged access to resources. The "how" question concerns how certain structural arrangements generate benefits and opportunities.

We view this tradition in network research as structural. Its advantage is the detailed mapping of social structures within and between organizations. A description of such social structures can convey patterns of communication, transactions and relations that organizational members are not consciously aware of. It can be argued, however, that this analytical network approach must be coupled with a better potential for predicting how structure facilitates or hinders change in order to be a useful tool in action research.

Another approach to "network" is more multidisciplinary and prescriptive, and views networks as a kind of organizing logic, a way of governing relations among economic actors (Powell and Smith-Doerr1994). This thinking leads to constructs such as inter-firm alliances, industrial districts, clusters, regional innovation systems and learning regions. This conceptualization was inspired by the rapid economic development in "The Third Italy". Studies of this development drew the attention to the importance of co-operation between small and medium sized companies in industrial districts, and between firms and local authorities (Brusco, 1982).

This gave rise to a number of efforts in other countries to create networks (Asheim 1996; Gustavsen 1998). Initiation and operation of network constellations is today a common means in macro level trade and industrial politics in Europe. Networking is a local strategy to achieve competitive power and developmental capacity.

The network as a form of governance approach has a clearer regional and contextual aspect to it than does the analytical approach. An advantage is that a regionally oriented approach seems to communicate well with policy makers, as a regional focus is considered important. Common for the two approaches is that they are based on a traditional philosophy of science. In a conventional social science analysis, network is a structure that creates action or exchange of resources, and the researchers seek to describe and explain this pattern. In a newer, and very different approach to network, the so-called actor-network theory (ANT), the issue of causal explanations is abandoned. "*An actor network is simultaneously an actor whose activity is networking heterogeneous elements and a network that is able to redefine and transform what it is made of*" (Callon 1987:93). Holm (2001) describes it like this: "*ANT sees science as attempts to construct and stabilize networks binding together the entities of many different kinds, be it material, machinist, textual, symbolic, human, legal, organizational, or whatever. Reality is thus composed of heterogeneous networks, hybrids or quasi-objects*" (Holm, 2001:132). ANT's mission is to understand how these hybrids are created and how they are stabilized. "The work of translation" is the key word in these processes. Applied to ED2000, this will refer to how an enterprise gets involved in a network with other enterprises, and which kind of identity this enterprise is given as a part of this network. Another central concept is "punctuation", referring to that actor networks have a tendency to become invisible when they get stabilized. Put differently: When a network stabilizes itself — important parts of it will be hidden. The attention is often paid to a few actors in the network who takes the praise for the success of it. The punctuation in the network hence comes to represent the whole network, which partly stands back and gets invisible. Aspects like power, communication, attention etc are elements that can be hidden when punctuation takes place.

The strength of using "network" as an analytical tool lies in the mapping of structures that facilitate action. This tradition builds on years of sociological research and methodological development in theory (Aldrich 1999; Burt 1992; Granovetter 1985; Granovetter 1973) and methodological tools (Scott 1991; Wassermann and Faust 1994). Its advantage is that it is a "good working theory", and a neat methodological apparatus for research. Rare in this tradition, however, is the use of a structural approach for understanding organizational change. This raises the question of bringing in a more dynamic view in this approach (Mønsted 1995). The problem with the approach, seen from an action-oriented standpoint, is that a pure description never can capture a movement or a change. Why actors act like they do, and what the content of the relations is, often remain unclear. This approach has no tradition in linking the result of research to the subjects of research. Revealing a structural pattern is a long way from using the results as input in an organizational renewal. In order to make this approach useful for action research, the link to development is necessary.

A network is prescriptive, in the sense that based on empirical knowledge, one argues that organizations joining a network are better off than "being alone". The strength of using "network" as a prescriptive policy concept lies in creating recipes for industrial restructuring and regional development, conceiving models for how companies and other agencies can join forces in development processes across organization borders. Little research has been done on the costs of joining a network and barriers to networking, as well on why firms do not collaborate with others. Networking is mainly seen as a solution for enterprises. There was no clear prescription in the ED2000 program on how these local network patterns should occur. This had clearly to do with the programs' link to HFB. It is the local social partners' own right to decide their needs for establishing networks between enterprises and the development of these. In this process, the researchers' main role should be to participate but not govern. It was therefore pretty open how researchers should relate to "network" as an organizational form in the ED program.

The strength of the ANT approach is the explicit constructivist element. ANT looks at science as local and contextual, something that fits well with the action oriented research paradigm. It allows for looking inside the network on the participants' (actors) own interpretation of the situation and their strategic action within these frames. In using this approach, one can learn why actors engage in networks, how they evolve, and the result of networks. ANT is a metatheory. It allows us to analyze researchers and modules as participants in constructing networks with their theories as a building tool. ANT is therefore an analytical resource for embodying the researcher and his/her theories in network as a research practice. They become a part of the issues to be studied. Whereas traditional sociology of science makes an analytical and normative division between science and other social institutions (Merton 1996), the scientific success criteria for ANT is not the "truth", but that the products of science are used. Science has to move from fiction to reality (Callon 1987).[1] This focus on the uses of research enables us to understand the local processes within the individual organizations, and to see how a network may mean different things to its different members, and how it becomes a resource for action. As also pointed out by Levin and Knutstad (2002) the literature on regional and business networks very seldom deals with the core of

1. Callon (1987:99) states: "To transform academics sociology into a sociology capable of following technology throughout its elaboration means recognizing that its proper object of study is neither society itself nor so-called social relationships but the very actor networks that simultaneously give rise to society and to technology."

the construction process. Here ANT fills an important hole in the role of networks in action research.

A weakness with ANT is that the emphasis on strategic and powerful actors seems to clash with the focus on democracy and participation in ED2000. ANT is no recipe for participatory development processes.

Network approaches in the field — Reflections over experiences

Dwyer, Schurr, and Oh (1987) argued that relationships evolve through general life cycle phases. Networks are not static arrangements. Instead they are changing constructions, where researchers continually have to define their roles according to the different lifecycle phases of the network-arrangements. Our *first question* therefore is to evaluate networking as an action research practice in terms of the construction process. In the construction of networks, the term arena is highly relevant. The network can itself be seen as an arena for communication, for sharing resources but also for exercising power or withholding information, for creating commitment, for reflection and for legitimization. From this point of view, the introduction of new activities and network arenas should certainly result in new kinds of construction processes and frameworks for network-based interaction. Our *second* question is therefore: How does a network serve as an opportunity for creation of different arenas? How do different arenas influence the processes of construction, action and reflection among the participants in networks? In an ANT perspective, this will include both researchers operating the networks and enterprises recruited in these networks.

A theme that is absent in the analytical approach, and in network as a form of governance, is the actors' own interpretation of being tied to their external constituencies. Actors have their own interpretation of what networks mean to them and what they "get out of it". This is especially important in the ANT approach and "network" as an analytical approach. How do networks imply awareness among the actors in the enterprises, and what is it that makes local actors adopt descriptions as a premise for their own action? If networks are to develop and "survive" as an action research practice, they must produce valued outcomes. What kinds of outcomes have networks produced?

Networks in ED2000 — "Brand new" or reconstructed "old ones"?

For the researchers in the Trondheim module, networking was not a stated interest at the outset. They had no prior experiences with running networks, and neither did the companies in the module. The networking activity came about because the program board forced its plans through. The network was a researcher initiative, very much an ED2000 construction. It developed, nonetheless, because the actors involved found it a worthwhile effort. Originally, neither the researchers nor the participating companies saw any need or interest in creating any type of network activity across the individual researcher-company contracts. The priority was to develop individual dyads: tight relationships to each of the core enterprises as the basic platform of our long-term research activities. The national level of the program saw the issue differently, however. Somewhat reluctantly, the researchers of the module started preparing for having their participating companies meet.

The Trondheim network was designed as an arena on which the various companies of the module could meet. Apart from being manufacturing companies, they had no preconception of having much in common. By and large, it was a rather loose alliance. It was not organized among actors in the same value chain. Neither did it focus on a shared challenge, such as a joint venture on export. It was not a regional network either: the distance between the northernmost and the southernmost participant company was more than one thousand kilometers. It consisted of medium-to-large-sized manufacturing companies of several industries. It was run as two-day seminars every six months. In the research team's own assessment, the first seminar was a flop. It created neither energetic company representatives nor engagement for a furthering of this practice. Judging it in hindsight, it was probably both poorly prepared and organized, and badly run. In the redesign, much more attention was given to careful planning, and it was decided to locate the seminars at the companies' premises. Also, professional issues of enterprise development work were supplemented with a social program at the seminars.

Gradually, this design worked out. Participants from the enterprises were managers (top and middle) and employee representatives. The network also grew through the period, from three companies to eight, and with broader participation from each. The agenda of the network seminars was to share experiences from development efforts and create new insights and skills in enterprise development. For each seminar, a particular focus was jointly set, based on emerging challenges in one or several of the participant companies. Seminar by seminar, the network planning and organizing became a shared responsibility.

Networking was a concept that the ED2000 program, in a way, forced upon the actors of the Trondheim module. On the other hand, much space was allowed to shape it and make it work locally. Used as an organizing logic, it could help us to strengthen the local development process at company level through the actors' sharing each other's experiences. Enrolled in the strategizing of the researchers of the module, the network was also used to develop an arena for shaping alliances between actors across organizational divides, and enrolling them in ongoing technological and organizational change processes. Some of the company actors took advantage of the network in this manner, developing alliances and interests around their agendas.

The RF module was in a better network-situation than Trondheim and Tromsø. The RF researchers had, prior to ED2000, established collaborative relationships with two formalized enterprise networks embedded in two different industrialized regions in western Norway. Even before ED 2000, these regional networks represented a formalized arena for collaboration and development between the participating enterprises. Asheim (1995) has characterized the collaboration and innovation activities within one of these networks, the TESA-network in southwest Norway, as a Norwegian example of flexible specialization within an industrial district.

The researchers' main challenge was initially not to construct networks, but to get acceptance for research and development issues promoted by the ED2000 program. In an ANT perspective, these reconstructed networks still gave the members a "new" identity, as there were new themes to be framed. The RF researchers therefore emphasized the creation of opportunities for introducing new agendas and new actors into the network.

The collaboration with the newly established IfS-network was characterized by one major enterprise playing a powerful and legitimating role in the initialization of the network project, as well as in the different developmental activities taking place later. Initially, the small participating enterprises within the IfS-network gave meaning to the network construction, and adjusted their strategic behavior in the light of this powerful and dominant actor. For them, acting within the network context meant positioning themselves strategically towards, and preferably also learning from, the main actor.

The introduction of the RF-researchers to the existing IfS network did not interfere with existing interpretations and positioning within the network. Even before ED2000, the dominant company had established a close relationship with RF regarding organizational development focusing on TQM. The ideas of TQM promoted by this company were highly congruent with the basic research ideas in ED 2000, and it was agreed to initiate processes of continuous improvement based on TQM in a number of core enterprises. Although there was no obvious pressure experienced by the enterprises in the network to join ED 2000, the fact that this major company strongly recommended the project was a driving force. Instead of changing existing ideas and appreciations of the network, the introduction of the ED2000 program reinforced them. From the researchers' point of view, their initial relationships with this influential actor within the network represented an appropriate alliance. By linking them to the most powerful and dominant actor of the network, the researchers' presence and ideas were accepted among the network participants. In addition, this intervention-based alliance created a legitimate foundation within the network for mobilizing participation among the other network participants as well.

The IfS-story illustrates the significance of viewing network arrangements in a life cycle construction perspective. The IfS was a relatively freshly formalized network. For several of the members in the network, including the secretariat, it was of importance to initiate common network projects that might contribute to the mobilization of the members within a common 'unifying' framework, and by that legitimate the usefulness and existence of the new formalized network. The ED2000 project and TQM represented such a common legitimating framework, which made it rather easy for the researchers to introduce their ideas.

The initialization of a collaboration between the RR-researchers and the TESA network was a more cumbersome process, caused by the long historical development of this network, including the recent incorporation of TESA companies into international corporate networks. Stronger corporate networks enhanced the linking of TESA enterprises to obligations outside the established network structure, and thereby caused a lack of commitment and involvement in the regionally rooted TESA-network. It seemed impossible to get a unified commitment to the TESA network.

Initially the researchers tried to change the network focus, from the aim of technological co-operation that earlier had served as a legitimating framework for the network activities, to a focus closely linked with management and strategic challenges facing the leaders in the different companies. This strategy was followed, despite the overall philosophy of ED 2000 placing decisive emphasis on both employees' and employers' participation. This strategy was perceived as necessary from the researchers' point of view, to create an essential trust that could be the basis for later commitment among the employees and their representatives. Inspired by their successful results from co-operation with the IfS-network, the researchers later stressed the importance of participation. Thereby they managed to introduce participation on the TESA enterprises' development agenda.

The whole approach related concerning TESA was in many respect markedly different from what happened in relation to IfS. The researchers expected to face rather similar challenges in their network interventions. Instead they realized that network arrangements may be regarded as changing constructions, where researchers continually have to redefine their roles, according to the different life-cycle phases of network arrangements. In the IfS network, researchers felt they were 'riding the wave' of an internal mobilization process, in TESA they had to be part of a reconstruction process. Still, owing to their simultaneous collaboration with the two networks, the researchers were able to play on their experiences and results from the respective networks in their collaboration with each of them. The relations between the networks evolved to a kind of symbiotic relationship, with the researchers continually acting as intermediaries between them. Lessons from one of the networks were in the next moment important experience in their acting within the other network.

As the researchers in the Tromsø module recruited enterprises from one industry in the northern region of Norway, the module got engaged in enterprises that already knew other enterprises in the same region and had informal contact with those. The enterprises did not find the network theme very appealing, and stated clearly that they were not interested in joining a network with other enterprises in the fishing industry, nor to participate on arenas were ED issues could be discussed. This resulted in that the researchers in the module could not lift the idea off the ground. The module accordingly did not construct a network of collaborating enterprises. As the project moved forward, the module sought to create connectedness where there was a clear possibility for learning. The module, with help from the HFB representatives in the program, arranged a couple of seminars in order to start a dialogue between union representatives and managers in the firms. The module was engaged in a construction of networks and arenas, as the researchers were asked to give lectures on a course for shop stewards arranged by the HFB. Most of the enterprises in ED2000 participated in this course. The module also lectured on "Management Roundtable", a roundtable discussion group between top managers in the fish processing industry and management researchers.[2] To sum up, we may say that the Tromsø module only indirectly and very imaginarily operated with the construction of networks.

Creation of new network arenas

The network seminars in the Trondheim module were planned as an arena for learning. The goal was to contribute to and to learn from the inter-organizational processes between different enterprises; arenas for dialogues between companies (managers and union representatives) and researchers. Dissemination from one case to broader populations has always been a challenge to action research. One of the ways ED2000 should contribute to work life development was, according to Gustavsen (1998), through dissemination: *"If one company has developed a new and more productive pattern of work organization, say, how can one get others to apply the same pattern?"* (op. cit., p. 2). The key ingredient holding the Trondheim network together, explaining its development and increasing durability, was its learning focus. There was a need for exchanging ideas and for learning across the module's companies. The network meetings created an opportunity for direct communication, across the company borders, unmediated by researchers or others. The companies had a lively exchange, where experiences and ideas were traded. Having

2. This forum is organized by NIFA, and holds two meetings annually where about 30–40 persons attend.

networked together eventually enabled the participants to directly contact other companies when the need was felt. The researchers' knowledge input was also a valued factor. Finding themselves in turbulent and rapid changing environments, the companies acknowledged the need for new knowledge in areas such as economics, management, organization and technology. Situating these knowledge inputs in exchange based seminars, this created a space where the participants both could learn from experience and be informed from research on other ways of thinking and acting. The network was more than a learning arena in the narrow sense. It was also at times a political process — an arena for negotiating the individual development agendas as happened in the IfS-network. All the participants had their own distinct agendas, goals and interests. The network seminars were arenas for reflecting together, but what each and everyone got out of it differed. The statement made by Greenwood about such processes is apt here: "*…the reflective process is a multiple, diversifying, sense-making process, even in close collaborations over long periods of time. Participants join in for differing reasons and leave with divergent lessons*" (Greenwood, 1999, p. 104). Since the start-up of the processes, conflicts of interests among the participants have been present. The researchers were familiar with this from the projects in the individual companies. Central to the modus operandi was a transdisciplinary interaction between diverse participants, and this inevitably invited differences and conflicts to surface. It has been focal in the approach of the Trondheim group to consider power and conflict as inherent ingredients, and even necessities of the dialogues at the local (enterprise) and network arenas. This resembles Greenwood and Santos (1992) who stress the importance of conflict, alienation, confusion and struggle in the experiments with industrial democracy, and Coopey (1995), who calls for a legitimating of political processes in the learning organization.

This is where the network arena came in handy, and just as in the individual companies, it was a process of different interests meeting and challenging one another. It was a different arena to handle development agendas. The network seminars provided an arena with a different set of prevailing models, thus an arena with the potential of creating change. We observed discussions on gender issues, engineers versus social scientists, management versus shop floor, shop floor union versus salaried groups; both within and across companies. Since the power distribution was different from the company situation, and perhaps unclear, the agenda setting was less straightforward than has been our impression of the local agenda setting. The network arena did not only offer more model multiplicity, it also offered a more distributed and at least less settled power and influence. Therefore, the network arena made different and more open discussions possible.

The ANT conceptualization shows that the coming into existence of a development project, is a product of the various actors' strategic interests and their ability to enroll others into their projects. They do so through forming networks, accumulating resources, reframing others' agendas and gathering allies everywhere. For an eager actor, the network seminar was a pool of potential allies and resources. He or she could seek out people from other companies who would hold interests compatible with his or her own, and use this actor as a support for his/her project. Similarly, a development project agreed upon by management and shop stewards in *one* company could be used by a strategic actor in a different company to strengthen a similar project in a *his* or *her* company. On several occasions, we could observe such processes at the network arena. Besides being an arena for reflection and learning, the Trondheim network also worked as an arena for conscious strategic activity, on which local development agendas could be renegotiated. The Trondheim-case illustrates the relevance of perceiving and treating network as an arena for communication, collaboration, and reflection. Working with networks in a development context may also be regarded as an opportunity for creating and utilizing new kinds of collaboration arenas within a network context.

The RFmodule emphasized the process of constructing appropriate collaboration forms, including defining appropriate roles for the researchers at the network level. The internal RFaim of the IfS-network was to support development processes in the participating companies, partly based on TQM-practice. From the RR-researchers point of view, they had to face continuity and commitment to the TQM-processes as their main challenges.

The arrangement of network based face-to-face arenas worked as an inter-organizational infrastructure that committed and motivated the companies in their development work. Having to stand up in the network forums and give face-to-face progress reports on improvements was an inducement to the companies. The network gatherings were also an important source of inspiration, and helped to motivate the participants to continue their improvement work, as well as building trust between the enterprises and the researchers, and between the enterprise participators themselves.

The employee representatives also contributed with positive and supportive attitudes to development processes in the companies. They were invited to the formalized network forums, and they also had the opportunity to discuss their own experiences with other participants. The network forums contributed to this by giving the collaboration more depth, by including various key participants in the companies. The network arenas also supported each other in generating mutual commitment in the follow-up process.

One of the main objectives of the IfS-network collaboration was to give the companies the chance to exchange experience and learn from each other. As time went by, mutual trust provided the basis for an open exchange of experience, replacing earlier scepticism towards presenting 'sensitive' information, and this gave a greater return in the form of learning. However, the common frame of reference for the exchange of experience, in this case expressed through the co-ordinate development processes using the TQM concept, contributed to a common foundation for the exchange of experience and learning. Common challenges in the process formed a unifying prerequisite for the exchange of experience. This played an important part in ensuring that the exchange of experience and the learning processes between the enterprises were relevant and recognized by the different participants.

As with the network of the Trondheim module, the IfS-network meetings also created opportunities for the participants to reframe and raise a new agenda for the development activity. By questioning traditional ways of perceiving enterprise development, the learning processes in the IfS network may be characterized as an example of double-loop learning (Argyris and Schön 1978), which evolved as a consequence of the network arrangements.

Network descriptions — A premise for action?

Networks involve human beings acting deliberately, and we want to reflect over whether researchers' descriptions of networks can be a premise for action for those involved. The enterprises in the Tromsø module were interested in internal organizational renewals, as they saw the ED2000 project as a tool to enhance their organizational structure and work environment. As the researchers' analysis pointed to that many of the problems the enterprises faced had to do with internal collaboration, the enterprises became interested in having their internal collaboration and communication patterns analyzed. In this process, the use of "network" as an analytical tool came in handy. The Tromsø module used the analytical approach first to map internal relations, and later the external relations in three firms. The motivation for the internal mapping was the companies' wish to have managers', middle managers' and staff's internal contact pattern analyzed in order to see if it was in accordance with the internal functional division of labor.[3] The motivation for the external mapping was sayings like "*we want to see how we use our time!*". This was specifically with regard to compare the contact pattern between individuals, so that one could discuss whether one had enough contact with the enterprises' external constituencies. A frame of reference for conducting these studies was research on managerial work (Hales 1986; Hannaway 1989; Mintzberg 1975), which portray managers as constantly involved in informal relations, internally and

3. In one firm the analysis showed that cultural distance and gender in addition to division of labor affected middle managers contact with subordinants (Foss and Gabrielsen, 2002).

externally. Based on self-reporting techniques in diaries, the researchers and representatives from the enterprises worked out a diary together.[4]

In order to feed the results into the development processes in the firms, a three-step procedure was followed. Researchers and enterprises decided that the researches should present descriptive results for the enterprise actors in a seminar. In these seminars, the members of the enterprices came up with comments, and together with the researchers, patterns were clarified, understood and interpreted. In depth interviews were performed to reveal individuals' own understanding of both internal and external contact patterns. These insights were then fed into the text that the researchers wrote in confidential reports to the firm.

One study (Otlesen, Foss, and Grønhaug, 2003) showed that many of the managers overestimated their contact with the customer but underestimated their contact with the suppliers. This result was much discussed at our follow-up seminars. The informants were unaware that their contact with their various suppliers occupied that much time. They estimated their contact with the customers much higher then the real time used. In one case, where the firm had a manager team consisting of three persons, a top manager, the second in command and a sales manager — they used the result from the study as an input in their further development of leadership roles and division of labor.

We claim that structures of internal and external communication patterns have cognitive implications. Network data can reveal issues that actors perceive and interpret as pertaining to the roles they have. In that way analysis of networks can create awareness of patterns of relations that become stimuli in an ever-changing process of organizational members' schemas of themselves and their roles. One of the staff members reflected around the external investigation in the following way:

> "Things got put in a perspective. We reflected over our own situation. This is something you do daily but never think about. Now you could compare yourself with others. I noted that we had very different roles. The pattern came out very clear out. That "the old one" (refers to the manager) had many external relations I sort of knew. But that the rest of us had it too I was not aware of."

That actors develop awareness of their time spent on contacts, what they "get out of" these contacts, how they see their own communication patterns in relation to

4. We decided to cover external contact with reference to what the firm viewed as important external constituencies (Pfeffer and Salancik 1978). 11 categories were chosen. In operationalization of under groups within these categories we were careful in not imposing any classification scheme on the informants (Grønhaug and Lines 1995). Each contact with these sectors was then characterized by relation (6 items), content (12 items) and result (6 items). The log period lasted for 24 consecutive days covering five weeks. The diary was a ring leaf book where each contact was to be filled-in on a separate sheet. The informants were given an instructors manual, which had been pre tested. Finally we visited the firm, in order to motivate and give instructions and a one-day test run of the diary was conducted.

other employees in the organization, can be a way to develop "network" as a tool in action research. Our experience is that there is potential for local actors to learn from structural descriptions, and use them as a premise for their own action. It requires, however, a democratic dialogue between researcher and user, and involvement throughout the process.

As we have seen in this section the Tromsø module's challenges in using networks were very different from Trondheim and Rogaland. The module ended up using a different approach, covering individual actors' relations to other organizational members and other actors outside the firm. This had much to do with the firms' need to develop their organization. The work with developing internal and external diaries created the awareness that much of the work in a fish processing firm is to communicate with other employees, handling relations, and giving and receiving information. In using networks as an analytical approach, the researchers came up with descriptions that local actors felt were a "scientific mirror" of their own behavior. Compared to Trondheim and Rogaland, the awareness aspect of networks was more intentional in the Tromsø module. It was the researchers' only way of applying the network concept on enterprise development, as they did not have a network arena to work on.

Outcomes of networks

In the Tromsø module, one outcome from using the perspective of networks as an organizational form was in investigating the co-operation between three firms in a fishing community. This town had a long tradition of co-operation between enterprises and local business life. This collaboration helped the community to survive many crises, which have emerged throughout the history due to lack of fish for processing. The result of the study was that the co-operation was not based on written contracts, but on trust and loyalty. These mechanisms are well known in the literature on co-operation and learning (Lundvall and Johnson 1995; Storper 1995). The co-operation between the firms was mainly based on practical issues, like exchange of fish, material needed for packing and the purchase of electrical power. More sporadically, the enterprises compared their internal control systems. The main finding, however, which also came to alter the enterprises, was that co-operation was mainly limited to the top leader level, where strategic issues were discussed. The top managers met daily and discussed issues daily over the telephone. The middle managers complained that they were not integrated in the co-operation. Several of the workers knew little about the co-operation, for which the community was known.

When networks get stabilized, they under-communicate elements that may make the network stand out as incoherent and heterogeneous. Success stories of networks are not necessarily the most interesting. According to ANT, it is more interesting to go beyond the immediate coherent surface and pull out the tricky parts, which are obstacles in a "smooth" organizational form. The above example shows how enterprises consist of power relations based on different hierarchical levels. In external network collaborations, all actors do not speak with the same tongue. Collaboration in a network is likely to be more effective if it is also built from a "bottom — up" approach, in addition to a "top-down" approach.

The result of this study was that the top managers were able to suggest new ways of co-operation, which to a larger extent was based on the competence of the middle managers. Furthermore, the top managers saw competence enrichment as a new way of building the new generation of leaders. Middle managers were sent to the School of Middle Management. Some years later, these firms asked the University of Tromsø to establish a competence enhancing educational program for their employees and other actors in the municipal business life. After 5 years work on enterprise development with the Tromsø module, the collaborating firms saw the need for a formal competence-enhancing program for their employees as a means for further development.

By using the network approach module was able to conceptualize collaboration between three firms as embedded in a community and its history. According to Huxham & Vangen (2000), a collaborative agenda is led by structure, processes, and participants. The result, that no formal agreements were needed in the network collaboration between these firms, shows that local actors use their local knowledge. Being tightly embedded in a hard working fishing community with an entrepreneurial spirit, surviving one crisis after the other, leave no place for formal arrangements.

The module, which worked to get acceptance and legitimacy in the industry, later served as a catalyst between the industry and the university. ED2000 became the vehicle for transforming the roles between the industry and the university.

The outcomes in the RFmodule was very much related to establishing a common understanding that the existing network infrastructure could be used as an enterprise development arena. A main result was that new participants, for instance shop stewards and middle management, got included in the established network arrangement. The established networks were thereby transformed to include new development issues as well as new members. The newcomers had also established their own informal networks *outside* the formal network structure. For the shop stewards, these new informal networks may be just as strategically important for them as the formal ones. This certainly is relevant when they have to deal with sensitive, union-related matters as part of the enterprise development processes. In this way, the networks participants have become more "conscious" and motivated for collaborating on development issues, but also for utilizing the different infrastructure within the networks in their enterprise development processes.

What effect did networking have on organizational development and integration between actors? There are powerful learning possibilities when arranging for experience-based exchange processes across companies. The Trondheim network's form and function shows the potential for constructing the network as a space for learning. Just as with the RF-networks, the Trondheim network also turned out to function as an arena for negotiating and developing new issues for the development agenda for the individual companies. In a way, the network functioned as a broker of agendas and interests in the individual companies. The network can play a role in setting the agenda, and giving priority in the development processes of the individual participating companies. The interaction in the network seminars can introduce and legitimize issues that the individual actors in a company are not able to bring into the internal discourse agenda. There are now signs of self-organization among the network participants. As happened in the IfS and TESA network, the union representatives have formed their own network, and some of the companies have taken initiatives to join forces in developing a management-training program. Although the ED 2000 program has come to an end, the companies regard the network as a vital arena for reflection and learning, and they want it to continue. Networks can function as change agents in the individual companies through learning and reflection, but also through negotiation and building of new alliances. It can be observed that the 'glue' of the network seems to be a multi-component mixture of individuals' and institutions' interests in issues like marketing, productivity and quality, technology and competence development, but also politics, and friendship and social well-being. However, this way of setting up a learning arena also shows a limitation in pointing to the need for network agency. It is for example not very likely that the Trondheim network would survive without having someone taking the responsibility for initiating, facilitating and providing inputs.

The seminars became arenas for learning and reflection, but also for forming alliances and negotiating issues, and how the network could be a resource base or incubator for the individual enterprises. This could be developed further if the networks were developed into more diverse constellations, not just consisting of companies and a network facilitator or agent, the latter being the role that the research group had. Other types of actors should be included in the network pool, such as local government, financial institutions, or trade organizations. When the resources of individuals or individual enterprises are limited, they can make the most of network resources, such as competencies, contacts (markets, suppliers), financial strength, capacity for development (such as process skills) and motivation.

It is important to realize that different network actors may contribute with different resources, all of which may be important in order to establish such extended network coalitions. The social partners and government bodies may contribute with financial support, political support and not the least through providing legitimacy for change processes. The role of the knowledge institutions could be to provide knowledge about technological development, finance, market developments, or current trends in the area of organization and management, and to provide competence in facilitating change processes. Enterprise development through network co-operation can be a way for companies to enhance their knowledge of how efforts to improve are fulfilled. It can also work as a pool of ideas, resources and allies from which the individual actors can create or strengthen the development agenda they bring with them back home.

Conclusions

We have identified three theoretical frames in network research: "network" as an analytical tool, an organizational form and as an actor-network perspective. The analytical approach can be used to feed results from a structural analysis into the development of the organizational structure and internal division of labor in enterprises. Networks as an organizational form can reveal patterns and processes between enterprises and enterprises and regions that in the next step can be broken down on a more concrete level and serve as input for further collaboration between enterprises. "Network" seen in light of ANT helps us understand how the process of networking is an activity of creativity and building local and inter-organizational alliances and pooling resources in order to shape local outcomes. This interwoven part of network frames would also be in line with the complexities at the enterprise level and the dynamic aspect of organizational development.

The experience from the modules demonstrate that both constructing networks and using them as an arena for enterprise development very much depend on the regional collaborative culture. It further depends on overcoming the reluctance to share such internal knowledge with one another within a network. Further the awareness of being included in networks is not something that one can take for granted, and this aspect needs to be developed if networks shall have the role of a development tool in research on enterprises.

As seen in this chapter, networks in enterprise development depends very much on process-based research (Van de Ven & Huber, 1990) This calls for longitudinal research and a wide range of methodological approaches to cover processes. The study of networks in enterprise development processes would probably gain from including methods that uncover the underlying structure in enterprises' networks. This should be given a voice, and preferably a narrative one, from actors in the field. We agree with Pentland who states: "Perhaps more than any kind of data, narratives can provide a window onto the values of a cultural group." (Pentland 1999: 715). Since networks are inherently contextual, narratives can be a useful tool to uncover the importance of values in networking processes. Further memory work (Widerberg 1999) can reveal how organizational members interpret a certain element in a network-development process, and how they collectively interpret each other's stories concerning these issues. This is clearly a method that helps articulate and communicate "consciousness" concerning being involved in networks.

Other challenges that have to be dealt with are the issues of democracy, participation and learning in networking. ED2000 is based on broad participatory development. Learning was a key focus for several of the networks discussed here, but what happens to learning under the constraints of power and conflict? How participatory were the communication processes in our networks? Bourdieu (1991) has argued that there is no such thing as a constraint-free dialogue. In any real-life communication, there is much more going on than explicit arguments that go back and forth. All arguments have an owner who has invested interests in them. The force of an argument, and thereby its 'truth', cannot be seen as isolated from the social context it is read into. The recipient reads the argumentation of an utterance also through an assessment of the authority and social position of the orator. Adding to these positional factors, the 'social competence' will play a role in determining the communication. Bourdieu suspends the distinction between knowledge and power. Knowledge gives you influence. But it also works the other way: power and influence give premises as to what it is worthwhile to know. Bråten (1973) touches upon the same when he argues that conceptual power asymmetries in communication creates a situation of so-called model monopoly: All issues debated are framed and they are named by someone, forcing strong conceptual constraints on the communicative participation of the others. To understand communicative action as interplay between arguments that are understood the same way by all participants seems a fragile position. If we admit that the application of knowledge always brings with it an execution of power, then any learning situation must be understood not just in terms of arguments, but also in terms of its social and political dimensions. In networking, we find ourselves away from home ground, facing different voices and interests. We did not find a conceptualization that could help us understand networks in the light of democracy and participation in any of the three approaches to networks used here.

Our experiences with networks as an action research practice can be seen as "scraping beneath the surface". There are still many challenges connected to developing network as an action research tool. More recent methods in process-based research and narratives would probably be effective in uncovering the underlying structure and processes of enterprises' networks. The often used dichotomy between qualitative and quantitative research should however be avoided. It is the longitudinal element that is important in networks as action research practice, allowing a variety of methodological approaches. Quantitative data reflecting a cross-sectional view of communication structures between firms, can be repeated (panel study) at another point in time and indicate changes in behavior. Our main point is that network as an action research practice ought to be methodologically more innovative than was the case in ED2000. According to ANT, the success of a research practice lies in that the "products" are used. The application of a methodological width, that allows for uncovering local actors' own voices as well as structures they are involved in over time, is necessary. The clue is that various methods should allow local actors to be able to recognize their own actions. By doing that, organizational members may grasp the researchers' descriptions as a premise for their own action.

We claim that several theoretical approaches to networks are needed in a program like ED2000. Action researchers claim that since there is no single theory dominating the field of organizational and workplace change, it is essential that theories of networks should support local development processes and provide understanding and ideas without dominating (Ennals and Gustavsen 1998a; Shotter 1993). They further view theories of networks as useful analytical tools in an action oriented research program, to be balanced against local experiences from actors in the field. In this chapter, we have seen that the ANT is the approach that to the largest extent considers the active role of the local actors. It is the application of scientific research, when its "products" are put into use, that makes research successful.

However, in order for networks to evolve and "survive" as an action research practice we advocate the need for treating networks as a multidisciplinary concept. As shown in this chapter, each of the modules was mainly based on one network approach. The network part of the ED2000 never got full attention in the modules. Neither the theoretical depth nor the potential of network as a developmental tool were shown in their full potential in ED2000. This is partly a result of the fact that network was only one of several themes in the program, and therefore could not require the full attention and resources from the modules. Researchers "grabbed" the nearest theoretical approach they were in command of, instead of educating themselves together in learning networks with researchers in other modules. As seen in this chapter, RR, in using networks instrumentally to pursue them as an arena for OD, did not have a vocabulary to explain which structures facilitated local actors to be successful in this. In the same way Tromsø, in using the analytical approach, has still a way to go in developing the diary as an ongoing development tool for enterprises. Trondheim, is a good example of how a "forced" network can develop into an organizational form that local actors in the end regard as "their" way, is firmly established in an epistemology of constructive social science. The fact that we seem to be able to make sense of the network through an ANT approach, should make us cautious because networking risks becoming a process by which clever and strategic actors are able to manipulate others and force their agendas on other actors.

Is a possible solution for the survival and development of networks as an action research practice that network researchers across modules develop the practice together? We would have been better off if we had done that in ED2000. In this way, networks should be treated as effective tool for ED2000. We think that researchers and enterprises would be better off if networks are not seen as one particular approach, but rather as a theme that needs to be analyzed from different theoretical and practical positions. However, the research environments in Norway are too small to allow each module to pay a sufficient amount of attention to networks. Writing this chapter together has taught us more about the modules' enterprises than our annual meeting arranged by the program committee in ED2000. The potential of the network in one module is likely to grow, when experiences are discussed with researchers and participants from other modules using different approaches. To allow for such collaboration in the future is likely to strengthen the position of network as an action-oriented tool in enterprise research.

By the end of the program, the concept of networks got more and more linked to the establishment of "development coalitions", that is, networks of enterprises and research institutions with a commitment to common development interest through shared activities. It was also envisaged in ED2000 that "such coalitions could link to other public development resources and, through this approach to the idea of broader learning networks and even learning regions" (Finne 2000). By using networks as the main means of organizing and managing the work reform process, organizations could support each other in developing and maintaining their own change and local reform efforts rather than relying primarily on external expertise. Significant innovation could be fostered through a collaboration between different organizations in the same branch or geographical area, learning about work reform from each other (Engelstad and Gustavsen 1993: 220). The researcher should be a partner in development coalitions. This implies that the focus of networks in the action-oriented approach is on a qualitative enhancement of social relationships in enterprises and between the research community and the field. As Gustavsen et al. (2000: 20) put it: "*There is a need for connectedness between the people with whom we work and it is a major part of an action research effort to help create this connectedness*".

We do not disagree with the statements above. In fact, we think that one thing we really managed as researchers in ED2000 was to create a connectedness between researchers and between the enterprises and ourselves. In order to link network as an action research practice to the well-established research field of networks, it would be wise not to start from scratch. The three approaches reviewed in this chapter, each with its limitations, have much to offer, and together they can be a holistic treatment of networks. As such, an action research practice inherently needs to pay attention to all of them. This may increase our knowledge of actors deliberate in networking, evolving structures, arenas for attention and changing roles for researchers and enterprises. We need to focus both on external networks and to pay attention to the enterprises' internal links. In our opinion, ED2000 focused too much on external networks, and had too little attention on how external networks impact internal work life processes in the enterprises. Structures of relations have no borders. For work life research, an internal focus on networks is also needed.

Chapter 13

Enhancing innovations

A core issue of ED2000

Morten Levin

Introduction

Enhancing innovation capacity was a stated goal of ED2000. In the English pamphlet presenting the program, a whole section is devoted to discussing innovations as a social process. "These (innovations) are primarily understood as a social, nonlinear process of interaction between employees within concerns, or between concerns and their environment, in which interactive learning is fundamental aspect of the innovational process" (ED2000 brochure 1995, p. 10). A central argument in these introductory statements was that innovations were social processes depending on the involved actors' skills, resources, imaginations and competencies. The conventional conceptualization of innovation as the application of scientifically developed knowledge in a practical situation is not perceived to be relevant for making sense of the innovation processes one could expect in the ED200 program. The learning processes and networking activity expected to be part of the day-to-day operation of ED2000 should create conditions that would support innovative capacity in participating companies.

A new potential for innovation and creativity was expected to result from the participative processes, involving new actors both at company level and in the research institutions in business development activities.

This chapter starts with a closer look at innovation processes, aiming at presenting an overview of this highly contested concept. The literature on innovations often delivers contradictory positions or its diversity is so broad that it is hard to find the threads that link the different positions. The aim is to create one (of many possible) frameworks for the empirical analysis of innovations in ED2000. The logic of this chapter is first to review the literature in the field. After this presentation, we present areas of the ED2000 program where we could identify innovative activities. This is the presentation of the achievements of the program.

On this basis, the last section is devoted to an analysis of how to explain how these innovations can be related to the operation of EED2000.

Innovation as an essentially contested concept

Innovation is one of those words that belongs both to everyday life and to the realm of researchers. At the outset, "innovation" seems to be pretty straightforward to make sense of. It deals with the challenge of creating something new, something that has not had any previous existence or something that is different from what earlier used to be the case. On the surface, this seems to be pretty straightforward. Alas — that is certainly not the case. Let us start with the simple issue of figuring out if something really is new. The first problem is that different experiences will determine whether something is considered to be new. To the general public for example, the Internet was a huge innovation some three to four years ago, but this same software system was well known and utilized in research environments 10–15 years earlier. With this perspective in mind, it is obvious that an innovation is context-bound and closely linked to experience. For the ordinary citizen installing connections to the Internet represented at least the same journey into the unknown as the scientists' inroad to the Internet in mid 1980s. Interpreting something as an innovation is certainly not a universal phenomenon, but is context-bound and culture specific. Hence an innovation becomes a fact when the involved social actors determine that it is something that is new, and different from what has existed earlier.

The second issue that makes innovations a difficult concept is simply the ability to identify whether something really is new, compared to the old. It would have been wonderful if the distinction between old and new had been clear cut and transparent. We of course know that this is not the case. Let us consider the example of the development of mountain bikes. Some will argue that this new bike concept is a radical innovation because it would make it possible to ride off the road. The counterargument focuses on the fact that a bike has two wheels and a set of pedals; hence it gives the rider the option to ride wherever he or she wants. The bike is only more or less suited for riding off road. The concluding remark here is of course that what is considered to be new, depends on the spectator or the user. More generally, it is obvious that the only way to identify an innovation is based on social judgement. An artifact or a new social arrangement (organizational design) is an innovation if a specific group of social actors agrees on its novelty.

Innovations are clearly not singular phenomena. Interpreting a phenomenon as an innovation is a social construction, given a specific context and environment. There is also an unclear distinction between something identified as innovative or merely as a slight development. Such human judgments are products of the local culture. The central point with innovations is, first of all, that what can be interpreted as an innovation is produced through social interaction. The central issue to investigate would then be to understand how these social processes bring innovations to the surface, and what causes them to be regarded as something new. What characterizes these exchanges in terms of involvement, power, resources and creative capacity? These questions will be dealt with in the next section.

Innovations as a social product

A traditional understanding of industrial innovations has been a linear conceptualization. Allen (1977) identifies a local "gatekeeper" as the central issue for a company in its effort to utilize external knowledge for developmental purposes. The gatekeeper envisaged the person in the company that had the connections and networking links to the knowledge producing institutions (Universities and research laboratories). The underlying idea was that new knowledge was developed in universities or research institutions. The crux of innovative capability would then have be to a close and effective communication link to these knowledge organizations, and hence also the ability to transform generic knowledge to specific product innovations. This is in essence the linear model of innovations. This has been the point made in the dominating literature on industrial innovations (see for example Utterback 1994).

In fact, this literature places little or no emphasis on understanding what actually supports innovative activity. The linear model conveys a mechanistic understanding of innovation processes, where organized social activity has a diminutive position, if visible at all. This position is basically challenged from two sides. Human creativity as a psychological process, where people have different capacities for being creative and where the physical and social environment are key factors stimulating creativity. (Grøhaug & Kaufman, 1988) This literature is rich and presents a broad array of important issues. We will not deal with problems of creativity in any more detail, but it suffices to recognize this field as important for innovations. In ED 2000, the focus was on social aspects of innovations. In other words, the focus of interest has been at the organizational level.

Turning to conceptualizing innovations as social processes, the first major strand of thinking we have to deal with is the Social Construction of Technology (SCOT) (Bijker et al. 1987). The essence of SCOT thinking is identifying that the construction of new technology depends on the involved social actors. They all bring knowledge, ideas and influence to the table, all of which are negotiated in the process of developing new technology. A new artifact, or a new technological solution, emerges as a process of closure where the involved actors develop an agreement on what the new product should look like. There is no one-dimensional technological logic that guides this process, but the available knowledge is interpreted and utilized by the participants in the design process. Hence, both social skills and technological knowledge are integrated in the same developmental activity, where there is no longer a clear distinction between what is technological and what is social.

If we add to this position a wish to understand the dynamic and strategic social processes involved in innovative processes, our attention is directed to the proponents of actor-network-theory (ANT) (Latour 1987, Callon & Law 1982, Law 1992). The vital idea in ANT is to study how actors construct networks in order to further specific points of view. The essence is the power play in the construction process, and the result can only be understood in terms of which actors had what power, and access to what type of resources for creating the "innovative" issue. A broad array of actors are involved through a process of translation, where goals and interests are mutually transformed (translated) to accommodate a broad coalition. In this process, material artifacts take on their own life as actants, with the same equal opportunity as actors have to impact the construction process. On the other hand, the ANT concepts do not contribute to an understanding of learning. The actors and the actants are pure political players without any developmental ability through learning in the network construction process. The only social change to be seen is the translation process of interests.

Let us start this theoretical development from a situation where one or more actors have an interest in joining forces in order to achieve something that is desirable. The participants might have differing interests at the outset, but in the process of negotiating for a joint action, individual interests are translated (Latour, 1987) into a platform acceptable for all participants. These interests might span from economic, political social and learning interests. A core point is to understand what constitutes these interests that the involved participants bring to the table. Innovation processes, both technological and organizational creations, depend on the involved actors, their interests, and their ability to create networks of actants and actors aimed at assembling enough power to support one's own perspective. Accordingly, no innovation will emerge as a natural solution. It is always a result of the interest and power of the involved network of actor and actants. It is only in the aftermath that an innovation appears as natural or obvious, because all controversies have then been settled.

Innovations are man made. Actors enroll in social processes where interests and power are played out in order to impact the decision on what the "innovation" should be. Understanding and impacting all those social processes are the core issues in terms of leadership and organizational design. That is the link to ED2000.

Organizational innovation processes

ED2000 was a program on enterprise development, not only focusing on organizational renewal, but equally on other development activities that could support the development of the whole business operation. This might for example be product development, development of new production systems or the creation of new logistics for fast delivery of products to customers. Whatever the focus of renewal is, the innovation process is always social. That constitutes the point of departure for the discussing ED2000 contribution to innovations.

The international literature on innovations that pays attention to organizational and leadership issues is quite disappointing. It is not because this literature does not pay sufficient attention to innovations, but it is a consequence of being so compartmentalized. A dominating strand of thinking is of course the whole field of organizational development (OD) (Cummings and Woreley 1993, French et al. 1994, Gustavsen 1992). In fact, the general idea in OD is to understand or model organizational change processes, but a lack of political and strategic understanding limits its fruitfulness in understanding innovation processes. On the other hand, the OD literature pays attention to what is missing in the SCOT and ANT tradition, namely an understanding of how to plan and support innovation processes. This normative approach, which is inherent in the Action Research paradigm (Greenwood & Levin 1998, Reason and Bradbury 2001) does not link theoretical positions on change processes with a thorough understanding of the politics of innovation. In particular, the field of organizational learning should be expected to have a focus on innovation, but that is hard to find (Argyris & Schön 1996, Senge 1990). What is even more remarkable now is how the literature labeled under knowledge management pays a stronger attention to knowledge than to innovation processes. Von Krogh et al. (2000) has the subtitle "How to unlock the Mystery of Tacit Knowledge and Release the Power of Innovation". This is a book which clearly belongs to the knowledge management tradition (Nonaka and Takeuchi, 1995), and hence it does not build a trustworthy picture of innovation processes combining knowledge development (learning) with a political and strategic position.

A more interesting take on innovations is the management-dominated literature on continuous improvement. The literature can be traced back to the quality assurance movement as formulated by for example Deming (1982) and Juran (1964). Flood presents this argument in his book Beyond TQM (1993). Today, it is this literature, emerging from production management, that sets the scene. The core arguments from this literature are to enhance processes that support small improvements. A continuous focus on, and attention to, small improvements is what creates the dynamic of organizational change. Many small steps make a long walk. Again, this literature does not pretend to deal with innovation processes per se, but forwards strong arguments for what is considered the most important process for change in business life.

Business Process Reengineering (BPR) takes on a very different position, as the central dogma in this tradition is revolutionary change. Hammer & Champy's (1993) missionary book preached revolutionary organizational change, but did not envisage any process for reaching that goal. Later writers in the field, such as Davenport (1993), have a more elaborate take on the change process, but again lack a conceptualization of the organizational politics of change.

Our general model for understanding innovations is built on an actor network perspective, where actors and actants participate in a process of creating a new artifact or new organizational designs where interest and power positions play a dominating role. The enrolment of actors in the innovation process is fundamentally the participation issue, because being involved is a fundamental prerequisite for making an impact in the closure of what an innovation should be. In addition, enrolment is not only limited to actors within a company, as the perspective makes it natural to look for anyone that can be involved. Organizational borders are not determinant for enrolment, which makes it easy to conceptually integrate external resources in internal developments. The secondary challenge is then how the involved group of actors can shape new and creative solutions. This is the translation process, where participation is increased and sustained, because the actors have sufficient gain to satisfy their own interests.

It is evident that participation in itself does not guarantee innovative solutions. In addition to depending on power and interest, it is also a question of how to create innovative capacity in this constellation of actors. Theories of individual creativity constitute one entry point to this, as the thinking framed as TQM and continual improvement constitutes another position. A third line of reference is that conceptualizations like BPR argue for the introduction of revolutionary ideas as the argument for change. The position advocated in this chapter is that the enhancement of creative capacity as the outside introduction of "revolutionary " solutions, has to be integrated in the larger picture of actors and actants, enrolled in networks, struggling to construct solutions to pertinent organizational issues.

Innovations are essentially contested as a theoretical concept, but identifying anything as an innovation in everyday life will be equally complex because of the inherent constructivist nature of innovations. The judgments underlying the identification of something as an innovation is purely social. When a group of actors identify an artifact or a new social (organizational) arrangement as new, it is de facto an innovation. Our main interest is to take a closer look at what "changes" could be identified in the view of ED 2000 activities. We will later discuss the complexity of making such direct inferences in a holistic real life situation. Many factors will of course operate at the same time, making strict inferences on remedy and result fairly difficult, but we will still argue that it is possible to trace results back to the impact of ED 2000. Our analysis will focus on how ED 2000 can be perceived to have introduced actors and actants to the innovation process, and how these actors and actants, through arguing from their perspective and interest position, translate interest that eventually could support the innovation process, leading to a closure where the outcome is judged as an innovation. The ANT perspective will be the guiding principle for this discussion. A central theme in this discussion will be how employee participation impacted the outcomes.

Innovation arenas in ED2000

ED2000 was flagged as a program in enterprise development. The degree of success of the program depends in part on the ability to create new innovative solutions, both technological and organizational, in participating networks and companies. The aim of this chapter is to investigate the innovative potential of ED2000, an effort that we will start by touring the modules in order to identify the innovative potential and the actual results from the participatory efforts in the program. The perspective will be innovative approaches to the organization of work, new forms of relationships between parties on the labor market, and to changes in leadership. The aim of the program was to support participative strategies for organizational change, and this directs our attention to joint union and management approaches to innovate in their own organizations.

In this section we will address six different types of innovations. They are all linked to the social dimension of new innovations. It is of course reasonable, in a project aiming at supporting trade union and management co-operative efforts in enterprise development, that new *innovative forms of co-operation* will emerge. In this perspective, it would make sense to look for two types of innovations. First, innovations might have resulted in new areas for co-operation or that co-operation might bring new issues of enterprise development activity into a participative forum. Thus, these organizational issues were both about creating new arenas, but also about which issues were open for participation. The second form of innovation will have a focus on *leadership development*. This is clearly something that emerged during the project period, and was hardly mentioned in the earlier days of the program. Leadership development had a participative touch, as it had a focus embedded in a long-term strategy for organizational change. The third arena where one could expect innovations to occur was shop floor work organizations. The Norwegian action research tradition was born as a strategy to change working conditions at shop floor level. The autonomous group that was envisaged forty years ago was an innovation that spread worldwide. Whether equally interesting innovations emerged from this project, was an interesting question. A more fundamental arena for development in ED2000 has been on *networks.* Much attention was focused on constructing networks in ED2000. Two types of networks were considered to be important. First, networks between participating enterprises were expected to shape learning opportunities and motivation for change at enterprise level. Through bringing companies together, staging a learning process, and motivating for local change, the expectancy was to see broad scale participative change processes. Second, developmental networks incorporating enterprises and knowledge institutions were considered an important instrument for regional economic development. This was identified as *developmental coalitions*, and these coalitions were expected to play an important role in local enterprise development. A central research question at the meta-level for this project was whether developmental coalitions really mattered. The program was constructed as a vehicle for enterprise development where the impact from coalitions of enterprises and research institutions are expected to be the driving force for development.

Cooperation between management and trade unions

ED2000 was a program with a major focus on participative approaches to company development. It was, in other words, expected that old arenas for participation should be revitalized, or that new arenas would be brought to life. Most of the modules report success in initiating and supporting co-operation between the social partners. In Norwegian work life, formal committee based co-operation was already institutionalized. One set of arenas was mandated by law, while others came out of the general agreement between the Confederation of Employers and the Trade Union Council. These co-operative bodies existed, but pure formal existence did not mean that they really were co-operative arenas. In companies where conflicts dominated the relationship between union members and the management, they could meet according to the law, but were not able to engage in real co-operation. In one of the companies where the Fafo/NHH module was engaged, these formally (by law) instituted co-operation bodies were given new meaning through the project. Instead of having a work council that made no impact, the transition to a developmental organization made it a powerful unit. This example showed how these formal institutions took on real responsibility in the change processes that the company encountered. The downsizing by 100 persons from the original workforce of 700 became the responsibility of this work council. They initiated a program to increase the vocational skill level. Every decision was made in this body, and the result was a downsizing process without forced lay-offs. The innovative aspect was here to give this work council real power and influence, and this also made it a real participative effort. The whole process rested on a cooperative agreement between the trade union and management.

The Agder module used the dialogue conference to bring the social partners together for planning future co-operation. This was done in one company that had an expressed hostility between the management and the trade union. The conference created a new experience in co-operation, which led to an agreed upon plan for joint efforts in developmental initiatives at the company. After the conference in this particular company, nobody took on the responsibility to follow up on the agreed plans. The researchers had to take an initiative to avoid the plan simply failing. Through strong involvement, the researchers managed to pull the process back on track, and they were able to establish a co-operative relationship. Here we can see that a strong engagement from the researchers' side supported the creation of new and deeper participation.

In the Rogaland module, they actively promoted participative issues in one of their three networks. The developmental strategy was to transform a very management-oriented network to an arena where participative issues had a stronger standing. Through long-term co-operation, they managed to put participation on the agenda, both for the network and for individual companies.

In all these examples, innovative forms of co-operation emerged as a result of a conscious strategy from the involved researchers. The actual participation took on many different forms, but in all cases the result was a new way of working that had not been practiced before ED 2000 came in operation.

Leadership development

Leadership development became an important issue in one of the companies participating in the Trondheim module. This company had already been running serious leadership training for quite some time. Over the last few years leadership training had been the responsibility of the corporation, but now the local unit took over the responsibility. Researchers from the Trondheim module were invited to take part in this activity, and they suggested a plan where leadership training was integrated in organizational development. The participation issue in this activity was to conceptualize leadership development as also involving the development of the participating leaders' department. This was probably an unconventional take on leadership development, as it also included subordinates in the process. Participation was of course on the curriculum in the training sessions, but the real participation issue emerged as the leaders had to involve subordinates in their own development. The idea of running a leadership program as a remedy for organizational change caught a lot of interest in the Trondheim module, and soon all participating companies had their own program running under the supervision of the research group. It seemed reasonable to explain the emergence of leadership programs as a productive merger of researchers' interests and actual challenges in the companies. The researchers' contribution was to link organizational development with leadership development. For the other two companies involved with the Trondheim module running an enterprise based leadership program, and to link that program to organizational development, were innovative measures. The results viewed as satisfaction with the program itself were quite promising, but it was not always easy to pinpoint how the local departments changed as a consequence of the leaders' development. To accredit leadership training as an innovation only makes sense from a local perspective. On the other hand, linking leadership development to organizational development is certainly not mainstream thinking in the field.

Networks

Networking is almost a trademark of ED 2000. This can be interpreted at two levels. First, the developmental activity was expected to be supported or run based on companies working with, and learning, from other companies in the same network. The second level of this networking was to create connections between companies and research institutions. This latter form of network was coined "regional developmental coalitions". The networking took on different shapes in each module. Every module emphasized developing or working with networks of companies. Only the Trondheim module paid little attention to supporting the creation of networks in the first years of operation. This was not included in their strategy, but by coincidence, networking later came to be one of the interesting developments in this module.

The Rogaland module based all its activity on creating or changing already existing networks. They succeeded in creating a network of smaller companies around the dominating company in the region. The network shaped a new arena for exchange of ideas, mutual learning, reciprocal motivation, and mutual empowerment. Network meetings were held regularly over the years, and they institutionalized an arena that had not been attainable before. A combination of direct networking and formalized meetings changed the organizational "world" of the participating companies. They shifted, from being isolated units in fierce competition, to companies understanding that they could both co-operate and compete at the same time. This is of course a pretty important innovation, changing fundamental attitudes and modes of operation in each company. This networking activity also introduced co-operation between the social partners in companies that had no tradition and prior experience in this field through networking. The small companies in the Rogaland module learned how the social partners should relate to each other. This insight would probably not have been this efficient if they had not been members of the actual network.

Developmental coalitions

In many respects, one could interpret the developmental coalitions as the meta-level research question of the ED 2000 program. In fact, developmental coalitions emerged in the later years of the program, probably caused by the greater focus on regional developmental activities in other European countries. In ED 2000 the researchers were expected to engage in the participating companies simply because this was an action research project. This also resulted in a situation where the researchers became members of the networks. This would de facto be the regional developmental coalition. The researchers engaged in different ways in those regional networks. Very often, the researchers took on a dominating role, being responsible for many of the initiatives. This was certainly what should be expected, and as such it was an important role for researchers to play in a developmental coalition. The challenge in the long run would be to let go of the researchers' potential dominating position and to transform the developmental coalition into a real participative forum. We have seen traces of this development, but it is too early to make any firm conclusions.

What is presented in this section, is a comprehensive overview of where innovative activity was to be found in ED2000. We expected of course to find new patterns of labor and management cooperation as well as new forms of networking. In addition we discovered innovative activity, in leadership development and as fragments of developmental coalitions. In the next section, we will take a closer look at two innovation dilemmas, both launched at the off set of ED 2000 as the main arenas for innovative activity.

The two central ED2000 innovation dilemmas

In the introduction we spent quite some time arguing for the difficulties inherent to the concept of innovation. It is a contested concept that both are theoretically unclear, and also difficult to study as an empirical phenomenon. It is of course a genuine social construction. Anything that is identified as an innovation, achieves this because a group of people (not always every body involved) agrees that this is new. It is obvious from the results produced in the ED 2000 that there has not been any breakthrough new organizational design that immediately caught international attention. However, that is only half the truth. People that are not insiders to the program often acknowledge the aspects of the program that they consider to be innovative. A general and quite consistent feedback that was given when ED 2000 was presented in international forums, was a marked and specific interest in the process of researching enterprise development based on co-operative agreements, between the social partners in work life, and researchers involved in company based developmental processes. This was an expression of a sincere interest in this genuine type of research, which for many also was an envied situation. The ED

2000 was in itself was a type of research program that is not mainstream. This was quite parallel to the Industrial Democracy Project (Emery & Thorsrud 1976), which was launched because Norwegian society had created a co-operative environment between trade unions and employers. This unique level of mutual trust and co-operation made it possible to experiment in Norway with something that seemed impossible in many other European countries.

The expressed international interest had probably less to do with judging the detailed innovative merits of ED 2000, but was caused both by the general structure of the program and the tight co-operation between the partners on the labor market. The central issues often revolved around the networks of companies, relating to research institutions where researchers played an active and direct role in the research process. The ability to work as action researchers was probably of less interest. More interest was devoted to the potential permanency of developmental coalitions, either being constructed in a region or as a networked coalition. The developmental coalitions, bringing the learning and developmental work of participants and researchers together, tended to be overlooked by the involved actors. It had in fact become a self-evident process. In terms of the ANT modeling of innovation processes, the developmental coalitions had turned into something that was taken for granted. We tended to disregard the fact that the whole program was based on the creation of networks for development, and that the concrete research and developmental activity have shown that this was a fruitful mode of researching enterprise development. There were few other ways available for recognizing this other than through the eyes of foreign spectators, who work in political economies where this kind of co-operation cannot prosper to the same extent that we have experienced in our own country.

If we narrow in our scope of interest to changes that actually were created on enterprise level and on network level, we face the problem of visibility and clarity. These changes in organizational design emerging from participative approaches tend to develop gradually. They sort of sneak into already existing patterns of work and leadership. When changes had taken place, they were not visible, and they were considered as an established fact by the involved actors. Again, this is fundamentally within the logic of the ANT theoretical position. This is also another explanation of why participative approaches to organizational design never need to be implemented, because they evolve discretely over time, and when new arrangements are instituted this happens because the participants judge them as a state of fact (the natural or logical way of working). In the following sections, we devote attention to the two main areas of activity in ED200 (participation and networking) in order to investigate the potential innovation capacity.

Innovation type I — working participation

Quite a lot of the work in ED2000 had a perspective of creating arenas where the social partners could "exercise" co-operation. Most of those structures had been named in the general agreement between the Federation of Employers and the Federation of Trade Unions, or in Norwegian legislation on work environment and worker's protection. Having created a formal body for co-operation does not automatically grant real co-operation. A situation could be identified where co-operative bodies were up and running, but without real content or impact on everyday business life. The intention in the law and the agreements were fulfilled, but the practical use would pretty much be zero. When organizational institutions passes through change processes that cause these structures to act on important issues and make a difference in the everyday life of the company, should we then call it an innovation?

The answer to this has to be twofold. If we deal with it at the conceptual level, the answer is pretty much self-evident. ED 2000 can certainly not claim that this program has introduced these formal co-operating bodies. They all belong either to the process of creating new laws in the Norwegian parliament, or they are a result of negotiations between the social partners. This is also connected to the general perspective of reform in working life, where no change is visible before it is lived by the actors on the labor market. Innovations in participative institutions will of course follow the same logic.

Much of the work in ED 2000 either started in the co-operative bodies or it emerged from these and subsequently invaded other arenas in the participating enterprises. A major effect of the work in ED2000 was the ability to vitalize or revitalize the participative organizational bodies. Almost all of the modules reported that such initiatives rendered successful results. One of the more successful stories concerned situations where one of these formalized work councils took on the process of downsizing the company. The important question related to innovations was whether making co-operative bodies to an arena for concrete and important co-operation can be counted as an innovation. Given a perspective of innovation as a social construct, it was obvious that when factual co-operation substitutes for pro forma participation it was an innovation. Thus, it will of course qualify as an innovation, even though it might seem to be a minor one. What value was there in having the social partners really co-operate compared to playing role games? From the perspective of work life experience, there was a huge gap between real participation and purely formal relations. In essence, that was what participative enterprise development is all about. Every company with respect for itself stated that they were either a learning company, a company that was process oriented, or a company that valued knowledge creation, but it was not self-evident that these activities was participative. On the other hand, the crux of enterprise development is actually to be able to create situations where employees take part in change efforts to make change an integrated part of everyday work life. Hence, vitalizing formal institutions to take on a participative role in enterprise development is a genuine innovation in the local context, because it reshapes peoples' way of working together.

How could we explain this process? Let us investigate the actual network at company level more closely. The social partners in the company were natural members of this network. In the context of a non-vital participative body, this network would not have been capable of making participation work. The institutionalized (and not working bodies) can be considered actants in this context. They are present and they might play a role in every decision-making as they are enrolled in arguments. The only new actor (or actors) in this situation is the outside researcher (or researchers) and a new actant — the ED 2000 program. In a successful situation, the ED 2000 and the outside researchers forces a new translation process to take place, whereby the involved parties sets new agreed upon directions for local work.

ED 2000 was an actant in participative enterprise development. The program underscores the point that the parties on the labor market valued participation, envisaged a strategy for enterprise development, and the ED 2000 funded part of the research and developmental activity. This was a very strong actant, and in turn it was important to enroll companies in participative change processes. The researcher(s) could then show up on the premises of the enterprise with the potential of building on three network actants, the legislative, the bargained participating structures and ED 2000. It was a very strong position, where participation became a "joint venture" between the social partners and where ED 2000 supplied money and research capacity. This was probably an offer that was hard to turn down. We could reframe this and ask: Why did some companies turn down such a proposal? From the Trondheim module, we learned that one company agreed to participate until it became clear that they also were expected to fund part of the local research and developmental work. Free money for experimental work was evidently welcome, but the company was not willing to bet their own money on such a process. This is obviously a situation where not even the three actants and the researchers could successfully recruit the management of the company. The local union never developed a position that had an impact. No enterprise development organized under the ED 2000 umbrella resulted from this activity. On the contrary, in all the companies that took part in ED 2000, the actor network consisted of minimally management, local union and researchers. In addition, there were three strong actants of ED2000, the program, the Law and the social agreement.

Innovation type II — Networks

Much of the activity in ED2000 took the form of networking between companies. This was a more complex network structure than in enterprise development activity. Obviously, more network actors were involved, and it was reasonable to look for more diversity of interest. These actors would come from different companies, some from large corporations, some from very small entrepreneurial types of companies, and the companies often differed in industrial area. The ED2000, the law on worker protection and quality of work life, and the agreement between the labor market parties were the dominating actants. In addition, the already existing networks were an institution that in themselves became actants. This is the situation with the TESA network in Rogaland. This network was in operation when researchers from ED 2000 enrolled it in the program. The researchers obviously had to adjust to the current modus operandi of the network, where participative approaches to enterprise development certainly were not on the agenda. The history and the image of what TESA actually should work on, was what created this actant. The researchers had to take this into account, and this resulted in a major transformation of interest seen from the researchers side. The core participative focus of ED 2000 was substituted by the ability to link up with TESA . The long-term strategy was to develop enough trust and mutual understanding, so that important values of ED 2000 could be reinstated. Later on in the program period, it became evident that TESA was ripe for working on participative enterprise development.

In the network of companies linked up to the Trondheim module, which was developed by strong engagement from the participants, the motivation to enroll was very much impacted by the need for an arena for sharing of experiences and mutual learning. The enrolment was in this situation based on identifying common interests, so the translation process was minimal. The research group initiated the network and took on the responsibility of running the first meetings. Later on, the further development of the network depended on interest and engagement from the participants. In this case, the actants supporting the development was the three basic ones, the law, the agreement and ED2000.

Development networks involving research institutions was essentially what ED2000 was all about. It was equally important at a company level, as it was at the regional or industrial level. Innovations in the program came about because actor and actants enrolled in the process of network co-operation. It was shown both through the module histories, and in the former sections, that many new networks were created through the researcher involvement in the ED 2000 program. A major point here is that the researcher(s) (actor) and the ED 2000 program (actant) were the initiating force. The resulting innovation was of course a consequence of the participative process, but it seems evident that few, if any, of the new networks would have seen the light of day unless ED 2000 had involved researchers to construct networks. Thus, the innovation capability of the program is demonstrated. The important point is that the program constructed both an actant (a program with funding options) and actors (the researchers) that in turn became the agents for innovations.

Finally, the single most important innovation in ED2000 was the networking dimension, both on creating a national network of research institutions and expecting that networks linking researchers and companies would be a vehicle for innovations.

Chapter 14

Democracy, participation and communicative change

When democracy becomes a means and not an end

Hans Chr. Garmann Johnsen and Tor Claussen

The purpose of this chapter is to see how the ED2000 process leads to a new understanding of democracy and participation. Although the guidelines of the ED2000 program are not specific about democracy, our reading is to see them as a trend towards the integration of democratic thinking in internal company developmental processes. In this respect, we can see a development different from the more classical understanding of democracy in the Scandinavian tradition.

In the classical understanding, democracy at work can be a way to reconcile tensions and asymmetries of power inside the company. Democracy can be viewed as a means that takes care of values overlooked by the structure of modern organizations or markets. In this context, debates about democracy are debates about how to make democracy more efficient. One of the main tensions in this debate is between direct and indirect democracy. Has the ED2000 brought this debate forward? However, ED2000 goes beyond this issue of the efficiency of democracy as such. Some new trends in enterprise development are less focused on the internal division of power, and more on knowledge sharing, development of competencies and broad mobilization in order to achieve results. In this trend, democracy becomes a mean to mobilize knowledge, to initiate critical debate and create an internal climate of development. Democracy becomes part of the developmental and strategic processes of the enterprise.

Industrial democracy and the ED2000 program

The ED2000 program was developed according to the idea that democracy is not just something that experts design and practitioners practice. Democracy is rather a characteristic of certain practices, as well as a consciousness and conceptualization of how "practices should be practiced". At the same time, ED2000 did not subscribe to any particular model of industrial and workplace democracy. Democratic development and participation was viewed according to more general criteria and guidelines. Among these where:

- Legitimacy in enterprise development should be established through both broad participation and representative indirect participation.
- Enterprise development processes should be based on specific challenges defined by the enterprises themselves. Identified change processes and improvements should be closely linked to the employees involved, and effected by the identified challenges.
- The process should be integrated into the ongoing development processes in the enterprise, either closely linked to the daily operations or organized in separate development organizations.
- The process should be based on the vision that future challenges are to be met by internal development coalitions that should become a permanent structure to handle new challenges.

The overall idea of the ED2000 program was to stimulate communicative processes based on broad participation and representative involvement inside enterprises.

Communicative arenas

One of the key instruments in the democratic process is the design of communicative arenas. These arenas might have many different forms depending on their purpose (Greenwood & Levin1998, Gustavsen & Engelstad 1995). Engelstad (1995) defines four categories of arenas depending on how comprehensive their task is and who it should include. Category 1 is a small meeting with limited participation and a specific task (project group). Category 2 is a large group with a specific task (working group). Category 3 is a small group with a wide span of themes (strategy forum). Finally, Category 4 is a large group with a comprehensive theme (dialogue conference).

These four categories of communicative arenas can be used in combination. They represent options related to tasks. However, they all require some general rules of dialogical interaction. According to Gustavsen (1992, p. 3), the democratic dialogue requires that the following criteria be met:

1. The dialogue is a process of exchange: ideas and arguments move to and from between participants.
2. It must be possible for all concerned to participate.
3. All participants are equal.
4. Work experience is the basis for participation. This is the only type of experience, which, by definition, all participants have.

5. At least some of the experience, which each participant has when entering the dialogue, must be considered legitimate.
6. All arguments, which pertain to the issues under discussion, are legitimate. No arguments should be rejected on the ground that it emerges from an illegitimate source.
7. A participating actor must make the points and arguments which are to enter the dialogue. Nobody can participate 'on paper' only.
8. The work role and authority of all participants can be made subject to discussion — no participant is exempt in this respect.
9. The dialogue must continuously produce agreements, which can provide platforms for practical action.

The idea of institutional design is taken from the theory of ideal regimes. In Habermas' theory that has inspired the communicative perspective (Gustavsen 1992; Johnsen 2001), there is a tension related to how far design should go, and Habermas has been reluctant to prescribe institutional design (Hjellbrekke & Osland 1999). The main tension is between reflexivity and freedom of speech on the one side, and design on the other. There is also the underlying idea that it should somehow be possible to neglect other structures (power, position), while taking part in the dialogue. McCarthy (1996) argues that this model is overly idealized. It might under-evaluate symbolic power (Deal and Kennedy 1982; Hjellbrekke and Osland 1999) and exaggerate instrumental rationality in communicative processes (Czarniawska-Joerges 1992). In real life, a dialogue, instead of realizing such an ideal regime and induce reflexivity, might come closer to the type of normativity that Kunda (1992) describes as a second control regime that reduces reflexivity.

Another question is what role the dialogue should have in the further process of selection of ideas, decision-making, and implanting of ideas that emerge through dialogue. It is not the idea of communicative organizational change to neglect the formal structure of the organization altogether. Dialogues therefore add to the formal structure and we have to find ways to reconcile with these structures. We will refer to this later in the discussion of whether a dialogical process should take place in a development organization on the side of the formal organization, or whether it should be part of the formal organization. The problem of having dialogical processes within the formal organization is that they are not equal in power. The dialogue therefore does not meet the ideal regime requirements. As Warren (1996) observes: "In such [functional] groups, there are often individuals whose personalities and skills of communication dispose them to act as mediators and facilitators, and who gain (discursive) authority within the group because they are good at listening, probing, drawing out opinions, interpreting, offering options, and restating them. Such persons often sense when positions have become polarized, say, as a results of threats to self-esteem and can recommend delaying decisions, allowing time to disentangle motives."

However, having presented these doubts, it must be added that dialogue arenas, although not ideal, are different from negotiating arenas. Furthermore, dialogue arenas secure a certain level of participation, and have a focus on communicative competence among its participants that secure a certain level of equality and legitimacy in the communicative process (Claussen 1999).

Communicative process

It is an important precondition for the communicative approach that the communicative process is different from a negotiation process. The communicative process is supposed to be an open-ended dialogue, where participants are willing to reconsider their arguments against better arguments. Gustavsen (1992) has prescribed principles for the dialogical process.

1. "The participation is not enough. Everybody should also be active. Consequently, each participant has an obligation not only to put fourth his or her own ideas but also to help others to contribute their ideas.
2. It must be possible for everybody to develop an understanding of the issues at stake.
3. The participants should be able to tolerate an increasing degree of differences of opinion.
4. Each participant must accept that other participants can have better arguments."

The fourth point can be either strong or weak. A strong condition means that a person is willing to reconsider beliefs and values. A weaker condition is that a person is willing to adjust or change an argument that is not essential to his or her existence.

The program of communicative change in a formal and functional relationship in the workplace can be perceived either as a socialization/decision process or as a dialogical process aimed at revealing differences in opinions and creating an increased rationality that does not necessarily lead either to agreement or to decisions. In the first perspective, the idea is that in order to make decisions that are respected or accepted, individuals need to have a common feeling of identity, goals and priorities.

In the second perspective, the communicative process is decoupled from the identity process and from decision-making processes. Our perspective on dialogical programs and communicative change is this second perspective. The challenge with this perspective, however, is how to retain a certain level of functionality (commitment, identity, authority) in combination with the plurality of the dialogical process.

The key to this balance is to acknowledge that the communicative process is not a decision process, but a process of reaching a higher level of rationality. This rationality is increased through critical discussion, reflexivity and the willingness to be convinced by a better argument. It presupposes that individuals involved in communicative action do not use strategic means in the communicative process.

The challenge is to decouple this communicative process of increasing rationality from the functional decision making process in the organization. In the decision making process, strategic action is acceptable only within the logic of the communicative process. If the communicative process is marked by honesty, the decision process must also comply with this norm. In this way, the communicative process will have a framing effect on the development in the organization. However, this implies the challenge of living with pluralism, accepting individual autonomy, and believing in the rationality of the communicative process.

The emphasis on communicative processes in the ED2000 program has therefore brought new aspects to the development of industrial democracy.

The Scandinavian tradition and workplace democracy

Participation in ED2000 rested basically on two different aspects of involvement. Each employee was involved in development activities. This is roughly covered by the term d*irect participation.* Direct participation usually emphasizes that each individual in an organization shall participate in enterprise development regardless of status, position, role, power, etc. On the other hand, *indirect participation* implies that involvement shall be based on more or less representative structures in an organization. Accordingly, employees, involved in developmental processes through indirect participation, have to utilize decision-making and negotiation structures to balance their differences of interest among employees to a common, representative expression.

The two forms of participation, direct and indirect participation, in enterprise developmental processes have their roots in classical democratic theory and controversies. Among the prominent classical debates, the views of Rousseau and Mill are well known. While Rousseau rests his view basically on broad participation in people's public democracy, Mill emphasizes representative democracy.[1] Major trends in democratic theory have also differentiated between positive democracy theory and classical constitutional democracy (Birch 1993). Positive democratic theory implies that part of the democratic process is to take care of the well-being of citizens, while classical constitutional democratic theory implies the use of democratic processes as a protection of individual rights against, for example, tyranny.

1. In the famous work of Pateman (1970), she refers to classical debates in her efforts to emphasis direct participation.

In the Norwegian tradition, these ideas and debates have taken up quite a lot of space both in theoretical aspects of the tradition, in controversies related to industrial democracy, as well as in action research. In the more recent trends, democracy as a communicative process has been highlighted.

Background

The conceptualization of the Scandinavian model of workplace co-operation was made in the early 1960s. The work of Emery and Thorsrud (1976) was partly inspired by the American functionalist Human Relation-tradition (McGregor 1960). The Norwegian activity had its parallels in Sweden and Denmark (Gustavsen 2000). The idea in this tradition was to adjust the organization and work routines to the psychological and physical job requirements of the employees. Furthermore, it assumed that these requirements were somewhat scientific, objective and general. However, work design should also allow for self-development and variation (Emery and Thorsrud 1976, p. 158). In this respect, it departed from Scientific Management. However, they were both in the tradition of making workplace organization scientific (Claussen 2000).

Large organizational development processes were started in private and public companies (Røvik 1998) based on the ideas of Emery and Thorsrud. However, Emery and Thorsrud also redefined this program based on Selznick (1957/1997). They argued for the complexity of the organizational processes, and launched the idea of the workers' collective as an important bulwark between those functional claims of the organization and the needs of the individual employee (Thorsrud and Emery 1976). The workers' collective forms in their model an alternative system to the formal power in the organization, and has the capacity to negotiate with the technical and economic system of the organization.

During the 1970s, the program initiated by Thorsrud and Emery led to the formalization of economic democracy. Economic democracy implied the establishment of awareness inside the organization of arenas based on equal representation of workers and management. The so-called asymmetry of power between these groups should be leveled out on these arenas. These arenas got dedicated issues to handle, mostly related to internal work conditions and health and safety issues. Workers were also given seats on the board, and the right to state opinions on issues like redundancies. These reforms implied the formalization of co-operation between employees and managers/owners at the workplace.

Gustavsen's (1996) introduction of the term *communicative turn* indicates both a descriptive and a prescriptive view on communication. In prescriptive terms, the communicative turn represents the possibility to activate inside the firm what Habermas have called communicative action (Habermas 1997, p. 285).

Communicative action implies being more involved, more committed to universal rules and individual reflexivity, and focused on reaching understanding.

The communicative turn

In the beginning of the 1990s, firms were increasingly challenged by the need for flexibility to meet changing market requirements. Formal co-operation between workers and owners was not in itself suited for this task. Organizations were increasingly faced by the need for internal diversity and to "live with pluralism" (Gustavsen 1998). The inherent antagonism that underlies the formal structure of co-operation had to be replaced by structures with more than one dimension. The perspective increasingly became communicative and social constructivist (Claussen 1998; Powell and DiMaggio 1991, p. 51).

However, more important was the new emphasis on practice as compared to analytical knowledge (Gustavsen 2000). Liberation comes not from theory but from practice. Theory can enlighten practice, but cannot take the leading role over practice. Practice is therefore the cornerstone in this perspective, and communication is the means by which practice is articulated, legitimated and spread. The perspective in this communicative turn is that truth is not objective, and it can not be found through analyses, rather, it is local, develops over time, it is subjective and based on continuous definition, redefinition and interpretation. Furthermore, the perspective is that development takes place in the network surrounding the organization, and not only within (Gustavsen 1996, p. 22). In prescriptive terms, it focused on creating arenas for dialogue, as well as increasing the communicative competence of the participants.

The communicative concept that has emerged from this initiative is focused on continuous improvement, participation, delegation, and bottom-up processes in addition to the particular communicative element, individual reflexivity and strong emphasis on dialogue. The underlying inspiration to this approach comes from Habermas (1997). But Habermas' general theory of communication in society is too general to be applied directly to organizational contexts (Gustavsen 1996; McCharty 1996). The Swedish and Norwegian programs therefore contributed to the development of a new organizational concept of communicative organizational change.

We shall however argue that the communicative approach in fact can be interpreted either as an organizational prescription, a management fashion, an organizational isomorphism, or a concept of organizational change.

Røvik (1998) argues that in order for these prescriptions to develop and spread, they need to be socially authorized, theoretically founded, and developed as a product. Furthermore, the prescription should be correctly timed, in line with general interests, and it would be easily communicated and able to be applied individually in the organization. DiMaggio and Powell (1991), Meyer and Rowan

(1991) and Scott (1995) argue that isomorphism occurs as a cultural process of adaptation based on general elements that find their local form. Abrahamson (1996) states that: "A management fashion, therefore, is a relatively transitory collective belief, disseminated by management fashion setters, that a management technique leads rational management progress."

The communicative concept of organizational change is rooted in general, or at least widespread, ideas that it will improve organizational performance. It is also rooted in a long tradition, although an elaboration of this tradition. It is general and allows for local variants. However, it is based on some strong beliefs in what counts for organizational development.

Direct and indirect democracy — Experience from the ED2000 process

ED2000 emphasized indirect participation, as the importance of the major working life parties in the creation of the program was an obvious fact. Their initiative in creating the program clearly manifested itself in the basic guidelines of the program. Involvement from both management and union was seen as an important aspect of the activities of each module. The involvement of both union and management in the developmental activities was followed up and checked by the working life parties.

Direct participation

On the company and network level, the involvement of union representatives and management varied quite a lot.

If we summarize the stories given by the modules, the rough picture is this: The AFI module was mainly focused on direct participation. They reported problems of implementing participation in the operations of the enterprises, and they argued that dialogical processes were to some extent non-instrumental. Direct participation, therefore, is not easily used as a management instrument in the strategic processes of the enterprise.

The Agder Module reported on their effort to develop a more instrumental version of direct democracy through dialogical processes. Their concept implied that dialogical processes were used instrumentally alongside, and as part of a broader strategy for development, and they reported on problems with involvement and participation in these processes.

The Tromsø module reported on the problems of moving from dialogical processes to broader participation. Many of their cases were management-driven. Dialogical processes were used strategically, but created little or no direct participation in the development processes.

The Fafo module was mainly concerned with indirect democracy. They focused on the impact of development on formal representative systems. They reported on the problem of creating broad participation, trust and involvement through this formal representative system.

The Nord Vest Forum module was mainly focused on the informal structure of participation in the enterprises. They launched a program to educate union representatives, and they anticipated that participation was a natural part of enterprise development.

The Rogaland module used dialogical conferences as part of a strategic process much in the same way as the Agder module. More than the other modules, they emphasized networking between enterprises. Some general implications of the Rogaland work were that there is a problem of developing real democracy inside enterprises. Democratic processes are part of the power structure and the formal structure of the enterprises. These structures represent countervailing forces in the development processes.

The Trondheim module gives few references to broad and direct development processes. Their focus was more on work design and the development of production systems. In this work they anticipated participation. They also had the bodies of the formal, indirect democracy (representative system) as a reference and legitimation for their work.

Many of the enterprises in the modules based their developmental activities on direct participation. Management involved themselves in the initiation processes and gave legitimacy to the different projects executed. Fewer actually engaged themselves directly in the activities in the projects.

On the other hand, few of the modules reported active involvement from the union representatives and shop stewards. This could be due to the size of the enterprise itself. In smaller enterprises, the legitimacy of the management could be sufficient due to the more personal contact between management and union. However, in one of the networks, the IfS network, the shop stewards actually played a significant role in the development activities. The importance of the involvement of the shop stewards and union in developmental activities, a significant feature of the IfS network, did give the process a necessary legitimacy. This legitimacy contributed greatly to the character of the developmental activities in the IfS network, giving them a thorough and long lasting profile. The importance of indirect participation was proved in many other aspects of the work in the IfS network as well.

Direct participation has dominated as the form of involvement and legitimization of the development work in ED2000. On the other hand, viewed more specifically, each module differed significantly in their emphasis on different forms of participation. In the Agder module, particular aspects of the main agreement between the working life parties concerning enterprise development were highlighted. Highlighting this aspect of the agreement was done partly to legitimize the importance of indirect participation, and the actual linkage to the representative system of participation. Specifically, this linkage concerned the attachment to the organizational structure responsible for daily operations.

The other modules in ED2000 based their linkages more on a variety of key persons in the organizational structure, in order to give the developmental activities legitimacy. Many emphasized the linkage and involvement of top management, in order to secure legitimacy. In its turn, this top management involvement was utilized to link each individual employee, in order to encourage direct participation in developmental activities.

Several questions can be raised in relation to these differences in ways of creating legitimacy and involvement of employees. Were these differences for instance due to mere coincidence? What effects did these differences have in relation to progress and results? In the developmental activities and action research conducted in ED2000, both forms of participation had major impact on the ways participants were involved, as well as the way the improvement projects were embedded in the organization. Direct participation was a way of involving each employee in order to achieve practical results. Each individual employee's direct participation was also aimed at creating a dynamic process, where creativity and the interplay between differences of opinions would ensure changes and improvements according to objectives. On the other hand, the actual results in the development activities in the program do not demonstrate any significant creativity and innovation. This could be due to reconciliation practices prominent in the development processes based on direct participation. Reconciliation processes are necessary in development activities based on direct participation, in order to prevent diversity and differences of opinions from hampering or destroying common understanding and co-operative efforts among the participants.

Indirect participation

Involvement of individual employees through direct participation can be a way of securing the involvement necessary to overcome possible resistance (Nord, 1994), when facing development and change in organizations. Direct participation then has to be guided by ways to reconciliate individual opinions and interests into a representative expression of all participants involved. Reconciliation practices have to reflect the main objectives of changes and development incorporated in the initial initiatives.

In ED2000, there were many examples of such reconciling practices. In the Tromsø module this, was both a task and a dominating effort among the researcher themselves. Reconciliation practices among the researchers themselves was necessary as a prerequisite prior to the actual action research taking place in the co-operating enterprises. Such reconciliation practices were also necessary prior to the action research conducted in the other modules. In the Agder module, a striking observation was the importance of negotiations of terms of involvement prior to the development process. However, both Fafo and Tromsø report that, in their cases, they did not succeed in creating involvement beyond the indirect representative system.

In the development research taking place in the different enterprises and networks, reconciliation practices were also necessary. They were based on different techniques and approaches. In the IfS network, a specific technique was utilized to reconcile differences of opinions and views into approved priorities on improvements to be executed. Indirect participation, in the form of union representatives, can encourage reconciliation through representative practices. This was the case of the shop stewards' participation in the improvements and developmental activities taking place at Aker Stord, one of the key actors in the IfS network. Less specified approaches and techniques characterized reconciliation practices utilized in the development activities in the other modules.

Legitimization of direct and indirect participation

Representative participation can be a way of ensuring a legitimate involvement in developmental activities. This has been the situation in many of the cases in ED2000. Although basically most of the cases involved in ED2000 highlight the importance of direct participation, many of the same cases more or less implicitly emphasize the important role of the local union and shop steward. The Agder module took a strategy process perspective on their activities. This implied the integration of communicative processes in the strategy process. Rogaland research in its approach highlighted TQM and direct participation in the initiation of enterprise development in the IfS network. On the other hand, it soon became clear that the major industrial partner already presupposed a strong involvement of the local union representative in its enterprise development program based on TQM. The role of the union representative in all stages of change was to transform an international management concept like TQM, with a weak link towards union participation, into a more Norwegian model, with strong emphasis on union involvement at every stage of change processes and program initiations. The role of the union was an important prerequisite for the direct participation of individual employees. Both direct and indirect participation contributed indivisibly to the participatory aspects of enterprise development in this case.

Representative participation has been a major aspect of involvement on program level. Actors representing the social partners in the HFB arrangement involved themselves in several program activities. They had a tremendous impact on the legitimization of developmental activities among managers, as well as employees and their representatives. In addition, these actors involved themselves directly in improvement projects, through their capacity as competent key persons related to participatory aspects of enterprises.

In addition ED2000 demonstrated several examples built more or less exclusively on direct participation. The AFI module demonstrates an approach built on direct participation based on the dialogue conferences. However, the AFI case also demonstrates the shortcomings of this approach in strategy development.

The linkages between direct and indirect participation in ED2000 were not without challenges. Representative participation has a possible legitimating aspect, which can be of great importance in enterprise development. On the local level, this was demonstrated through to the involvement of the local union representative, together with representatives from the central HFB arrangement. For the program and its overall initiatives, the representatives from the central HFB arrangement contributed to give ED2000 its necessary credibility.

The legitimating aspect of representative participation in ED2000, on the other hand, could involve an ideological aspect. Having too much confidence in the initiated developmental activities could cover the possible differences of opinions and interests with a "veil of ignorance" (Rawls, 1971). This in turn could equalize diversity and creative resistance, destroying the possible inherent creativity in the existing differences and inequalities. The existence of such possibilities does not seem to have been highlighted significantly in the different case studies and discussions in ED2000 so far.

In the ED2000 program, the challenges and possible linkages between direct and indirect participation has mainly been dealt with theoretically.[2] Many of the practical implications from these challenges have not been a systematic focus in the research conducted. Among these are the possibilities and obstacles related to resistance, reconciliation, diversity, etc., in a more innovative approach to enterprise development.

Resistance and opposition in democratic processes

There are great challenges related to reconciliation practices conducted in enterprise development. As differences of opinions are important in democratic practices, reconciliation practices could hamper or destroy differences of opinions in the efforts aimed at reaching a common understanding and approval of each participant. Creating a common understanding and consensus inherently runs the risk of overruling diversity and multiplicity of interests and opinions. It might just

2. See above. For a more thorough discussion see Claussen (2000).

be diversity and multiplicity of interests and opinions that represent the creativity and possibilities of innovations in modern industrial organizations (Claussen, 2000). One major question in this respect will be whether direct participation, aimed at overcoming possible resistance, becomes a way of eliminating constructive and creative criticism inherent in differences of opinion, opposition and resistance. Overcoming resistance could violate a fundamental aspect of democracy, where the role of opposition and criticism is just as important as the majority opinion in any democratic process.

In a critical review of ED2000, the question is whether the creative, innovative and dynamic aspect of the program, and its developmental activities, have been given the necessary attention. The different program and improvement activities have emphasized consensus driven minor changes, at the expense of more creative and innovative developments and improvements. The overall consensus on communicative actions, based on for instance Habermas, runs the risk of reconciliation and elimination of differences of opinions, as the contest of the best argument finalizes the existing diversity and differences of opinions.

Representative participation and reconciliation practices/techniques run the risk of eliminating the inherent innovative and creative capacity of diversity and differences of opinions. Here there is a risk of making and manipulating a consensus and agreement based on direct participation. Direct participation (and indirect participation) could then become "mystifying processes creating overlapping consensus" (Rawls 1971) disrupting diversity and creativity in developmental processes. The possibility then remains that democracy and direct participation become ideological constructions lacking real involvement in decision making processes and related activities concerning enterprise development.

Experiencing participation and involvement as more or less obvious ideological constructs could turn employee involvement into different forms of resistance. Many developmental initiatives are met with different forms of passive resistance or resistance through distance. On the other hand, more active forms of resistance could be the case, especially if individual or collectively agreed basic rights and obligations are violated (Collinson, 1995).

ED2000 was characterized by different forms of resistance on different levels and among different actors. Resistance built on different research perspectives took place among the researchers in many of the modules. This form of resistance hampered many of the research initiatives in the initial phase of the program. Some of the modules finally succeeded in giving these differences and diversities a beneficial outcome for the research conducted. Other modules experienced devastating conflicts and obstacles, hampering or destroying progress. This explains the experiences reported by the Fafo, Tromsø, and AFI module.

Resistance seems mostly to be termed as a reaction against, or passive neglecting of, efforts to make changes. It can be termed as positive and legitimate or hostile, negative and illegitimate. In the resistance literature, the term anyhow implies some form of reaction or passive neglecting. There are few examples where resistance is viewed as creative and innovative. Viewing resistance as a possible creative and dynamic potential of an organization might give a very different perspective. Such a perspective will form part of the background framework building the point of reference for a critical analyses of the research done in ED2000.

Judging whether participation, resistance, and necessary reconciliation work one way or the other, is a major issue in enterprise development and industrial democracy. This has not been the case in the research conducted in ED2000. The consequences of missing out on these major issues is also part of the critical discussions conducted in this chapter.

Democracy in strategy processes — What have we learned?

What characterize the democratic practices and processes prevailing in ED2000? What have their contributions been, and what were the challenges? Did any particular aspect cause major deficits in the processes and practices of democracy and participation in ED2000?

These are large questions and no final, comprehensive analysis of the ED2000 program has been made in order to answer them. However, we argue here that the ED2000 program has contributed to some progress in our understanding of these questions.

Democratic process and incremental change

Many of the cases show that there is major emphasis on direct participation in the developmental activities conducted in the different modules. On the other hand, there are many examples where representative participation is more or less prominent alongside direct participation. At first sight, there seems to be no indication that the different participatory aspects have any impact on the actual character of the development activities as such.

In the case material from the Rogaland module representative and direct participation were present in different degrees in the improvement projects that were organized. The character of these projects and the improvements made did not vary significantly. None of the improvements had great change potentials or significant impacts on the overall development of the enterprises or the actual workplaces of the individual employees. Mostly small identifiable and minor changes occurred that were closely related to daily operations.

Neither direct participation nor indirect participation managed to stimulate any noteworthy change of the capacities in the organizations. It is also difficult to grasp any articulated resistance that could give birth to changes and processes not outlined by the initiators of the developmental activities. There seems to be little or no (democratic?) opposition and alternative perspectives articulated in the different cases in ED2000.

However, other experiences and analysis point in a different direction. In analyzing communicative processes in six enterprises in the Agder module with a detailed examination of one of the cases, Johnsen (2001) found that participation, communicative processes and strategic development did follow some interrelated patterns. It was revealed that participation took different forms in the different stages of the strategic process. In an early stage of legitimization, participation was broad, direct and general. Later in the development stage, participation was indirect, and more functional, while in the implementation stage of the strategy process, participation again was broad but targeted.

This last finding indicates that communicative processes and participation is meaningfully integrated into the ongoing strategic process in the enterprise. These are promising findings that point out directions that could be explored further. However, Johnsen (2001) also found that change agents and key actors played a very important role in the process.

Implications for further research

After the ED2000 program, we are left many unanswered question. Why was there a high degree of suspicion towards researchers and consultants, specifically among the employees? What were the advantages of researcher participation in action research? Was a special legitimacy involved, trusting that the researcher would give neutral and equal emphasis on the different opinions and interests in an organization regardless of status, positions and place in an organization?

On the other hand, what has been pinpointed here is the possibility of important improvements in the further development of industrial and workplace democracy. These improvements could be related to questions like:

- To what extent could one expect more diversity and creativity in the involvement of the participants?
- What would have to be the prerequisites and conditions for more advanced forms of democracy in ED2000?

In relation to what has been stated previously, a more principal question would be whether the democratic processes in ED2000 indicate a rudimentary industrial democracy in the different enterprises involved. If opposition and differences of opinion in a democratic process is as important as the majority rule, does the absence of opposition, resistance, etc., indicate that the necessary dynamic aspects to be fully democratic are missing? Are we then experiencing a less developed and rudimentary form of democratic process in the examples and enterprises involved in ED2000?

ED2000 demonstrated very advanced participatory arrangements compared to previous arrangements and initiatives, both compared to other Nordic examples as well as according to international examples. In several respects, ED2000 created new opportunities and arenas for direct as well as indirect participation, indicating important milestones in the overall development of industrial and workplace democracy.

These questions occur, because in enterprises, democracy is not primarily a means to secure basic rights and to adjust asymmetry of power, but rather a means to motivate employees and to activate and utilize knowledge and learning. This points to the need for broad direct participation. However, there is also a growing need for co-ordination and rules of just conduct at modern workplaces that calls for a comprehensive, democratic and representative system. As we have asked more questions in this chapter then we have answered, although we also have given some tentative answers, we indicate that the ED2000 program has not provided us with theoretical and empirical support for a comprehensive, up to date understanding of industrial democracy.

CHAPTER 15

Epilogue
Research on Enterprise Development

Lessons learned

Tor Claussen, Lene Foss, Hans Chr. Garmann Johnsen, Henrik Kvadsheim, Morten Levin, Jarle Løvland and Johan E. Ravn

Introduction

Enterprise Development 2000 lasted for five years. It was a program with no clear starting point and there was no clear ending date. The program was officially launched in 1995, and had a planned closure by the year 2000. A committee consisting of members from the Confederation of Employers and the Trade Union Council, together with researchers, developed and lobbied for the realization of . The program was expected to get off the ground by 1995, but it took more than a year until all research modules were in operation. The closure of the program was equally diffuse. The closing conference was in fact held in March 2001, but all modules still have a modest activity, awaiting the next generation program, "Value Creation 2010". Writing up the research is in process. The lessons from will hopefully create a backdrop for continuing this type of research and developmental activity in organizations. In Chapter 1, "Researchers on Research " we signaled five major issues of concern reflecting and systemtizing the findings from

The first area of interest was on the key *issues at stake in creating a national program, involving several semi autonomous research groups.* These different groups were expected to operate pretty much on their own, given their regional economic context. The expectation that the seven modules were to create some kind of co-operation and hopefully possibilities for mutual learning was however not clear. The core issue of knowledge development would be to question whether a program that integrated modules in a national program would turn out to be something more than just the sum of independent research groups. Was it worthwhile calling it a national program on enterprise development? Program leadership was expected to be a core factor, either leading to a disintegrated program, or to research that integrated experiences and knowledge from the different modules. Attention was accordingly focused on the leadership structure, in order to understand its governance structure.

The second area of interest was on the *creation of action research capabilities in the seven participating modules.* Two obvious major challenges emerged. The modules were expected to become proficient in action research, and there were expectations that the modules should be able to integrate researchers with different professional background in researching enterprise development. Some of the modules had former experience from 30 years in action research, while others were embarking on this kind of research for the first time. The expectation posted to each participating module was both to support practical problem solving, and to create research based texts for the scientific community. Hence, the experiences from created very rich material, which enabled an understanding of the possibilities, problems and pitfalls for researchers moving from values and models of research learned through their initial graduate work, to new and different research paradigms. The third focal area in focus was the *situatedness of the regional political economy in enterprise development and research.* Each research module created networks involving local companies and public institutions, that became an integral part of the local action research activity. The posted challenge was also to create research activity that no longer was built on one single researcher, but integrated several researchers in a co-operative activity, both in research and in developmental work. anticipated and supported close networking among the participating researchers, both integrating different professional backgrounds and locations. The networking activity was very much a clear break with orthodox social science's inherited individualistic character. The fourth area of interest was on *innovation potential.* It was clearly stated in the program proposal that the enhancement of innovation capability in the participating companies was important. The ability to create new patterns of work and new organizational structures was emphasized . A key question in this connection was whether the program gave room for radical innovations, or whether it only supported incremental innovations? Finally, the fifth area of interest was on *the enhancement of democracy at work.* ED2000 as a program created on the basis of a long time involvement with industrial democracy. The Norwegian industrial democracy program was launched in the late 1969 (Emery & Thorsrud, 1976), and elements of this ideology are reconstructed through this program. At that time, democracy at work was considered a value in itself, while the rhetoric of integrated participation and democratic structures in business development, to create profitable and sustainable organizations, was new. It was important to investigate to what extent ED2000 could support democracy at work, and what forms it would take in the new century.

Constructing and leading a national program

ED2000 was expected to become a program that integrated the activities in the different modules in order to create a national program. The modules had a varied background in research. Some modules had former experience in enterprise-based research, while others had little or no former practice related to development work accompanied by research. This created quite a challenge for the governing body of ED2000, as they initially were forced to work with a diverse set of research groups. The task for the governing body of ED2000 was to shape the ground for a broad and integrated regional research activity, aiming at supporting participation in enterprise development. In the perspective of "conventional" funding for research, where applications are evaluated and grants are either refused or given, the active involvement from the board in the process of developing the individual modules was a new dimension. In order to meet this goal, the governing body of the program had to exercise leadership, and not only distribute money based on judgment of the quality of a proposal. The challenge was in fact to develop the modules working capacity (research capacity), in order to enable them to meet the demands of the program. All this was to take place within the overall context of a research program that should enhance participative change processes in work life.

The program board took on the task of creating a leadership intended to shape the program in a desired direction. In retrospect, three different strategies can be identified. First, the governing body of applied pure pressure by giving specific directions on how local research should be carried out. This was a genuine application of pressure, and the power was clearly in the hands of the governing body. This forceful induction of a research agenda was important to set the tone and the focus of the research activity, making it clear that the action research was expected both to create tangible practical results and research publications.

The second stage in managing the program was to use monitoring as a remedy for impacting the development of the program. The mid-term evaluation of the program became the turning point and the end of the power strategy. The bench-marking exercise created a constructive conflict between the modules and the board, rendering the unintended outcome of a closer cooperation between the modules. This was probably the first sign of an emerging national focus on the part of the researchers. Later in the program the monitoring function was successfully extended through extensive traveling by members of the secretariat, creating their own understanding of, and judgment about, how the research and development work progressed. Their observations were passed on to the governing body, but it also created an interesting learning opportunity for the modules, as the same information was passed on to them. The result was a leadership style, that through monitoring the operation of the program managed to create learning at module level, which in its turn enabled improvement in the local work.

The third model of leadership style was more based on participative approaches, where active researchers in the program obtained a larger space for involvement. Meetings between all researchers were a success, and stronger involvement in operation and planning from the researchers' side was possible.

The important aspect of the leadership of ED2000 was the willingness to take on the task of really leading a research program, building the leadership on different modus of operation judged to be relevant for that particular problem focus, and to be able to let go of some of the control as the participating modules found their own research identity. We consider this an important experience from this program, and it should certainly be modeled in future programs.

Creating a new research practice

ED2000 confirmed the rigidity of the disciplinary barriers embarking on module based action research. Many of the "new to action research" modules were living examples of how previous education and departmental and institutional loyalties made it difficult to put the enterprises' need for practical problem solving first, and the narrow disciplinary agenda second. Mastering a profession's "normal" research paradigm creates a strong identity, and it reveals the individual's scientific capacity. To become a professional researcher is to work hard to comply with the standards set by the profession, and it also involves a lot of pressure to stay within the conventional boundaries.

Exceeding the boundaries set by the professions involves making oneself vulnerable, both in terms of access to conventional career patterns and to negative judgement by peers. That happened to many of the researchers in ED2000, as they felt that they were externally controlled by the program board, by their institutions, and by their disciplinary belonging. Living with other researchers and enterprises for almost five years, the participating researchers slowly developed a new identity and started advocating transdisciplinary knowledge creation embedded in practical problem solving (Gibbons 1994). However, there is a reason for advocating a different path for the next generation of researchers participating in programs like ED2000. It is important to acknowledge the strong impact of initial training, and a major improvement would be to train the next generation of researchers to handle action-oriented enterprise research. In this regard, it is important to sponsor an engagement in graduate training with the specific purpose of training researchers to handle transdisciplinary action oriented problems. Some positive results were created in ED2000 with regard to re-aligning research, but in future programs, this issue must be given much more attention.

Regional research networks

The regional embeddedness of ED2000 was certainly a strength as it primarily created co-operation between regional enterprises and stakeholders, and local research institutes. When the co-operation between researchers and enterprises started to function, it also gave results for both parties. We argue that one premise for the regional modules was the ability to identify enterprises and to work out collaboration practices. A prerequisite for enterprise development is to recruit researchers that know their local culture, history, practices, and the context from where the employees are recruited.

The local context of enterprise development, embedding researcher and enterprise, was important for the success of ED2000. Enterprise development has to be based on the situated knowledge of the actors in participating companies, combined with researchers' inclusion of theoretical knowledge in concrete problem solving.

Regional research modules, in co-operation with local enterprises, have positioned situated knowledge on the research agenda. Regional coalitions between enterprises, local work life actors and research institutions have proven to be important for regional economic development. Knowledge and skills from different disciplines have been made available in a regional context, and in addition practical problems from local companies have entered the sphere of research. These mergers are potentially the most promising factors for future development of regional competence and economy.

The networks that were constructed under ED2000 were the research modules. The modules themselves were actors in a network structure With few resources available for collaboration in the initial phase of the program, the ties between the actors were weak, and mainly related to exchanging information on the module leader meetings. As time passed, and their self-esteem grew, trust between the actors increased, and more sensitive information was exchanged. Stronger ties between the modules were also developed by collaborating in the writing process of this book. In that way, weak ties were transformed to strong ties.

Networks can be a resource base for the individual enterprise. This implies bringing in other types of actors into the network pool; such as local government, financial institutions, or trade organizations; but also further attempts at creating multi-disciplinary research teams as vital actors in these constellations. Different network actors may contribute with different resources, all of which may be important. Collaborations among private enterprises in networks have been exemplified in a number of ways in ED2000. Some networks have been loosely connected, while other networks could be characterized as "quasi" enterprises, as they in fact were companies, owned by shareholders, with the business purpose of connecting participating companies.

Historically, this utilization of network collaboration represents a fundamentally new aspect in enterprise development. Broad participation was an outstanding feature of the earlier mentioned enterprise development projects taking place in Norway in the 1960s and 1970s. ED2000 demonstrated, in addition to broad participation inside the enterprises, a way to encourage enterprise development among participating enterprises. This is one of the important results from the program and the project activities within the different modules.

Innovations

We have already dealt with what in the aftermath of can be identified as an unintended innovation, namely the leadership strategy. It is a fair conclusion that ED2000 modeled a leadership style that created desired outcomes, as it was both flexible and forceful, depending on the actual context. This innovation will just be noted here and not discussed further.

Most of the innovations that came about as a consequence of ED2000 can in retrospect be seen as minimalist. In the aftermath they are considered obvious and only modest in range. One should be cautious not to overlook the process by which a new organizational practice or institutional arrangement, in being integrated in the daily routines, is no longer judged as an innovation. The rhetoric of key figures in ED2000 changed as the program went on. An interesting transition took place as regional networks gradually were substituted by regional developmental coalitions. First, this change occurred as the concept of regional development coalitions entered the international discourse on regional economy, and this implied a shift of vocabulary in ED2000. Second, with few exceptions, the modules tended to create work patterns that easily could be described as coalitions involving local businesses, regional research and education institutions, and public and private regional economic actors in the same developmental process. Thus, the whole strategy of ED2000 became a successful experiment in constructing regional developmental coalitions. The problems, pitfalls and possibilities that are described in this book reveal this process.

ED2000 created a structure at company level that facilitated new forms of co-operation between management and local trade unions. This is not by any means an innovation, in terms of breaking the ground for something that has not taken place in other organizations, but it was a major innovation in the local environment. In this perspective, it is probably fair to state that did not result in any ground breaking innovations, but that it shaped the ground for many incremental developments. The results were valued by the participating companies in their battle for survival and growth. The program also shows roads whereby international management concepts could be integrated successfully into the Norwegian tradition of co-operation between the parties in the labor market. It is worth mentioning that the very existence of ED2000 facilitated developments in participating companies in terms of management — union cooperation that had not been in place before engaging in ED2000. The program itself was the factor that made this move possible.

Democracy

ED2000 used the language of participation to communicate the underlying democratic values. Democracy at work was traditionally considered as a value in itself, but in ED2000, the language focused on participation for improved innovation capability and enhanced economic performance. The enhancement of democratic ideals is seen as dependent both on representative democracy and on direct influence on daily working conditions. The core strategy for promoting a democratic work life was closely linked to developmental processes that utilized communicative approaches as a vehicle for promoting change.

It was obvious that in many of the participating companies direct and indirect participation functioned alongside each other. The formal representative system, both mandated through Norwegian legislation and through agreements between the parties on the labor market, operated in an ordinary fashion. Participative structures supplemented this activity, and there were few examples of overt controversies. The effect of participation was not equally obvious in the investigated modules. First, it is important to notice that it is very difficult to single out one specific factor in "real life" experiments that could account for the results. It is important to acknowledge that participation had an obvious effect on the day-to-day improvement activity in the companies, but there was also an indication that participative approaches to strategic development benefited from direct participation. It seemed like participation on strategic issues in the early stages functioned as a legitimation of the participative process, ED2000 has demonstrated that a very elaborate scheme for direct and indirect participation can be implemented. One major effect has been promoting employee motivation for learning and engagement in development work.

ED2000 was a program with a broad perspective. The program was intended to build research capacity for enterprise development in several regional research institutions. The main issue was to establish developmental coalitions that could create a mutual learning situation, both for the involved companies and for the committed researchers involved. In this respect, the program involved researchers in everyday business life, while actors in participating companies got access to knowledge organizations. ED2000 was in itself a factor that promoted developmental processes in companies, as it supported participative activities in order to improve the operation of the involved enterprises. It created and supported an ongoing dialogue between labor and management, making enterprise development an effort worth continuous engagement.

References

Abrahamson, E. (1996) Management fashion, *Academy of Management Review. vol. 16, pp. 586–612.*

Alasoini, T. and M Kyllønen (eds.) (1998). *Crest of the Wave.* Helsinki: National Workplace Development Program, Ministry of Labour.

Aldrich, H.E. (1999) *Organizations Evolving*, Thousand Oaks: SAGE Publications.

Allen, T.J. (1977) *Managing the Flow of technology*, Cambridge: The MIT Press.

Andersen J.A. (1995) *Ledelse og ledelsesteorier*, (Leadership and theories of leadership), Oslo: Bedriftsøkonomenes forlag.

Arendt, H. (1958) The Human Condition, Chicago: University of Chicago Press.

Argyris, C. and D.A Schön (1978) *Organizational Learning: A Theory of Action Perspective*, New York: Addison-Wesley Publishing Company.

Argyris C. and D.A Schön (1996) *Organizational Learning II*, New York: Addison Wesley.

Asheim, B.T. (1996), Industrial Districts as "Learning Regions": A Condition for Prosperity, *European Planning Studies 4: 379–400.*

Asheim, B.T. and P. Cooke. (1998). *Localized Innovation Networks in a Global Economy: A Comparative Analysis of Endogenous and Exogenous Regional Development Approaches*, 199–240 in Comparative Social Research, vol. 17: JAI Press.

Barnes, J.A. (1954) Class and Committees in a Norwegian island parish", *Human Relations 7, pp. 39–58.*

Bijker W.E., T. P Hughes. and T Pinch (1987) *The Social Construction of Technological Systems*, Cambridge, The MIT Press.

Birch, A.H. (1993) *The Concepts and Theories of Modern Society*, London: Routledge.

Bourdieu, P. (1991) *Language and Symbolic Power*, Oxford: Polity Press.

Brusco, S. (1982), The Emilian Model: Productive Decentralisation and Social Integration, *Cambridge Journal of Economics 6, pp. 167–184.*

Bråten, S. (1973) Model Monopoly and Communication: Systems Theoretical Notes on Democratization, *Acta Sociologica 16, pp. 98–107.*

Burt, R. (1992) *Structural Holes: The Social Structure of Competition*, Cambridge, MA: Harvard University Press.

Callon, M. (1987), Society in the Making: The Study of Technology as a Tool for Sociological Analysis. In *The Sociological Construction of Technological Systems: New Directions in the Sociology and History of Technology*, pp. 83–103, edited by W.E. Bijker, Hughes T.P., and Pinch T.J. Cambridge: MIT Press.

Callon, M. and Law, J. (1982) On interests and their transformation: enrolment and counter-enrolment, *Social Studies of Science*, Vol. 12, no.4. pp. 615–626.

Callon, M. and Law J. (1997) After the Individual in Society: Lessons on Collectivity from Science, Technology and Society, *Canadian Journal of Sociology* 22, pp. 165–182.

Claussen, T. (2000), *Bedriftsutvikling, arbeidsmiljø og filosofi.* (Enterprise development, QWL and philosophy), Bergen: Unipub forlag.

Coopey, J. (1995) "The Learning Organization. Power, Politics and Ideology, *Management Learning 26, pp. 193–213.*

Cummings, T. G. and G F Worley. (1993) *Organization Development and Change,* Minneapolis/ St.Paul: West Publishing Company.

Czarniawska-Joerges, B. (1992) *Exploring Complex Organizations: A Cultural Perspective,* Newbury Park: Sage Publications.

Davenport, T H. (1993) *Process innovation: reengineering work through information technology,* Boston, MA: Harvard Business School Press.

Deal, T. E. and Kennedy, A. A. (1982) *Corporate cultures: The Rites and Rituals of Corporate Life,* Reading, Massachusetts: Addison-Wesley Publishing Company Inc.

Deming, E. W. (1982) *Quality, Productivity and Competitive Position,* Cambridge, Ma: MIT Press.

Dwyer, R. F., P. H. Schurr, and S. Oh (1987), Developing Buyer-Seller Relationships, *Journal of Marketing Vol.51 (April 1987),* pp. 11–27.

Eikeland, O. and Finsrud, H. D. (eds.) (1995), *Forskning og handling: Søkelys på aksjonsforskning* (Research and Action: Searchlight on Action Research), Oslo: Arbeidsforskningsinstituttets skriftserie no. 1.

Elden, M. and R. F. Chisholm. (1993). Emerging Varieties of Action Research: Introduction to the Special Issue. *Human Relations 46, pp. 121–142.*

Elden, M. and M. Levin. (1991). *Cogenerative Learning. Bringing Participation into Action Research,* Pp. 127–142 in Participatory Action Research, edited by W. F. Whyte: Sage.

Emery, F. and E. Thorsrud (1964), *Industrielt demokrati.* Oslo: Universitetsforlaget.

Emery, F. and E. Thorsrud (1970), *Mot en ny bedriftsorganisasjon* (Towards a new enterprise organization). Oslo: Johan Grundt Tanum Forlag.

Emery, F. and Thorsrud, E. (1976), *Democracy at work. The report of the Norwegian industrial democracy program,* Leiden: Martinus Nijhoff Social Sciences Division.

Elvemo, J. and I. Munkeby. (Planned published 2003). *Boisterous diversity: towards transdisciplinairy co-operation at the offshore construction yard,* in Team-based Action Research, edited by J. Elvemo and I. Munkeby.

Engelstad, Per H. (1995) *Fra dialogkonferanser til utviklingsorganisasjon,* in: Eikeland, O. and Finsrud, H. D. (eds.) 1995: Forskning og handling: Søkelys på aksjonsforskning. Oslo: Arbeidsforskningsinstituttets skriftserie no. 1.

Engelstad, P. H. and B. Gustavsen (1993) Swedish Network Development for Implementing National Work Reform Strategy, *Human Relations 46, pp. 219–248.*

Ennals, R. and B. Gustavsen (1999) *The Emergence of the Idea of Development Coalitions,* in Work Organization and Europe as a Development Coalition, vol. 7, edited by R. Ennals and B. Gustavsen. Amsterdam/Philadelphia: John Benjamins.

Flood, R. L. (1964) *Beyond TQM,* New York: John Wiley and Sons.

Flood, R. L. and N. R. A. Romm. (1996) *Diversity Management.Triple Loop Learning,* Chichester, UK: John Wiley & Sons.

Foss, L. and H. C. Gabrielsen (2002). Like barn leber best! Om betydning av kultur og Kjønn for kontact mønster i organisusjoner. (Birds of a feather should play tegether: The significance of culture and gender for contact patterns in organizations) Nordiske Organisusjonsstudier, 4.

French, W. L., C. H. Bell and R. A. Zwaki, (1994) *Organization Development and Transformation,* Irwin, Boston.

Gibbons, M. (1994), *The New Production of Knowledge.* The Dynamics of Science and Research in Contemporary Societies. London: Sage.

Granovetter, M.S. (1973) The Strength of Weak Ties, *American Journal of Sociology 78,* pp. 1360–1380.

Granovetter, M.S. (1985), Economic Action and Social Structure: The Problem of Embeddedness, *American Journal of Sociology, 91, pp. 481–510.*

Greenwood, D.J. (1991) *Collective Reflective Practice Through Participatory Action Research: A Case Study from the Fagor Co-operatives of Mondragòn,* in The Reflective Turn. Case Studies in and on Educational Practice, edited by D.A. Schön, pp. 84–107 New York: Teachers College Press.

Greenwood, D.J. and M. Levin (1998) *Introduction to Action Research Social Research for Social Change,* Thousand Oaks, CA: SAGE Publications.

Greenwood, D.J. and L.G. Santos. 1992. *Industrial Democracy as Process. Participatory Action Research in the Fagor Co-operative Group of Mondragòn.* Assen: Van Gorcum.

Greenwood, D.J., W.F. Whyte, and I. Harkavy.(1993) Participatory Action Research as a Process and as a Goal, *Human Relations 46: 175–192.*

Grønhaug, K. and R. Lines (1995) Managerial Focus in Changing Environments, *Scandinavian Journal of Management 11, pp. 283–293.*

Grønhaug, K and G Kaufman. (1988) *Innovation: A Cross-Disciplinary Perspective,* Oslo: The Norwegian University Press.

Gustavsen, B. (1992) *Dialogue and development: theory of communication, action research and restructuring of working life.* Assen: Van Gorcum.

Gustavsen, B. (1996) *Development and Social Sciences: An uneasy relationship.* In: Toulmin, S. and Gustavsen, B. (eds.) 1996: Beyond Theory: Changing Organizations through Participation. Amsterdam: John Benjanins Publishing Company.

Gustavsen, B. 1998*: Enterprise Development 2000: A program for distributive and interactive learning,* in Gustavsen, B., Colbjørnsen, T. and Pålshaugen, Ø. (eds.) 1998: Development Coalitions in Working Life. Amsterdam: John Benjamins Publishing Company.

Gustavsen, B. (1998) *Enterprise development 2000: A program for distributive and interactive learning,* in Dialogues on Work and Innovation, vol. 6, Development Coalitions in Working Life. The "Enterprise Development 2000" Program in Norway, pp. 1–22 Amsterdam: John Benjamins.

Gustavsen, B. (2000) *Theory and Practice: the Mediating Discourse,* in: Bradbury, H. and Reason, Peter (eds.) 2000: Handbook of Action Research. Thousand Oaks: Sage Publishing, inc.

Gustavsen, B. and P.H. Engelstad (1995) *The design of conferences and the evolving role of democratic dialogue in changing working life,* in: Eikeland, O. and Finsrud, H.D. (eds.) 1995: Forskning og handling: Søkelys på aksjonsforskning, (Research and Action: Searchlight on Action Research). Oslo: Arbeidsforskningsinstituttets skriftserie no. 1.

Gustavsen, B., H. Finne, and B. Oscarsson (2001) *Creating Connectedness. The Role of Social Research in Innovation Policy,* Amsterdam: John Benjamins.

Habermas, J. (1972) *Knowledge and Human Interests,* Boston: Beacon Press.

Habermas, J. (1973) *Legitimation Crisis,* London: Heinemann Education Books.

Habermas, J. (1981/1984) *The Theory of Communicative Action: reason and the Realization of Society,* Cambridge: Polity Press. Vol. I and II.

Hanssen-Bauer, J. and C.C. Snow (1996), "Responding to Hypercompetition: The Structure and Processes of a Regional Learning Network Organization", *Organization Science,* Vol. 7(4): 413–427.

Hjellbrekke, J. And O Osland (1999) Den symbolske dominansen og "det kommunikative mistaket": om Bourdieu sin praksisteori i studiar av det politiske feltet, (The Symbolic dmoninace and the "communicative failure) in *Norsk Statsvitenskaplig Tidsskrift.*

Hales, C.P. (1986). What do Managers Do? An Critical Review of the Evidence, *Journal of Management Studies, Vol.23, No.1, pp. 88–115.*

Hammer, M..and Champy, J. (1993) *Reengineering the Corporation A manifesto for Busienss Revolution*, London: Nicholas Brealy Publishing.

Holm, P. (2001) *The Invisible Revolution: Reconstructing Institutional Transition in the Fisheries*, PhD Thesis, The Norwegian College of Fishery Science, University of Tromsø.

Huxham, C. and S Vangen (2000.) Leadership in the Shaping and Implementation of Collaboration Agendas: How Things happen in a (not quite) joined up World., *Academy of Management Journal 43*, pp. 1159–1175.

Johnsen, H.C.G. (2001) *Involvement at Work* (delivered PhD dissertation, unpublished). Copenhagen: Copenhagen Business School.

Juran, J.M. (1964) *Managerial Breakthrough*, New York: Mc-Grawhill.

Kunda, G. (1992) *Engineering Culture: Control and Commitment in a High-tech Corporation*, Philadelphia: Temple University Press.

Kuhn, T.S. (1962) *The Structure of Scientific Revolutions*, Chicago: Chicago Press.

Kvadsheim, H. (2001) *Integrering av arbeidsmiljø i et bedriftsutviklingsprogram*, (Integration of QWL in Enterprise Development), Stavanger: Rogaland Research.

von Krogh, G., Ichijo, K. and Nonaka, I. (2000) *Enabling Knowledge Creation. How to Unlock the Mystery of Tacit Knowledge and Release Power of Innovation*, Oxford: Oxford University Press.

Latour, B. (1987) *Science in Action: How to Follow Scientists and Engineers Through Society*, Cambridge: Harvard University Press.

Law J. (1992) Notes on the Theory of the Actor-Network: Ordering, Strategy, and Heterogeneity, *Systems Practice, Vol. 5, No. 4. pp. 379–393.*

Levin, M. and G. Knutstad (2001). *Construction of Learning Networks — Vanity's fair or realistic opportunities*, To be published in Systemic Practice and Action Research.

Levin M, Ø. Fossen og R Gjersvik (1994) *Ledelse og teknologi* (Leadership and Technology), Oslo: Universitetsforlaget.

Luhmann, N. (1989). *The Differentiation of Society*, New York: Beacon Press.

Lundvall, B.Å. and Johnson B. (1995) The Learning Economy, *Journal of Industry Studies 1, pp. 23–42.*

McCarthy T. (1996) *Pragmatizing Communicative Reason*, in: Toulmin, Stephen and Gustavsen, Bjørn (eds.) 1996: Beyond Theory: Changing Organizations through Participation. Amsterdam: John Benjamins Publishing Company.

McGregeor D. (1960) *The Human Side of Enterprise.* New York: McGraw-Hill.

Meyer, J.W. and B. Rowan (1991) *Institutionalized Organizations: Formal Structure as Myth and Ceremony*, in: Powell, Walter W. and DiMaggio, P.J. 1991: The New Institutionalism in Organization Analysis. Chicago: The University of Chicago Press.

Merton, R.K. (1992) *The Ethos of Science*, in On Social Structure and Science, edited by Sztumpka P. and Merton R.K., pp. 267–276, Chicago: The University of Chicago Press.

Mitchell, J.C. (1962) *The Concept and Use of Social Networks*, in Social Networks in Urban Situations, edited by Mitchell J. C, Manchester: Manchester University Press.

Mitchell, J.C. (1976) The Concept of Use of Social Networks, in Interorganizational Relations, edited by Eran, W.M.: Hamundswerth, Penguin books, pp. 293–306.

Mønsted, M. (1995) Processes and Structure of Networks: Reflections on Methodology." *Entrepreneurship & Regional Development 7, pp. 193–213.*

Nashold, F., Cole, R. E., B. Gustavsen and H. van Beinum (1993) *Constructing the New Industrial Society*, Assen: Van Gorcum.

Nonaka, I. and K. Takeuchi, (1995) *The Knowledge Creating Company*, Oxford: Oxford University Press.

Northouse P. G. (1997) *Leadership Theory and Practice*, Thousand Oaks: Sage.

Ottesen, G. G., L. Foss and K. Grønhaug (2003) "Exploring the Accuracy of SME Managers, European, Journal of Marketing (under publication).

Pentland, B. T. (1999), Building Process Theory with Narrative: From Description to Explanation, *Academy of Management Review 24, pp. 711–724.*

Pfeffer, J. and Salancik, G.R (1978*). The External Control of Organizations: A Resource Dependence Perspective*, New York: Harper & Row.

Powell, W. W. and DiMaggio, P. J. (1991) *The New Institutionalism in Organization Analysis*, Chicago: The University of Chicago Press.

Powell, W. W. and Smith-Doerr L. (1994), *Networks and Ecnonomic Life*, in The Handbook of Economic Sociology, vol. 15., pp. 368–402.

Scott, J. (1991) *Social Network Analysis — a Handbook*, Thousand Oaks: Sage.

Pålshaugen, Ø. (1992). Aksjonsforskning: En nyttig vitenskap? Et innspill i fire satser.(Action research: A useful science? A communication in three movements), *Tidsskrift for samfunnsforskning 33: 231–251.*

Rawls, J. (1971) *A Theory of Justice*, Cambridge, MA: Harvard University Press.

Rapoport, R. N. (1970). Three Dilemmas in Action Research, *Human Relations 23: pp. 480–513.*

Reason P. and H. Bradbury (2001) *Handbook of Action Research*, London: Sage.

Røvik, K. A. (1998) *Moderne organisasjoner: Trender i organisasjonstenkningen ved tusenårsskiftet*, (Moderen organizations: Trends in organizational theory at the miullenium change) Bergen: Fagbokforlaget.

Scott, R. W. (1995) *Institutions and Organizations*, Thousand Oaks: Sage.

Selznick, P. 1997 (1957) *Leadership in Administration: A sociological Interpretation*, in: Foss, N. J. (ed.) 1997: Resources, Firms and Strategies. Oxford: Oxford University Press.

Senge P, (1990) *The Fifth Discipline*, New York: Doubleday.

Shotter, J. (1993) *Conversational Realities*. London: Sage.

Storper, M. (1995) Territorial Development in the Global Learning Economy: The Challenge to Developing Countries, *Review of International Political Economy 2, pp. 394–424.*

Sørensen, A. B. (1992*) Evaluering av norsk arbeidslivs- og aksjonsforskning. Fokus på Arbeidsforskningsinstituttet (AFI) og Institutt for industriell miljøforskning (IFIM)*, (Evaluation of Norwegian worklife- and action research. A focus on WRI and IFIM) Oslo: NORAS.

Trist, E. L. (1981). *The Evolution of Sociotechnical Systems as a Conceptual Framework and as an Action Research Program. Perspectives on Organization Design and Behaviour*, in Perspectives on Organization Design and Behaviour, edited by A. Van de Ven and W. F. Joyce, pp. 19–75, New York: Wiley.

Trist, E. L. and. K.W. Bamforth (1951) Some Social and Psychological Consequences of the Longwall Method of Coal Getting, *Human Relations 4: 3–38.*

Utterback J. M. (1994) *Mastering the Dynamics of Innovation*, Cambridge: Harvard Business School Press.

Van de Ven, A. and G. P. Huber (1990), Longitudinal field research methods for studying processes of organizational change, *Organization Science. Vol. 1, No. 3, pp. 213–219.*

Warren, M. (1996) *The self in discursive democracy*, in: White, Stephen K. 1996: The Cambridge Companion to Habermas. Cambridge: Cambridge University Press.

Wassermann, S. and Faust K. (1994), *Social Network Analysis — Methods and Applications*, Cambridge: Cambridge University Press.

Weber, M. (1964) The theory of social and economic organizations, New York: The Free Press.

Whyte, W. F. (1991) *Participatory Action Research*. Newbury Park, CA: Sage.

Widerberg, K. (1999) Alternative Methods — Alternative Understandings: Exploring the Social and the Multiple "I" through Memory-Work., *Sosiologisk Tidsskrift. Scandinavian University Press 2*, pp. 147–160.

About the authors

Tor Claussen is senior researcher at Rogaland Research. He holds a Ph.D. in social anthropology and philosophy. Claussen's main research interest is work life research, research on enterprise development, work environment and a general interest in social sciences issues. He is headed the Stavanger based module ED2000. Claussen has a special interest in topic from classic philosophy and their relevance for the linguistic turn and social constructivism.

Eivind Falkum is Research director at the Fafo (Institute of Applied Social Science) in Oslo. He holds a master degree from Institute of Administration and Organisation Science at the University of Bergen His field of work is organization analysis within industrial relations and enterprise development. He is heading a group of scientists focusing correlations between labor relations and value adding.

Lene Foss is associate professor of entrepreneurship and enterprise development at the Norwegian College of Fishery Science, University of Tromsø and adjunct associate professor at the Norwegian School of Management. She received her Ph.D. in organization and management from the Norwegian School of Economics and Business Administration. Her research interests include networks, leadership, gender, emerging industries and action research. She is a reviewer in Academy of Management Journal and Journal of Organizational Change Management.

Jon Hanssen-Bauer is a social anthropologist who is at present managing director for the Fafo (Institute for Applied International Studies). He has previously held positions as researcher at the Work Research Institute and as project director at the Norwegian Work Life Center. He has been studying and publishing on work organizations and working environment issues, and has also been working and teaching on social development challenges in the third world, in conflict areas and in post-conflict countries in the Middle East, in Asia, Latin America and in Africa. He has functioned as an advisor to the Nordvest Forum learning network.

Bjørn Gustavsen is professor at the National Institute for Working Life in Sweden (part time), adjunct professor at the Norwegian University for Science and Technology, and research director for the Enterprise Development 2000 program and its successor Value Creation 2010. Bjørn Gustavsen has together with the labour market parties in Norway and Sweden, helped organise several workplace development programs. Alone and with others he has written or edited about 25 books and about 250 articles, the majority of both in English. Main themes are the relationships between knowledge and practical development in workplaces, enterprises and society.

Hans Chr. Garmann Johnsen is research director at Agder Research. H e holds an MBA from the Norwegian School of Economics and Business Administration and a Master in political science from the University of Bergen and a Ph.D from Copenhagen Business School. Before joining Agder research, Johnsen worked as a manager in a trading company. His has done research service management and published a book on service quality management in the public sector. Later his focus of interest has been in communicative processes in organization development.

Harald Knutsen is a professor of management at Agder University College. He holds an MBA and a Ph.D. from the University of Oregon. He is professor of strategic management at Agder College and he is now Dean of the Faculty of Economics and Social Science at Agder University College. Harald Knudsen also has a deep interest in philosophy and ethics. Recent teaching and research activities have been in the areas of leadership development, international management and organizational learning. He is the author of several books focusing on leadership.

Henrik Kvadsheim hold an MBA from the Norwegian School of Economics and Business Administration and is currently senior research scientist at RR — Rogaland Research. His research and publications has specially focused on issues related to strategies for industrial development and innovation, employee participation and work-life development.

Morten Levin is professor in the Department of Industrial Economics and Technology Management at the Norwegian University of Science and Technology. He holds graduate degrees in engineering and Sociology. Throughout his professional life, he has worked as an action researcher with particular focus on processes and structures of social change in the relationships between technology and organization. He has developed and been in charge of Ph.D. programs in action research. He is author of a number of books and articles.

Jarle Løvland is research director at the Norwegian Institute of Fisheries and Aquaculture Research. Løvland is educated in management science and enterprise development. He has research interests in exploring the development of employment relations, human capital resources and relevant management practice during the ongoing restructuring in the Norwegian seafood industry.

Ida Munkeby is senior research Scientist at SINTEF Industrial Management, New Praxis, in Trondheim, Norway. She holds a master degree in sociology from the Norwegian University of Science and Technology and is currently working on a PhD in sociology at the Norwegian University of Science and Technology. Her main research areas are industrial relations, leadership, ownership and organization of work.

Håkon Raabe holds a Ph.D. from the Norwegian University of Science and Technology. He has a MBA the Norwegian School of Economics and Business Administration. He has worked for several years holding different management positions in the finance industry. He is now associate director of Nordvest Forum AS, a regional learning network organization based in the industrial core area of North-Western Norway.

Johan Elvemo Ravn is a senior research scientist at SINTEF Industrial Management, New Praxis, in Trondheim. He holds a Ph.D. in Organization Behavior and Business Management from The Norwegian University of Science and Technology. His main research interests are action research, transdisciplinary research, enterprise development and leadership.

Øyvind Pålshaugen is researcher at the Work Research Institute in Oslo. He holds a Ph.D. (Dr. Philos.) in sociology. His filed of study include action research, organization development, the rhetorics of science and the science of rhetoric. He is co-editor of the journal *Concepts and Transformation.*

Name index

Subject index

D

O

P

Q

R

In the series DIALOGUES ON WORK AND INNOVATION the following titles have been published thus far or are scheduled for publication:

1. NASCHOLD, Frieder and Casten VON OTTER: *Public Sector Transformation: Rethinking Markets and Hierarchies in Government.* 1996.
2. TOULMIN, Stephen and Bjørn GUSTAVSEN (eds): *Beyond Theory. Changing organizations through participation.* 1996.
3. GUSTAVSEN, Bjørn, Bernd HOFMAIER, Marianne EKMAN PHILIPS and Anders WIKMAN: *Concept-Driven Development and the Organization of the Process of Change. An evaluation of the Swedish Working Life Fund.* 1996.
4. MERRELYN, Emery: *Searching. The theory and practice of making cultural change.* 1999.
5. PÅLSHAUGEN, Øyvind, Bjørn GUSTAVSEN, Dag ØSTERBERG and John SHOTTER: *The End of Organization Theory? Language as a tool in action research and organizational development.* 1998.
6. GUSTAVSEN, Bjørn, Tom COLBJØRNSEN and Øyvind PÅLSHAUGEN (eds): *Development Coalitions in Working Life. The 'Enterprise Development 2000' Program in Norway.* 1998.
7. ENNALS, Richard and Bjørn GUSTAVSEN: *Work Organization and Europe as a Development Coalition.* 1999.
8. GREENWOOD, Davydd J. (ed.): *Action Research. From practice to writing in an international action research development program.* 1999.
9. VAN BEINUM, Hans (ed.): *Ideas and Practices in Action Research. An institutional journey.* n.y.p.
10. KALLIOLA, Satu and Risto NAKARI (eds.): *Resources for Renewal. A participatory approach to the modernization of municipal organizations in Finland.* 1999.
11. LJUNGBERG VAN BEINUM, Ingrid: *Using the Lamp instead of Looking into the Mirror. Women and men in discussion about the relationship between men and women in the work place.* 2000.
12. MUNTIGL, Peter, Gilbert WEISS and Ruth WODAK: *European Union Discourses and Unemployement. An interdisciplinary approach to employment policymaking and organizational change.* n.y.p.
13. GUSTAVSEN, Bjørn, Håkon FINNE and Bo OSCARSSON: *Creating Connectedness. The role of social research in innovation policy.* 2001.
14. LEVIN, Morten (ed.): *Researching Enterprise Development. Action Research on the cooperation between management and labour in Norway.* 2002.